D1095620

BEYOND

ALSO BY CATHERINE WOLFF

Not Less Than Everything:
Catholic Writers on Heroes of Conscience from Joan of Arc to Oscar Romero

BEYOND

How Humankind
Thinks about Heaven

Catherine Wolff

RIVERHEAD BOOKS

NEW YORK

2021

RIVERHEAD BOOKS
An imprint of Penguin Random House LLC
penguinrandomhouse.com

Library of Congress Cataloging-in-Publication Data

Names: Wolff, Catherine, 1952– author.
Title: Beyond : how humankind thinks about heaven / Catherine Wolff.
Description: New York : Riverhead Books, 2021. |
Includes bibliographical references and index.
Identifiers: LCCN 2020037564 (print) | LCCN 2020037565 (ebook) |
ISBN 9781594634451 (hardcover) | ISBN 9780698405110 (ebook)
Subjects: LCSH: Heaven. | Future life.
Classification: LCC BL540 .W65 2021 (print) | LCC BL540 (ebook) |
DDC 202/.3—dc23
LC record available at https://lccn.loc.gov/2020037564
LC ebook record available at https://lccn.loc.gov/2020037565

Printed in the United States of America
1   3   5   7   9   10   8   6   4   2

Book design by Amanda Dewey

For my family,
the great cloud of witnesses

In paradox and story

Parable and laughter

Find I the glory

Here in hereafter

Madeleine L'Engle,
"The Glory"

CONTENTS

PART IV. CHRISTIANITY

PART V. ISLAM

PART VI. HINDUISM AND BUDDHISM

PART VII. WE SHALL NOT CEASE FROM EXPLORATION

At the Horizon of the Known

In every man's life there are moments when
there is a lifting of the veil at the horizon of the
known, opening a sight of the eternal.

We do not leave the shore of the known in
search of adventure or suspense or because of
the failure of reason to answer our questions.
We sail because our mind is like a fantastic
seashell, and when applying our ear to its lips we
hear a perpetual murmur from the waves beyond
the shore.

· ABRAHAM JOSHUA HESCHEL

My father lay dying after ninety-five full years. Family members kept vigil during those last days as he slipped in and out of consciousness. Dad spoke only twice. First he said: "Well, I've stopped trying to figure it all out." Then a day or two later he came round again and said: "But the thing is, I don't know where to go from here."

My sister, keeping watch, replied: "Straight ahead, Dad, straight ahead."

Straight ahead, yes—but where exactly? As years have passed, and friends and relatives have gone straight ahead, I find myself wondering where they might have gone.

I have always believed that our path through life does not end at death. And like all of us, I want to see friends and close family again. I especially want to drink a bottle of good red wine with my brother Bill, and see if we've figured anything out yet. I have both apologies and thanks for my parents, and would dearly love to meet Mary Magdalene and Rumi and William James and, dare I say, God.

But who am I to undertake a quest for life beyond this one, given the heroes and visionaries who have traveled there throughout the centuries—Gilgamesh; Enoch; Julian of Norwich; Dante; Black Elk; the Buddha? I am neither heroine nor scholar, prophet, mystic, or priest. I am simply a woman with enough curiosity and faith, family and friends to sustain me in this effort. All visions of life beyond are reflections of the ideas and practice of a given culture and a given time, but thanks to my moment in history, I can explore both historical and contemporary belief.

THIS BOOK IS NOT a comprehensive history of how humans have sought life beyond—such a thing would be impossible. Rather, it is a record of my own search for knowledge and hope for continued life. I have drawn from many fields—theology and history, anthropology and psychology—to understand the beliefs of individuals, communities, and faiths. I have learned a great deal from scholars, but their theories and explanations are framed by the limits of their fields, and by their own interest or personal engagement. Thus I came to rely on believers for my sense of how we think about life beyond life.

There were as many views as there were believers. Some might see this lack of uniformity as an indication that faith traditions are losing their appeal and their authority. But I suspect that if I had been working in the third or the fifteenth century, I would have found a similar range of speculation and belief. And the very fact that I could find so many people willing to share their visions with me, in what is a fast-paced, intellectually sophisticated, highly secular environment, is testimony to the continuing relevance and vitality of our quest for life beyond our earthly existence.

Part I

IN THE
BEGINNING

Seek and Ye Shall Find

I learn by going where I have to go.

• THEODORE ROETHKE

W hen I started imagining life beyond, I called it heaven. Most of the people I knew growing up did. My earliest visions were those of a little kid enduring frigid San Francisco summers: heaven would be a bright, sunshiny blue-sky place where each person had her own cloud with a swimming pool in it. God did not figure much, nor did my noisy family. I would be alone in the sunshine (and the pool!) forever.

In the ensuing years, I came to see heaven as a state of bliss in union with God and the blessed departed, a state I would earn through a life lived by the conventional moral code. I figured that was as far as one might legitimately speculate. I had no idea the extent to which my ideas of heaven were a product of my time and my Christian tradition, as "heaven" turned out to be only one of the many ways we humans have envisioned life beyond.

To make sense of it all, I had to make my way through a thicket of competing, even contradictory, information, argument, belief, and expression. And at every turn I was faced with the flawed and whimsical nature of my efforts, the folly of describing something beyond time and space in terms limited by those realities. But that's what we have to work with.

Life beyond may exist in time, or in eternity. It may be where we come from—as Plato believed—or where we may go in mystical experience; our destination when we die, or even later. There may be a progression of stages through which we mature spiritually so that we might escape the cycle of rebirth, as in Eastern religions, or we may have just one shot at redemption. We may reach life beyond as soon as we die, or have to wait until the end of the cosmos.

Life beyond is generally characterized as good, although with the need for social order and the development of moral codes it came to have darker regions as well. We may require salvation for our sins, or we may be predestined in some way. There may be a messiah, as in the Jewish and Christian traditions, or we may have to save ourselves. In a rare instance of agreement, most people hold that the way we live our lives on earth affects our prospects for life beyond, through good deeds and compassion for others.

Some believe that we will be fully aware, even that our consciousness is the very bridge to another reality. Others suggest that our individual identities may not carry over, and that we will lose ourselves in the divine. We may be alone, or with others, or one with the universe. Life beyond may be a "place" or "state" of universal gratification, or we may simply get what we want. Which may include final death, complete cessation.

Finally, there is the question of a God or gods, whom we may or may not encounter in this life or in the next. The divinity may be a loving Person or an all-encompassing Mind or the ultimate mathematical harmony.

The wonder of it all is that, despite not knowing where we are going or what it might be like, we keep yearning for life beyond. In this we are fueled by the terror of death, of the loss of our selves; by the desire to be free of suffering and rewarded for our struggles. But our hopes seem also to be fueled by an intrinsic sense of a reality that transcends our limited earthly existence and that beckons to us. From the first stirrings of human spirituality to present-day exploration of the frontiers of our minds, we have sought to respond, and in doing so we have found meaning in our lives that goes beyond the limits of self and survival, and of death.

———

FOR MUCH OF HUMAN HISTORY, we have found meaning through belief in God, interwoven with hopes for ultimate union with him. For believers, God is the reason there is anything at all, the source and sustenance of the universe, our world, you and me. It is God who beckons to us, and God in whom we shall find our eternal home.

The existence of God or gods has never been a foregone conclusion, however. There was a rich array of viewpoints among the ancient Greeks. The Older Sophist Protagoras wrote, wistfully, "As regards gods, I am unable to know either that they exist or that they do not, or what form they have. For there are many obstacles to knowing: the obscurity of the matter, and the shortness of human life." The philosopher Epicurus embraced an empirically based, naturalistic view of the world and human societies. If there are gods, they have no interest in us; we have no soul, and death is the end. The atomists espoused the intriguingly modern view that the basic components of the universe are simple, indivisible, indestructible particles and that every phenomenon is due to random motions of these particles coming together to form complex entities in space. The gods themselves were, like us, born of pure chance.

On the other hand, there is a considerable body of Western thought that makes the case for the existence of God. One argument holds that there must be a God because from the beginning of the universe there is an observable, orderly chain of causes that can only be accounted for by a first cause, a self-created Being who simply *is*. Another demonstrates the existence of God through the fact that the universe is ordered in a purposeful way so as to sustain life—as G. K. Chesterton put it, "One elephant having a trunk was odd; but all elephants having a trunk looked like a plot." Other arguments are based on the existence of a moral law that cannot have its origin in the natural world, or on miracles, which exceed the power of nature and violate its laws and can only be explained by supernatural intervention, which is to say God.

But religious faith does not rest on reasoned arguments alone. When believers explore the realm of religious thought—certainly when they pray—their horizons open wide, and the existence, the immanence of God, becomes a distinct possibility. And through myth and ritual and community, believers find inspiration and solace and a way of life that will lead them to a rendezvous with God. For the mystics of every religion, this takes place in the here and now. For the rest of us, it will come at the end of our lives or at the end of the cosmos. Until modern times, the beliefs of religious faith traditions were the main repository of our hopes for heaven and union with divinity, and we look to them to teach us why and how it is that such hopes are continually renewed.

I WAS ON A TREK across the Sierras one summer with a group of friends, including a number of soulful burros who carried our equipment and provisions. When night fell we'd face the dilemma of whether to leave them tied up. If we did, they'd be ready to go the next day, but they'd have methodically eaten everything in reach. If we left them free, we'd hear a rustling around four a.m.: they'd be drifting off, uphill or down, through trees or open space, always east, sometimes for a mile or two, following some deep calling. They were seeking the light slowly dawning on the world.

Those who recognize themselves as creatures of God instinctively seek the light, and its source. Indeed, as the ancient theologian Longinus wrote, "The extensive reach and piercing speculation of the human understanding passes the bounds of the material world, and launches forth at pleasure into endless space." But God also seeks us. In the last months of his life, before he died of brain cancer, my brother Bill—the one I want to drink that bottle of red wine with—was often told by well-meaning people that he was going to God. But in prayer he discerned something altogether different, and spoke wonderingly of his sense that God was coming toward him. He was not so much being wrenched out of this life in his prime as being approached by God moving into his life, calling to him.

We must seek if we are to find, and the search to find God in this life, and thus to join God in life beyond, can be daunting. But we have all been called. As Saint Augustine prayed, "You have made us for yourself, O Lord, and our hearts are restless until they rest in you." And we are guided by "the Spirit that comes from God, to teach us to understand the gifts he has given us." Finally, we are not alone: there are prophets and saints in every faith tradition. Moses led his people in the desert; Muhammad is his people's moral exemplar; Siddhartha taught the way; Jesus is the mediator, embodying the human and the divine.

Whatever path we take, we must search using all our ways of knowing—philosophy and theology, science and experience. But when our accustomed ways of knowing do not suffice, religious believers turn to faith, and it is through faith that we reach beyond this existence. In turn, we find another way of knowing, which is nothing less than "collaboration with the mind of God."

A cautionary note here. The fullest religious quest is grounded not only in the intellect and in the soul but also in the body, and everything and everyone we encounter in our lives. Too much religious belief is dualistic: the mind and spirit are innately pure while the body is innately degraded. But we come to knowledge and understanding through our bodies, through our senses and emotions and the sheer wear and tear of life. We leave our bodies behind (for a while, or for good) at death, but we live our earthly lives in them, and should cherish the ways in which they lead us to God.

The very effort to follow the path of faith, to find God in the moment and in our ultimate rendezvous, enhances our ability to do so. There are times when we are confident, but also times when we are in the desert—world-weary, despairing. And yet so many saintly people—Mother Teresa, Abraham Joshua Heschel, Dietrich Bonhoeffer—say that when God seems far away, when we cannot find him, we can still be faithful to the times when we have felt faith. The wise course is to find peace with questions, with doubt, rather than through prefabricated conclusions; to pursue clues of the divine without feeling obliged to prove anything. As the poet

Christian Wiman writes, "Truth inheres not in doctrine itself, but in the spirit with which it is engaged, for the spirit of God is always seeking and creating new forms."

RELIGIOUS FAITH provides a pathway to life with God, during our time on earth and after our death. But along with the challenges of pursuing such a path, we are faced with the stark limitations of our earthly existence, bound as it is by space and time. How can we conceive of something we've never experienced directly, that by definition lies beyond us? That has always been sought, but never quite found? All the information gathered, all the arguments considered, are not enough for us to glimpse what lies beyond this existence. If we can do so at all, it is through the alchemy of the imagination.

Author John Cornwell told me of an old friend who sought the divine not through creation or revelation but through understanding the self. He believed we are born with the notion of an ideal self that has a whole range of virtues and qualities that we are conscious we don't measure up to. This ideal self springs from the imagination and is nothing less than the reflection of the divine in the world. It is through the creative, one might say sacred, exercise of the imagination that our very souls arise.

The workings of the imagination are mysterious. Samuel Taylor Coleridge described the imagination as the power "to shape into one," so that unconscious elements emerge into consciousness, making a meaningful whole of sensations, language, memory, and perceptions. We moderns are accustomed to applying a scientific standard to reality: a given phenomenon must be objectively verifiable, preferably through measurement. But the imagination gives rise to interpretations—maps, poetry, paintings, creeds, diagrams—that can be just as valid. Such figurative language and representation, symbol and ritual, express the dynamic connection between the human mind and the universe and point us toward things beyond. Indeed, the history of belief in heaven (or hell or transcendence) is the history of our imaginings about it. We are authors of an ongoing story whose conclusion, if it has one, lies beyond our natural horizon.

The imagination is what a creative person lives on, and so I asked the author Tobias Wolff (with whom I converse regularly, as he is my husband) how it works for him. He was emphatic: all the things we think and do are entwined with the imagination, as it creates in us the capacity to decide what to do going forward, whether meeting a friend for lunch, planning a trip, or writing a story. He does not make the common distinction between the imagination and reason, which often carries the implication that the imagination is just froth, lacking the substance of observable concrete reality. Wolff points out that it is convenient to divide things that way but that our lived experience tells us otherwise. Still, he understands the distinction might be comforting: "The thing about imagination is that it represents a potentially riotous and uncontrollable part of your life, and some people fear that."

One can appreciate the risk, but then there is the adventure. The imagination provides a way to escape from everyday reality, to move beyond the self. And it can take us in unexpected directions. Wolff described *The Stranger* as a novel its author, Albert Camus, did not mean to write. In public statements, Camus spoke of the character Meursault in heroic terms, and framed his impending execution in such a way as to recall Jesus's crucifixion. But the Meursault in the novel is a self-justifying liar and murderer. This Meursault is actually a much more interesting, complex figure than the simple truth-teller Camus described, and the novel accedes to greatness precisely because of those complexities.

What accounts for this difference between the intention and the achievement? Wolff believes that "in the creation of art, if you're lucky, something unexpected happens—you do something even better than you intended. The greatest work somehow has taken a step beyond what you imagined it would be."

Wolff does not take the imagination for granted, however. "It is a gift, and gifts can't be commanded. They come when they are given." He believes most artists understand that there is something inexplicable about the imagination, and that to try too hard to figure out where the gift is coming from can compromise it. "An open and welcoming heart is the best way to invite imagination, and a grateful heart when it comes. I see why people think of it as a sacred gift, because it's like grace." It is no surprise that Wolff believes that imagination can be a path to spiritual experience.

WE CAN EMBRACE A HIGHER REALITY, and we can be moved and inspired by ideas of the soul and of God and a heavenly destination. But we can never describe them directly. Concepts are too abstract; sensory impressions are transient. The imagination, through its language of symbols, implies things beyond; what we see through a glass darkly is not illusion but another realm of reality. But as the psalmist wrote, deep calls to deep and through disciplined spiritual practice, through the dedicated use of the imagination, we may ourselves participate in that reality. The hope for union with God may be realized—however fleetingly—in this life, a taste of what is to come.

TWO

Origins

Another world to live in—whether we expect
ever to pass wholly into it or not—is what we
mean by having a religion.

• GEORGE SANTAYANA

The historical religions that have played a central role in inspiring
and preserving ideas about what might lie beyond earthly existence have flourished for some five thousand years. But how is it
that we came to have such ideas at all? What is it about human nature and
our capacities developed through evolution that gave rise to our sense of
other realities?

The origins of our belief in life beyond lie in the fact of death and the
fears we hold in common with our remote forbears. There is evidence of
ritual disposal of the dead in caves from at least 200,000 years ago, and
possibly as long as 2.5 million years ago.

We share an ancestor from 500,000–750,000 years ago with Neanderthals, whose genes many of us still carry. (In fact, one of my most highly
evolved friends recently found that he is 3 percent Neanderthal.)

Still, there is an ongoing debate as to whether Neanderthals were a
subspecies of *Homo sapiens* or a more distant relative. Modern human su-
premacists regarded them as savage and stupid. We now know otherwise:
Neanderthal anatomy suggests that they could speak; they vanquished rhi-
nos and made jewelry and tools, ate chamomile and marine mammals and

used toothpicks. And they buried their dead. Grain and flowers (indicated by pollen traces), flint pieces, stone axes, remains of food offerings have been found at burial sites. Were these things just gifts, or could the Neanderthals have been provisioning the dead to continue life on the other side? We have no evidence of ceremonies performed at Neanderthal graves, but they concocted paint and used special feathers that may have been used in rituals.

If Neanderthals buried their dead with deliberate offerings as supplies for the next life, would that be a convincing argument that they were more than lower-class relatives? Indeed, why can't preparation for the afterlife, which implies hope and expectations, be a defining characteristic of humans?

We were successful at keeping our numbers up, enabling the spread of innovations that helped us survive, while groups such as the Neanderthals faced insurmountable challenges and eventually died out. Or they became part of us, and passed down not only their genes but also their intimations of an afterlife.

HUMAN FACULTIES THAT ARE the cornerstones of religion and our orientation toward life beyond evolved slowly. Archaeologist Steven Mithen locates their origins in the brain, describing a process where we went from all-purpose learning and decision-making to specialized intelligences such as social interaction, dealing with the natural world, technical intelligence for making and using tools, and linguistic intelligence. Over a long period—from 30,000 to 60,000 years ago—we developed what's called "cognitive fluidity," the capacity for knowledge and ideas to flow freely between these areas of specialized intelligence, which in turn provided us with new ways to think and act. As for consciousness, it too arrived gradually, but eventually we woke up.

While Mithen finds the roots of our capacity for religious belief and ritual in the brain, sociologist Robert Bellah makes the case that they are based in social interaction. Even though evolution has required an ongoing struggle for existence, humans have always engaged in play as well. It gives rise to a wide range of physical and behavioral capacities such as communication, innovation, and creativity, and enables us to push our horizons beyond everyday life. Bellah believes that playful nurturance is the earliest manifestation of what we call love, and that play can become ritual that sustains and enriches a culture. Indeed, it was play that opened up for our remote ancestors the first alternative reality, leading to our discovery of "possible worlds, multiple realities" whose "consequences we could not live without."

The origin of language is still a matter of debate. Some locate it in the communication involved in play, while others emphasize the anatomical development that enabled us to learn new sounds and to control our vocal tracts, cavities that filter those sounds. It was relatively recently, roughly 100,000 years ago, that we began to speak the way we do now, and as for writing, that came much later during the fourth millennium BCE.

SOMEWHERE IN THESE VAST STRETCHES of time, humans began to seek meaning, and therein lies the dawning of spirituality and eventually religion. Many consider this development a product of evolution as well, as seeking meaning pushes us toward understanding, which leads to increased mastery over our environment. Through his encounters with the inhabitants of Tierra del Fuego at the tip of South America, Charles Darwin came to believe that the notion of a god was generated in our evolving minds, arising from the fear that came from living in a harsh and hostile world and the sense of a lofty divinity manifested in an oceanic feeling. Darwin did not consider such feelings to be evidence for the existence of God, but he acknowledged that there was another argument for belief that had more weight, one we can take to heart. The argument "follows from the extreme difficulty or rather impossibility of conceiving this immense & wonderful universe, including man with his capacity of looking far backwards & far into futurity, as the result of blind chance or necessity."

Darwin seems to have longed for a creator, a source of the wonder he observed in the natural world. His writings reflect a growing sense that evolution was not just about physical entities, that it had religious and moral implications. But they held no place for philosophy or a divinity—God was a projection that crystallized rules to be passed on. Nevertheless, Darwin was intrigued by the notion of immortality and acknowledged that such instinctive belief could be found all over the world.

THERE CAME A TIME, some 40,000 years ago, when human culture exploded, either through a kind of "big bang" or as the result of a gradual process among different populations. The evolution of our brains and social interactions brought about the transformation of our relations with each other and with the natural world. And we began to express ourselves through art.

Art is manifest in all areas of human life: it is in our nature to create and express symbols to communicate meaning. This involves planning and executing works so that the meaning that inspires us will be accessible to others. It is impossible to say when art began, because we have no evidence as to the function of certain prehistoric artifacts, but we can speculate that some already served this expressive purpose. Certainly artifacts at burial sites give us clues about the origins of religion, the result of the integration of many different forms of intelligence in the early human mind.

Consider the gravesite in Sungir, Russia, from about 28,000 years ago. The bodies of a young girl and an old man were decorated elaborately with beads and pendants that indicated their status, their relationships with other people, and their group affiliation. These artifacts are both aesthetically valuable and rich in social information, and their inclusion in their owners' burial is also a clue that their death may have been seen as a transition to a subsequent life. And belief in survival after death leads to belief in nonphysical, spiritual beings and another world to live in.

Anthropomorphic images in cave paintings, which may have been the site for ritual activity, indicate stirrings of such faith. Human attributes were given to objects and animals, and eventually to gods. Cave paintings reflect a mythological world we glimpse in late Paleolithic paintings in a cave in France, Les Trois Frères. A human figure with animal features set high above a mass of animals may well be a shaman who communicated with supernatural beings or who was himself regarded as supernatural. Such inspired ones, messengers who moved between worlds, were empowered to enact rituals that have direct bearing on our lives, and our deaths. A passage beyond had been established.

THREE

The Sacred Fire

They had what the world has lost: the ancient,
lost reverence and passion for human personality
joined with the ancient, lost reverence and
passion for the earth and its web of life. Since
before the Stone Age they have tended that
passion as a central, sacred fire. It should be our
long hope to renew it in us all.

• JOHN COLLIER, U.S. COMMISSIONER OF
THE BUREAU FOR INDIAN AFFAIRS

R eligious belief among indigenous, primal peoples, transmitted
orally for untold generations through myth and practice, reflects a
worldview that many of us today have lost. Still, we can speculate
in an informed, imaginative way about how primal religions came about.
The British politician and scientist John Lubbock, a protégé of Darwin and
a pioneer in the study of prehistoric humans, proposed five stages in the
evolution of religion. The first was atheism, but the experience of dreaming, in which one left one's body at night, and the sense of one's shadow
being a soul of sorts, may have prompted the earliest religious stirrings. If
there was life beyond death, it would have been only for a few days as the
soul lingered.

The next stages were fetishism, wherein one caught a deity in an
object—a rock, an animal—and made it do one's bidding; and totemism, a
view of nature as a repository of good and evil spirits. The emergence of

shamanism was for Lubbock a sign of a transition to higher forms of religion. At this stage, gods lived in a separate realm, where only shamans could visit them so as to serve as conduits for messages from the gods to the people.

The final stage, idolatry, involved fashioning gods in human form. Lubbock believed that this stage arose when royal power became linked with divine power: at his death, a human king would become associated with the gods. Lubbock concluded that in the earliest manifestations of religion, theological notions about a soul, a creator, an afterlife, or a supernatural realm would have been vague, but eventually there emerged belief in "universal, independent, endless existence."

Another set of stages has been set forth by Merlin Donald, a psychologist, neural anthropologist, and cognitive neuroscientist who draws on a century's worth of scientific research beyond what was available to Lubbock. Donald sees the roots of religion reaching back long before humans arrived on the scene. As long as two million years ago, there emerged in primates and eventually humans a "mimetic" culture that was pre-language and based on gesture and imitation. It gave rise to ritual, which is so very effective in making beliefs feel real—and though it predated religion, it still lies at its very heart. Early people participating in ritual likely experienced a "collective effervescence" arising from the sense that those gathered were special, bonded in the moment. We still do: it's that electrical current that courses through a gathering of people in St. Peter's Square when we witness the pope hugging a child or whenever we hear a powerful exhortation such as Martin Luther King's "I Have a Dream" speech.

In addition to ritual, mimetic culture enabled the development of language anywhere from 100,000 to 250,000 years ago. It was about that time that our ancestors realized they had a past, a present, and a future, and they started telling stories, first through oral and much later through written expression. Eventually we reached a theoretic stage when we began to question our old narratives and beliefs. This development made possible the Axial Age, an era midway between the development of writing and our own time, a time of great cultural, philosophical, and religious innovation manifested in Greece, India, and China between the eighth and the third centuries BCE. It was during that time that we began to think about how we think and gave birth to the world's great historical religions that are still alive today.

BUT WE ARE GETTING AHEAD of ourselves. There is scant available evidence from Paleolithic peoples, who lived as early as 3.3 million years ago, that indicate there was music, possibly song and dance and ritual. Thus we need to reconstruct how religious belief developed, weaving together the living evidence of contemporary primal peoples with that of long-gone primal cultures.

In *The World's Religions*, scholar Huston Smith set forth guiding principles: primal peoples are neither backward nor uncivilized; they are apart from us, and their oral mode of expression is different from, not inferior to, our literacy. In preliterate societies, anything that must be remembered must be spoken among people. Memory is collective, and its accumulation and refinement of information serve as an "ongoing, empowering seminar."

The beliefs of primal peoples do not emphasize an afterlife, although there are many stories about where we might go after death. Their sense of time, place, and nature is firmly rooted in the present. Time is based not on chronological sequence but on causation, so that what is "past" is what is closer to the origins of things. The cycle of the seasons is a constant backdrop untouched by time, for each year the world is renewed in its original sanctity. Primal peoples are present in many different dimensions, which they regard as "everywhen." We moderns are used to the notion of "everywhere" but not that of "everywhen." We have lost this rich way of apprehending and experiencing reality.

Primal peoples are embedded in a concrete place in which all things have their rightful position in the sacred order. They are embedded in their tribal relationships, in every aspect of their lives together, as well as in nature. They recognize a common, shared life between humans and animals—and even the inanimate—that is sustained in harmony with the "living womb" of the cosmos. Such embeddedness leads to religious expression that is not so much worship as participation in a sacred order in which they join with each other and with their ancestors—venerated as being closer to the source of things—and with nature itself. Everything is sacred; there is no need to define it as such through religion. Nor is there any need to focus on another life separate from this one—life is everywhere, and everywhen.

THE LONGEST CONTINUOUS HISTORY of any human culture—going back 50,000 to 65,000 years—is that of aboriginal Australians, who are firmly embedded in the sacred order. Their religion is Tjukurrupa, the Dreaming, which exists before and after life on earth. Dreaming stories are passed down, following the precedent of the ancestors, and told in many ways, through music, dance, and art. Images of the Wandjina, powerful cloud and rain spirits, are repainted regularly, image over image over image. The expression of the Dreaming in rituals is an essential responsibility and source of virtue for Dreamers, and is known as "looking after country."

The religious world of Dreamers is populated not by gods but by legendary figures who originated hunting, love, maleness, and femaleness. A primal person engages in these aspects of life with a sense of profound identification with an originator such as Warramurrungundjui. Human life began when she emerged from the sea, gave birth to the first people, and endowed them with language. She planted food and made waterholes for her offspring, and then turned into a rock.

The ongoing process of identification with the originators serves to link people to their land, their past to their present, in a ritualized life wherein the "everywhen" becomes the now. Not surprisingly, death is not seen as a cessation of life, which is a never-ending cycle. Rites conducted over the deceased are aimed at moving her along to her next phase of existence. There is a sense that the life subsequent to this one will be lived out in a remote location—under the ground or the sea, or in the sky-world. It may not be much different from the life the deceased person just concluded, although some part of her may merge with ancestral figures or even become a spirit trickster.

SUCH RADICAL INTEGRATION with the natural order of things is seldom encountered in the modern world, but now and then we get a glimpse. The priest and social psychologist Diarmuid O'Murchu tells a story of the Moken tribe on the west coast of Thailand. Theirs is a nomadic, sea-based culture; they can see dolphins seventy-five feet underwater. Early one morning in 2004, they observed that the waters were receding and that fish were leaping up and down. Their leaders quickly discerned a great disruption in the order of their world. The Moken fled the area and survived the horrific tsunami that engulfed that part of Southeast Asia. O'Murchu marvels at their indigenous wisdom that we moderns have lost. "It was immersion in the Earth, not escape from it, that defined our sacredness," he wrote. "The Earth itself was perceived to be a living organism pulsating with the heartbeat of God."

IN EVEN THE EARLIEST MANIFESTATIONS of religion, there are stories and practices in which certain living people visit the spirit world, indicating belief in life beyond this one. James George Frazer, a father of modern anthropology, studied the concept of immortality among primal peoples in North America, Asia, and Oceania. In all three places, people believe there are two different souls or spirits. They make the distinction between a "free soul" that leaves the body during a dream or trance and a "body soul" that stays behind. They also distinguish between a life soul that provides vitality for the body and a "death soul" that is freed at death.

The ultimate fate of souls varies in these religions, and there are no distinctions between heaven and hell, or nirvana and the cycle of reincarnation. Souls might be reborn or not, or may fail a trial of ordeals and never reach the land of the dead. The manner of one's death might affect one's fate in the afterlife as well. On one island in Micronesia, lots were drawn among the living to decide whether the soul would continue to exist in felicitous circumstances or disappear from both the living and the dead by being smashed between two rocks.

In some belief systems, pleasant or unpleasant afterlives served as rewards or punishments for a person's behavior during earthly life, an early manifestation of what would become powerful teachings on salvation and damnation in religions such as Islam and Christianity. But what was considered good or evil conduct varied considerably. Frazer recorded several ways in which one's fate could be decided: only those Fiji warriors who had killed and eaten many enemies could achieve paradise, while everybody else went underwater to Murimuria, where the dead pounded mud with clubs. Bachelors were prone to get caught by monsters and have their souls smashed on rocks. Women who did not have tattoos were tortured.

What was considered to be sinful and what constituted an appropriate punishment may seem bizarre or amusing to us. Why these were matters of such great importance may not be something we can comprehend, but what is clear is that sin can be socially constructed to fulfill some purpose.

Different fates based on this life could also be the result of social status, which would be galling to most of us. The afterlife could be the abode of aristocrats, with souls of commoners being destroyed by death. Sometimes aristocrats got to go upward to heaven while commoners went down to hell under the earth. We find many of these characteristic beliefs among the Mapuche, an indigenous people living in the far reaches of Argentina and Chile who remained independent until the late nineteenth century. The Museo Chileno de Arte Precolombino in Santiago has a display of *chemamulles*, small wooden statues that the ancient Mapuche placed on the tombs of their loved ones. The *chemamulles* assisted the spirits of the deceased in their journey to the afterlife. Warriors and chiefs went east to roam in Kalfu Mapu, a blue land of volcanoes. Everybody else headed west to eat bitter potatoes beyond the sea. Interestingly, there is some evidence that sweet potatoes had been introduced into the Mapuche diet around 700 CE by travelers from Polynesia. Thus the common folk's fate of eating bitter potatoes seems punitive, although the fate of the head honchos does not seem altogether attractive, either. In any case, neither group is transported to another world.

Indeed, there is no distinct line between this world and some other in the worldview of primal peoples, unlike what we find in historical religions where the line is clear and definitive. The land of the dead, the world beyond, may for primal believers be distant or close, hidden by rocks, beyond the sea, in our universe or a parallel one. People did not have to be dead to visit the Ghost Land, although as the inhabitants of the island of Yap have it, we are losing our ability to do so, for we have lost the secret of ascent.

I ENCOUNTERED PEOPLE who have made otherworldly journeys in many religions, as well as in the contemporary paranormal practice of out-of-body experience. Such exploration dates back thousands of years. In the caves of Lascaux, there is an Ice Age–era painting of a wounded bison and a dead man who may be a shaman in a trance. And the bird on top of a pole might refer to the ascension and flight of shamans. Such early visual art may have portrayed not only hunting and fertility figures but also transcendence of death.

The shaman is a special character in primal religions, a spiritual savant who perceives spiritual reality directly, and in turn affects physical reality through spiritual means, such as healing the sick through exorcism. He— or she, as a shaman is often a woman—makes contact with the parallel universe through a trance, summoning spirits to this world and traveling to the spirit realm. Performing for an individual, family, or tribe, the shaman enacts symbolic encounters with death, through seizures, illness, or ritual.

Among the Inuit, there is a process called "soul pursuit," made necessary by the loss of various spirits, or souls, in a human. A family might request a shaman to heal a loved one who has lost her soul, and the shaman

Cave painting of bird-headed man at Lascaux

searches, recovers, and reinstalls it in her body. There are Australian tribes where the shaman is dismembered by spirits in a dark cave, after which he ascends to the sky with the help of magic crystals. Iglulik Inuit shamans journey down to the ocean floor to placate the erratic mother of sea creatures who rules over the dead. Among the peoples of the Altai Mountains in Mongolia, the shaman flies up through the smoke hole in his tent or climbs a pole in a symbolic ascent through the seven levels of heaven.

In the 1960s, American anthropologist Ellen Basso lived among a tribe in central Brazil, the Kalapalo. Their shamans undergo rigorous training and are invested in a public ceremony. In their rituals, they "sing into being" powerful figures who were present at the beginning of things. They then reenact the mythical relationship between these beings and humans. Kalapalo shamans use their power for good, although there are also witches who use it for evil, for which they may be killed. As in other primal religions, Kalapalo shamans journey beyond the earthly realm, to the sky village near the sunrise where their powerful ancestors, the Dawn People, dwell.

Basso gives us a rare glimpse of a primal people's version of the afterlife. After death and burial, the shadow of the deceased makes a goodbye visit to her family, eating food they have prepared for her. She then travels eastward toward the sunrise, up into the sky to the village of the dead. A relative there helps her to navigate a slippery bridge after which she comes to a central plaza where she meets Sakufenu, whose body is the source of all people. Sakufenu nurses new souls until they are strong enough to join others. Souls do not have to work for their food in this heaven, as there is a magical silo in the plaza, so they are free to sing and dance into eternity.

BLACK ELK WAS A LAKOTA SIOUX SHAMAN who straddled primal and modern worlds. His visions took him to the sky-world that is the destination of the Lakota after death. At the age of nine he was taken by thunder beings to the world beyond, where he met the grandfathers from the four quarters of the universe, the earth, and the sky. They gave Black Elk powerful gifts of healing and spiritual insight: a cup of sky, the power of life; a cleansing wind and herbs of power; a peace pipe, and the friendship of the wings of the air, the winds, and the stars. Black Elk also received a bright red stick that burst forth with leaves, branches, and singing birds. It stands at the center of the Lakota sacred hoop, their circle of life.

The ancient grandfather of the east gave him courage to face the troubles that his people were to encounter. A great voice told Black Elk to join a gathering of his people, who were dying, and to place the red stick at the center of his people's hoop, the sacred circle of their community. The voice declared the hoop to be holy and endless, and directed the people to take to the road, where the grandfathers would walk with them. But the way was difficult; their hoop was breaking and their holy tree was dying. Chaos ensued, but Black Elk, with his new powers, drew the sky horses together into a great hoop around a magnificent black stallion. The stallion sang, all creation danced, and the universe grew silent.

Black Elk found himself on the highest mountain, above the whole hoop of the world. He received a revelation of the sacred order of things: "While I stood there I saw more than I can tell and I understood more than I saw, for I was seeing in a sacred manner the shapes of all things in the spirit, and the shape of all shapes as they must live together like one being. And I saw that the sacred hoop of my people was one of many hoops that made one circle, wide as daylight and as starlight, and in the center grew one mighty flowering tree to shelter all the children of one mother and one father. And I saw that it was holy."

Black Elk continued to have visions of his people and their travails, and revelations of the true nature of things, which he saw as darkened dreams, shadows cast on the earth from the bright heavens. He practiced as a medicine man and cured the sick, although he declared his power to be from "the outer world"; that "the visions and ceremonies had only made me like a hole through which the power could come."

After a jarring interlude during which he goes on a road show to England, performing for Wasichus (greedy people), Black Elk returned to find his people broken and exiled after the Black Hills Treaty of 1889. He learned the Ghost Dance, a ceremony said to bring back dead Indians, return the buffalo, and restore the native way of life. When he danced, he saw the sacred hoop of his people and a beautiful flowering tree. He had entered the land of the departed, but his people sent him back to earth. There he saw that the dancing people were silent, and the tree dead. He had failed to follow his great vision, and not long after there came the massacre at Wounded Knee.

Black Elk recounted his story "as from a lonely hilltop." "I, to whom so great a vision was given in my youth . . . you see me now a pitiful old man who has done nothing, for the nation's hoop is broken and scattered. There is no center any longer, and the sacred tree is dead." But he remains faithful to the vision, "for such things are of the spirit, and it is in the darkness of their eyes that men get lost."

Black Elk took no credit for his extraordinary experiences. They were gifts from the powers that ordered his universe, he said, and his part in that order was to be open to where they led him, to life beyond and back again.

Part II

ANCIENT
RELIGIONS

FOUR

An Imagined World

You save the one in the netherworld.

• A PRIEST OF AMUN, C. 1330 BCE

I n Egypt, early glimmers of hope for life beyond are found in Neolithic graves stocked with provisions. Beginning around 2200 BCE, there is evidence of beliefs about divinity and the afterlife in the ancient pyramid texts. Still, ancient Egypt, as archaeologist Barry Kemp confesses, is very much an imagined world: "The more I try to make sense of the facts, the more what I write is speculative."

Egyptian religion was a rich tapestry of beliefs rooted in nature, with myriad figures and overlapping, sometimes contradictory stories. The sky was a goddess, and the earth a god, as was their ruler: Horus, "the one on high." Rituals dating back to the third millennium BCE did not feature humans reaching for the gods; instead priests played the roles of gods, uttering their sacred words. Through such rituals the pharaoh, the god/king, maintained the cosmic order, the daily passage of sun and yearly flooding of the Nile.

Although much of Egyptian religion remains a mystery, belief and practice regarding a life beyond were from the beginning its most pronounced feature. At its heart is the myth of Isis and her devoted husband, the beneficent king Osiris. After Osiris's evil brother Seth killed him and scattered parts of him all over Egypt, Isis found all but his phallus, which had been thrown into the Nile. She put Osiris back together along with an artificial penis and restored him to life through mummification. Alas, mummification could not bring back Osiris's powers of regeneration, so Isis impregnated herself with his relics and gave birth to Horus.

Osiris became lord of the underworld, while Horus stayed on earth to fight Seth, and ultimately prevailed. The Pharaoh was seen as both Horus and Osiris, avatar of this world and of the next. As Horus, he was obliged to govern the living well; as Osiris, the dead. The priests of Osiris accompanied the pharaoh to the afterlife and were actually more powerful than he. They decided who would attain immortality: those who amassed wealth to bring along, those who had proper funerals involving ritual mummification and burial, and those who had observed correct behavior.

By the second millennium BCE, there is clear documentation of religious belief in an afterlife. Stories, hymns, and a body of literature known as wisdom texts explore the nature of divinity as well as the relationships among the gods, morality, and human social conditions. In considering the afterlife, there was a sense that there might be consequences for good and bad behavior, which led to the emergence of moral values and the idea of a final judgment. This was a signal development in the history of religion: we humans came to see ourselves as part of a moral universe. But already there was a sense we might need a messiah to bring about our salvation. As a priest of Amun wrote around 1330 BCE: "You came to save me . . . you save the one in the netherworld . . . you are the one who comes from afar."

THERE ARE SOURCES BESIDES TEXTS—tombs, mummification, funerary objects—that help us understand Egyptian belief about the afterlife, which was not so much a separate world as a continuation of this one. Spells found in pyramid texts describe pyramids as ladders for the pharaoh to ascend to heaven, made for him by his father Ra (associated with Horus). They were constructed according to geographical and astral features, as at Giza, where the pyramid complex was laid out in the directions of the compass and lined up with stars that represented immortality. Eventually, stars that periodically rose and set in the sky—stars that never rested—came to symbolize regeneration, guiding the dead toward immortality. The tombs themselves were symbols of prosperity and harmony between this world and the next, full of supplies for a life that was clearly expected to be physical, and pleasurable.

Egyptian burial practices have been reconstructed from tombs and their contents. As far back as the third millennium BCE mummification was an essential practice, reflecting the belief that survival of the body is essential to survival of the soul. The process began with the removal of internal organs, which were placed in jars representing the four sons of Horus. The heart was mummified and put back into the body, while the brain was discarded as being unimportant. This is both amusing and ironic to those of us living in the age of expanded consciousness, rooted in our brains— they may be all we'll need to survive in future times when death may not be so final.

But the Egyptians counted on the survival of the body, and that would require manual labor. Dating from the early second millennium BCE, mummy-like figurines were included in tombs to assist their owner in the afterlife, many inscribed with a spell to bring them to life as needed. At first, just one servant was installed in a tomb, but eventually burials contained one for each day of the year. There were commercial models, too: little granaries, breweries, bakeries, and butcher shops. For further provisioning, there might be a "soul house" at the entrance to the tomb shaft, where offerings to the dead could be made by loved ones left behind.

Rituals were as important in ensuring immortality as tombs or mummification. They acted out processes such as revivification, imparting new life after death. Spells mirroring the rituals of royal funerals guided the deceased to the final resting place. Properly enacted funeral rituals would inspire the mummy to make the voyage to Abydos in Upper Egypt, the sacred area belonging to Osiris. This accounts for the boat models included in tombs; they symbolized that final journey, or perhaps conveyed the soul to its next life.

———

THE ANCIENT EGYPTIANS BELIEVED that a person had various forms: a body, which was not expected to rise physically from the dead; a shadow that we would call a soul; and one's name, which was the form of soul that would exist as long as one was remembered. The heart contained emotion, will, and thought, and its mummification ensured their survival.

The *ka* was the spiritual aspect of a human that could exist after death through a surrogate, an image of the deceased such as a statue or painting on the tomb wall. The *ka*'s house was the tomb with the mummified body in a sarcophagus, although it could also dwell in the sky. The *ka* still needed food, drink, clothes, even entertainment—thus the provisions supplied through models, images, and spells. Such efforts to ensure the physical survival of the *ka*'s surrogates are unique among the world's religions; soon enough we would separate the soul from the body.

Only slightly less mystifying than the *ka* is the *ba*, another part of the soul that represents the personality and power of the individual and can fly between the tomb and the world beyond. In early times only the pharaoh had a *ba*, so that he could become divine after death; later the nobility and royal bureaucrats acquired *bas* so as to participate in the afterlife. As for common people, they eventually gained access as well: texts found inside coffins describe the concern a god has for the poor as well as the rich, taking care of them by sending them winds and floods, a care that may have continued through the passage of death and beyond.

Finally, there is the *akh*, the transfigured person in the afterlife, which maintained the person's identity. One became an *akh* as the result of proper burial rituals and continued to play a part in lives of the living who made offerings to them with pleas for help. The grim alternative to achieving *akh* status was to be dead forever.

As religious belief evolved over time, more and more people became eligible for an afterlife, and the idea of final judgment of the individual took root in Egyptian thought. If one was not royal, one needed to be morally upright.

In the judgment hall, the heart of the deceased, its seat of intelligence, would be weighed on the scales of justice, to be deemed worthy of joining Osiris or being devoured by the monster Ammut. Some accounts tell of a series of challenges—such as gates guarded by demons, caverns, and threatening spirits—that the deceased must face before reaching the judgment hall. In others the challenges come after judgment as he makes his way to the afterlife. By the sixteenth century BCE, help was available in *The Book of Going Forth by Day*, a compilation of ancient funeral practices, helpful spells, and instructions on how to reach the afterlife and to live in the day, not just at night like ghosts.

And what did the afterlife hold for an ancient Egyptian? There was some variation depending on which cult one practiced and when one lived. Some looked forward to Ma'ati, a land presided over by Ma'at, goddess of justice and faith whom only the pure of heart could see. For reasons that remain mysterious, the departed brought with them flames and crystal scepters and buried them there. A more common version was A'aru, the Field of Reeds, a perfected reflection of this life, although not so perfect if you hadn't brought servants with you to do the work, or if you were one of the servants, as the earthly social order remained intact. But earthly life was seen as worth living forever. One could look forward to bountiful harvests, to banquets where "cakes of Osiris" were served, and to floating on the Lake of Flowers, fanned by pleasant breezes. One would live forever with family, friends, pets, and with Osiris and the other Egyptian gods.

IN CONTRAST TO THE TEXTS left by the Egyptians, those of the Sumerians, who arrived in Mesopotamia around 3300–3000 BCE, are a treasure trove describing fantastic sights and experiences in the abodes of the gods.

The oldest story of the Sumerian afterlife that we know, from the second millennium BCE, is that of Adapa, a famous exorcist whose powers were held to be comparable to the king's, and a trustworthy guide to the afterlife. Adapa goes fishing one day, and the wind overturns his boat. In a fury he breaks the wings of the wind. The Sky God Anu is angry and orders Adapa brought to him. Fortunately, Adapa is protected by Ea, the god of water, who instructs him to be humble and unkempt, and seemingly in mourning. Ea meanwhile tells the gatekeepers of heaven that Adapa is grieving for them. Thus when Adapa arrives, they receive him warmly and send a good account of him to Anu, who in turn extends to him the hospitality of heaven. Adapa is given clothes and oil, as well as bread and the water of life, which will make him immortal. But Ea has told him not to eat or drink in heaven, and in being obedient to Ea Adapa violates Anu's hospitality and loses his chance at immortality. Alas, so does the rest of humanity.

There are similarities between the story of Adapa and that of Adam and Eve, who lose immortality as a result of succumbing to the temptation of forbidden knowledge. Adam and Eve are granted moral discernment, while Adapa acquires great knowledge, and they all are granted clothes. (Unfortunately, the Sumerian text breaks off at this point, so we do not know how Adapa later fared, but both stories teach us that we cannot live forever.)

THE SUMERIAN GILGAMESH EPIC is the oldest recorded story about human life beyond death in the Western world, dating back as far as 3000 BCE. While the pharaohs stepped up into the sky that humans shared with the gods and Adapa passed through a gate into a different realm, the hero Gilgamesh roamed an expanded universe with three domains: the heaven of the gods, the earth of humans, and the underworld. Gilgamesh's story served as a guide to the grieving in Mesopotamia, where the prevailing attitude toward death was one of resignation. There may have been some notions about an afterlife, but there was no system for reward and punishment that would have provided different experiences for different people. It was nothing but a house of dust.

Gilgamesh was fashioned in part by gods, so he was, weirdly enough, two-thirds god and one-third mortal. He was an impetuous, violent man whose behavior concerned both gods and men, and his trials recorded in the epic served as his education for ruling his kingdom of Uruk. The gods made a twin/friend for Gilgamesh named Enkidu, who lived wild among animals until he was initiated into human sexuality and lost his ability to speak with them. He was educated to become a worthy companion for the king, and they grew close.

The epic (of which there are many versions) tells of the adventures (not all heroic) through which the two bound their friendship. Their pillaging angers the goddess Inanna, and to make things worse Gilgamesh kills her special bull and spurns her amorous advances. He clearly prizes the male realm of war and adventure over the female realm of marriage and family, and to accept her proposals might trap him in the underworld. Inanna vows that either Gilgamesh or Enkidu should die. Enkidu succumbs to illness, but before dying he dreams of his final destination, the House of Dust, from which there is no return. There he finds priests of purification and of ecstasy, Ereshkigal, the Queen of the Netherworld, and other gods. Its human inhabitants, who wear garments of feathers, live in darkness, drink dirt, and eat clay. All around are heaps of royal crowns of mighty rulers who now wait on Anu, the father of the gods, and Enlil, the god of storms and of destiny, serving them cooked meats and sweets and cool water. When Enkidu dies and reaches the underworld, he turns into a bird-like creature, a sign that he has become a ghost.

Gilgamesh observes the rites for honoring the dead: He lays aside his good clothes and head coverings and allows himself to become dirty and unkempt. He fasts and flagellates himself and performs ceremonies of purification before returning to his normal ways. But he is still grief-stricken at the loss of Enkidu and sets out to find the land of immortality. Traveling westward, Gilgamesh tunnels through the underground realm where the sun travels at night, crosses the corrosive sea of mortality, and struggles toward the ends of the earth where Utnapishtim, the flood hero, resides. This Noah-like character and his wife are the only humans ever to have been granted immortality by the gods, for having saved human and animal life in their great boat. Gilgamesh undergoes trials and fails the test of staying awake for six days and seven nights. Alas, he is unfit for eternal wakefulness. Only gods live forever: humans can become wise but not immortal.

FIVE

The Realm of Endless Light

The soul of the Righteous . . . has the feeling of
abiding in the middle of plants and breathing
fragrances. It feels an intensely fragrant wind
blowing from the south.

• FROM THE HADOKHT

From Mesopotamian otherworld travelers we turn to Zoroastrianism, the official religion of Persia from 600 BCE to 650 CE. Its founder, Zoroaster, was appointed to preach the truth by the god Ahura Mazda, creator of the spiritual and the material worlds and sovereign lawgiver in his kingdom of justice. Ahura Mazda was surrounded by beings called Beneficent Immortals who represented godly qualities and led humans to Ahura Mazda, bringing the spiritual and material worlds close together. But there was an ongoing challenge to this order in the person of Angra Mainyu.

In the beginning, there had been a great convocation of the offspring of Ahura Mazda where the Beneficent Immortals freely chose to be in favor of life, while Angra Mainyu chose the opposite. These choices were the origin of good and evil, which informed two dominions: one of justice and truth and one of lies. Every individual human and spirit was required to choose freely which to belong to, and the decision was a final one. The result was a universe of warring dominions, but in the end Ahura Mazda would prevail over Angra Mainyu, thereby ending both moral and cosmic dualism.

Zoroaster's teachings were based on this cosmic history, addressing death, judgment, and the afterlife, as well as the significance of our every thought, deed, and word for our ultimate reward or punishment. As humanity made moral progress, it would cease to be interested in food. Eating was associated with dying, so giving up food meant perfecting oneself, becoming free from digestion and corruption, and this freedom signaled the ascent to immortality. Purification took place at individual death as well. Corpses were left out in the sun, first on stone outcroppings but later in a high enclosure called a tower of silence. The body belonged in the air, not in the ground with demons who, according to the Law Against the Demons, would "rush . . . to defile him from the nose of the dead, from the eye, from the tongue, from the jaws, from the sexual organ, from the hinder parts." Such an unfortunate person would be unclean forever. A year in the sun led to a much more felicitous fate: the body would eventually be resurrected.

In Mesopotamian belief, even before Zoroastrianism, the soul hovered around the corpse for three days before beginning its journey to the next life. First it would travel to the Bridge of the Requiter, where the person's deeds would be weighed in a balance, and the soul would have to make its way across the bridge. For evildoers, the bridge would become so narrow that falling was inevitable. A soul might also meet its own deeds through its daena, or conscience, which would appear as a beautiful maid or an ugly hag who guided the soul to its proper reward or punishment.

Zoroastrians believed that souls would be judged by Ahura Mazda, and sent either to the kingdom of everlasting joy and light or to the region of horror and darkness. Those who had chosen evil would be condemned not only by Ahura Mazda but by their own consciences as well. "Thus does the evil one's conscience forfeit the assurance of the straight path; His Soul stripped naked shall be afraid at the Bridge."

At the end of time, the forces of good and evil would do battle, and good would triumph. All souls would have been punished sufficiently in the time since their death, and there would be a general resurrection on the great day of Pahlavi. The Zoroastrian resurrected body would be spiritual and perfected. This notion of a resurrected body is mysterious, or at least paradoxical—how can the decidedly physical body become spiritual? The nature of the resurrected body would be described in various ways in later religions, but to date there is no clear consensus among believers.

FOR A FIRSTHAND ACCOUNT of the Zoroastrian afterlife, we look to the Righteous Viraz, whose story originated in ancient times, reached its final form in the tenth century CE, and is charmingly depicted in the late-eighteenth-century Rylands Persian Manuscript. The story is rooted in a tradition pre-dating Zoroastrianism, in which brotherhoods of warriors underwent shamanistic ecstasies and made journeys to a heaven full of ritual singing. Zoroaster targeted these brotherhoods for reform, but such practices continued, including the use of various drugs to unite the traveler with the Beneficent Immortals in an ecstatic union that would yield knowledge beyond perception and language.

In Zoroastrian tradition, a righteous seer could serve as a link to the afterlife, giving the living a glimpse of what lay ahead. Viraz is elected by an assembly of priests to test the truth of Zoroastrian faith by taking a seven-day trip beyond, during which time his body will be watched over by his seven sister-wives and the priests of Ahura Mazda. After saying farewell to his sister-wives, Viraz makes out a will and performs funeral rituals for himself. He then lies in a fire temple, perfumed and clothed in new garments, and drinks a potion of wine and henbane.

The soul of Viraz leaves his body and is met by divine guides. They take three steps, corresponding to good thoughts, words, and deeds, to the Bridge of the Requiter. Viraz stays there until the third day, as do all righteous souls who spend the first three nights beside their bodies rejoicing in liberation. At the end of the third night, he has "the feeling of abiding in the middle of plants and breathing fragrances. [He] feels an intensely fragrant wind blowing from the south. The soul of the Righteous breathes this wind through [his] nostrils."

Viraz then meets his daena, who is, due to his own virtue, great, good, victorious, without blemish, and she smells nice. He crosses the Bridge, which has grown wide to accommodate him, and is granted a vision of the god Rashn. In the Rylands Manuscript, Viraz waits patiently as his deeds are weighed in a golden balance in his hand. He goes on to purgatory, where people whose deeds were equally good and bad undergo alternating waves of heat and cold as they await resurrection. He is then guided to the three levels of heaven: the stars where those who had good thoughts dwell; the moon, for those who spoke good words; and the sun, for those who did good deeds.

The fourth level is the realm of endless light, the paradise of Ahura Mazda, where Viraz finds a place already prepared for him. He is introduced to courtiers of the sovereign god—including Zoroaster—and finally to Ahura Mazda himself, who orders that he be shown the rewards for the good and the punishments for the wicked. Viraz encounters the souls who make it to heaven: for example, people who have killed lots of reptiles and women who have "satisfied their husbands and lords, and were submissive, respectful, and obedient to them." These virtuous souls can be seen in the manuscript enjoying themselves in a heavenly garden. Viraz also learns that no tears should be shed for the departed, as they flow into an afterlife river, swelling it so that it is difficult for souls to cross.

The second part of Viraz's story reveals the starkly dualistic Zoroastrian cosmos in which Ahura Mazda is opposed to Angra Mainyu. Accordingly, paradise is opposed to hell, good to evil, and this dualism is expressed in fragrant vs. foul scents. Viraz returns to the Bridge and is overwhelmed by a frigid stinking wind that blows from the direction of Angra Mainyu and his demons. In this evil wind Viraz sees his own daena "in the form of a naked whore, rotten, filthy, with crooked knees, with projecting buttocks."

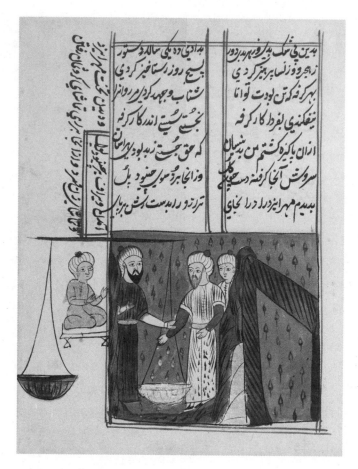

**Illustration of the Righteous Viraz
from the Rylands Persian Manuscript 41**

The structure of hell mirrors that of heaven, with four underground levels. Sinners suffer for deeds that to us might not warrant damnation. Along with the usual apostates and witches, Viraz sees women who had touched water and fire while menstruating, and people who had peed standing up. There is a pervasive emphasis on pollution, accompanied by great olfactory and gustatory woe—indeed, the damned are all gorging themselves on excrement. The Rylands Manuscript provides vivid depictions of such punishments—one shows people being eaten by demons for not wearing a sacred girdle, another a woman being hung upside down for disobeying her husband. The very bottom is Angra Mainyu's hell, for the most abominable sinners, such as a woman who licks a red-hot oven for having been sharp-tongued and not consenting to sex with her husband, and women who wore makeup.

Eventually, Viraz is led back to Ahura Mazda, and his journey culminates in a vision of the divinity as pure light. He then returns to this world to recount his tale.

ZOROASTRIAN THOUGHT WAS WIDELY INFLUENTIAL from the mid-third century BCE to the mid-third century CE, a time of greatly enhanced communication enabled by the international use of the Greek language and the flourishing of both the Roman and Persian empires. The resulting cosmopolitanism enabled religions to spread and to influence each other. The Persians ruled over the Hebrews for two hundred years, and thus there would have been contact between their two religions, particularly during the Babylonian Captivity of 597–539 BCE. Certainly, there are many common elements in Zoroastrian and Jewish theology. Both feature a personal God, revealed by prophets, whom humans will ultimately encounter face-to-face. They tell similar stories of a dualistic cosmos, of cosmic battles between good and evil, of travelers to the world beyond. And both look toward final, bodily resurrection, and a communal afterlife.

SIX

As Though It Were a Dream

Souls of Poets dead and gone
What Elysium have ye known . . .

• JOHN KEATS

The origin of ideas about the afterlife among ancient Greeks and Romans lay in the division of the kingdom of Kronos by his triumphant sons. Zeus took the sky, Poseidon the sea, Hades the underworld, and they shared the earth and its inhabitants. Over the course of time and the spread of Greek civilization, various notions of the gods and the afterlife emerged in myths, epics, essays, and philosophical and travel writing. The evidence shows conflicting views of what the Greeks believed happens after death. Is there a shade that separates from the body? If so, where does it go? Does it retain its individual identity? Does its fate depend on the life it lived on earth? What will the afterlife be like? And what role do the gods play in the fate of humans?—a question that gave rise to stories still bursting with life.

The *Iliad* and the *Odyssey* were composed in the eighth century BCE. They described the Greek gods as living in a world seemingly as real as ours, and often manifesting themselves to us. As writer Roberto Calasso describes it, "The gods of Olympus agreed to appear as entirely human. It was the first time a group of divinities had renounced abstraction and animal heads." They would visit us as "Unknown Guests" and feast with us at important weddings; go adventuring with our young men and ravish our young women. And we would visit them: there were tales of ascents to heavenly realms and a vast body of myths and mysteries that described the gloomy underground realm of Hades, some with maps to find the way.

There was also articulate opposition to any notion of life after death among various schools of Greek philosophy. Epicurus was adamant: *non fui, fui, non sum, non curo*: I was not; I was; I am not; I do not suffer. There was no reason to be afraid: "The most terrifying of evils, death, is nothing to us, since when we exist, death is not present. But when death is present, then we do not exist. It is nothing, then, either to the living or to the dead, since concerning the former it does not exist, and concerning the latter, they no longer exist." The Stoics (beginning in the third century BCE) were more willing to speculate. They believed that "the soul is both corporeal and survives death; but it is perishable, while that of the universe is imperishable. . . . Cleanthes believes that all souls exist until the Conflagration, but Chrysippus that only the souls of the wise remain."

Fortunately, such gloomy perspectives did not dissuade the Greeks from imagining life beyond and devising ways to get there. The mystery cult of Demeter held out the promise that its devotees would fare well in the afterlife. The cult was grounded in the story of Demeter, goddess of fertility and the harvest, and her daughter Persephone, who was kidnapped by Hades, the ruler of the underworld. Demeter was able to free her for six months every year, rendering the earth fertile during that time. She was in mourning for her daughter for the other six months, and the earth lay fallow. The story reflects not only the cycle of seasons but also the ritual concern for the dead, and it inspired the Eleusinian Mysteries. The mysteries involved the use of a barley brew to produce an altered state of mind, sacred processions, and purification rituals—all designed to provide the initiate with an experience of overcoming death and being reborn. As the Hymn of Demeter tells it, "Happy is he among men upon earth who has seen these mysteries; but he who is uninitiated and who has no part in them never has a lot of good things once he is dead, down in the darkness and gloom."

———

HOMER WAS THE FATHER of a long Western literary tradition about travel to other worlds. In the eleventh book of *The Odyssey*, Odysseus is ordered by Circe, goddess of magic, to travel to the underworld to consult the prophet Tiresias about his future. Guided by Circe, he crosses the river Oceanus and digs a trench on the shore into which he pours various libations as well as the blood of a sheep he has sacrificed. Swarms of "poor feckless ghosts" surround him, and Odysseus allows them to feed on the blood for strength to speak. One is Tiresias, and he promises Odysseus that although the journey will be arduous, he will reach his home in Ithaca, and "your life shall ebb away very gently when you are full of years and peace of mind, and your people shall bless you."

Scores of other figures appear, and Odysseus's trip to the underworld becomes a tale of encounters with the dead; we are given no glimpse of what it might be like there. When he does describe a setting it is the back-drop of a vision of a particular person such as Minos in his spacious house, attended by ghosts as he sits in judgment on the dead, or Tantalus standing in a lake that dries up whenever he attempts to drink, or Sisyphus endlessly rolling his rock up the hill only to have it thunder down again.

The most touching passage tells of Odysseus meeting his mother, Anti-clea. It is steeped in the longing to be reunited with lost loved ones that lies at the heart of human imaginings of life to come. They speak of his wan-derings, of family, and how Anticlea died pining for her son. He ponders this in his heart and tries to embrace her, but she slips through his arms, saying: "All people are like this when they are dead. The sinews no longer hold the flesh and bones together; these perish in the fierceness of consum-ing fire as soon as life has left the body, and the soul flits away as though it were a dream."

Orpheus traveled to the underworld as well, a story full of love and, once again, loss. Celebrated as the greatest of poets and musicians, he could charm beasts, move trees to dance, and cause rivers to change course. At their wedding, his bride Eurydice fell into a nest of vipers and died from a bite on her heel. Orpheus was overwhelmed when he found her body and played such mournful music that even the gods wept. He made the journey beneath the earth determined to bring Eurydice back. Hades and Persephone, moved by his music, allowed Eurydice to follow Orpheus on condition that he not look at her until they had reached the land of the living.

But could a human lover obey such a command? When Orpheus reached daylight, he anxiously glanced back at Eurydice, and she vanished forever. Thereafter Orpheus roamed the earth, forsaking the company of men, playing piteous music on his lyre.

Not everyone was sympathetic to his plight, though. Plato's Phaedrus excoriated him for being a coward, for trying to bring Eurydice back to life rather than giving up his life to be with her in Hades. And he suffered an awful death at the hands of a band of female followers of Dionysus who tore him limb from limb.

WE TURN FROM STORIES of encounters with the afterlife to philosophy that seeks to understand our nature and our fate. The Greek philosopher Plato, using the voice of his teacher Socrates, advised that a great deal can be learned by thinking about death, for which philosophy is a preparation. His philosophical concepts have had a profound effect on Western views of the soul and of life before and after this one.

In the *Apology*, Plato set forth his theory on the soul. He argued that life and death are opposites, like waking and sleeping. And as waking leads to sleeping and vice versa, so does life lead to death, and death to life. There must be something even more basic, something that underlies these changes, and that is the soul.

The soul preexists our birth, and this accounts for what Plato called recollection, through which we have innate knowledge of basic categories such as time and space: we have known before what we learn in this life. Recollection is necessary for abstract thinking, forming ideas, and gaining knowledge. Through recollection, thinking becomes a transcendent act. For Plato, this process demonstrated the immortality of the soul.

Plato's ideas about immortality, based on logical analysis, are clearly a departure from those that involved heroes and cultic ritual. There is a world of difference between the mythical hero Odysseus, who fought with great cunning through whatever it took to get home, and Plato's philosopher in pursuit of wisdom. His ideas also presented a challenge to the common belief, expressed in myth, that souls forgot everything upon crossing the river Lethe on the way to rebirth.

THE *PHAEDO*, known to ancient readers as *On the Soul*, reflects the profound dualism in Plato's thought: our soul is of the invisible, immortal, incorporeal realm, whereas our bodies are of the visible, mortal, corporeal realm, to be discarded at death. Plato describes the journey of the soul, which was embodied as punishment for a fall, but which still harbors an innate affinity for the divine. It longs to return to heaven to live forever in ecstatic contemplation. "After having got rid of the foolishness of the body we shall be pure and have converse with the pure, and know of ourselves the clear light everywhere, which is no other than the light of truth . . . what is purification but the separation of the soul from the body?"

Plato envisions the soul as winged, capable of flying high to where the gods dwell, and thereby nourished. But all souls fall back to earth eventually and as a result become embodied as humans. At the end of the first life, souls follow a familiar path: they are tried and sent either to prison beneath the earth or up to the heavens to pass their time in a manner worthy of the lives they lived as mortals. But after a thousand years, both groups choose a second life. The soul can pass into the life of a beast, and the soul of a beast can take human form. But a soul who has never seen truth at all, who has never been in the company of gods, can never become human. The soul who has lived a good life grows wings again, a process that takes about

10,000 years, and is rewarded by reincarnation into the higher rank of human beings.

However, those who have chosen the life of the philosopher three times in a row have learned to separate the soul from the body and to seek the divine. They have recollected "those things which in times past our soul beheld when it travelled in the company of the gods, and looking high over what we now can see, lifted up [their heads] into the region of eternal essence." Thus they are able to reincarnate in only three thousand years. The ensuing ranks of souls awaiting reincarnation, in order of privilege, include kings, statesmen, doctors, prophets, and poets; after them come manual laborers, sophists, and tyrants. Plato thought women were ontologically inferior, so they are ranked after tyrants but, fortunately, before beasts. We have seen this before, and we will see it again throughout the history of religion: the standard for human nature is male human nature, and women are either denigrated for their feminine nature or ignored.

At the end of the *Phaedo*, Plato describes this common journey of humans toward the divine, pushing off from the earth into the sky. If we can pass through its upper limit, like fish from the sea, we come into the realm of "the true heaven, the true light and the true earth, for the earth here, these stones and the whole region, are spoiled and eaten away."

IN THE *PHAEDO*, Plato explores his vision of life beyond in universal terms, or at least universal male terms. In the tenth book of the *Republic*, he tells the story of a particular man sent on a mission to reveal to humans the secrets of the afterlife. A soldier named Er dies in battle and travels with other souls to a magnificent place where judges decide the path of souls on the basis of how they lived their lives on earth. In a complex process, the good souls are sent through a door to the sky, the bad through another to the earth. Two other doors are for the return passage from the sky and the earth. Clean-looking souls emerge from one, dirty souls from another.

The clean and dirty souls gather on a plain and tell stories of their last millennium. The clean tell of lovely sights and great happiness; the dirty speak of torments tailored to their sins. Er is told to observe all this so he can report back to humankind. After seven days, they all proceed to a place where the Sirens' song echoes with the harmony of the spheres, and they can see the whole universe, including the Spindle of Necessity and her three daughters, the Fates.

The souls, who were supposed to have learned the difference between a good and an evil life, then choose their next lives. Er witnesses animals changing forms and men changing into beasts: Orpheus chooses to become a swan. Er realizes that the clean-looking souls from the sky, who have not been punished, sometimes make bad choices. And the dirty-looking souls, who have been punished, sometimes make good choices: they have learned from their suffering. The moral of the story is that a soul must live an examined life, in whatever phase of existence, to turn its fate toward the good. There are echoes here of the *Phaedo*: in each of our lives in this world, as well as during the periods of reward or punishment in the afterlife, we are to grow wiser and more spiritual.

Their choices having been made, the souls are led to drink from the river Lethe, to forget their former lives. Having fallen asleep, they speed upward like shooting stars to be reborn. Er does not drink from the river and returns to his body, which has not decomposed during the time he has been traveling, and he is now lying on a funeral pyre. His fellow soldiers save him from the fire, and he tells his story of the afterlife to them, and to us.

THE ROMAN POET HORACE WROTE that "captive Greece took captive her savage conqueror, and brought civilization to barbarous Latium." The Greek influence on Roman culture was profound, affecting everything from architecture to philosophy and religion and literature, and was in turn transformed. The sixth book of Virgil's *Aeneid* followed the form of book 11 of Homer's

Odyssey, but Virgil's Roman social context shaped his version of the next life. Cicero in *Scipio's Dream* had encouraged young Romans to become involved in politics and administration, promising eternal reward to those dedicated to the welfare of others. In Virgil's day, as a result of the moral reforms of Caesar Augustus, such service to state was regarded as highly virtuous. Virgil wrote Aeneas's witness of their rewards as proof that a glorious afterlife was available not only to the rich and the well born but also to those who did the basic work of the Empire. The gates of the afterlife had opened wider.

Virgil also incorporated Platonic thought into his vision of the afterlife by adding judgment to Homer's Hades. The afterlife has become a place with different fates for different souls. Heavenly reward or punishment according to one's way of life on earth points to an understanding of an individual self, one that will endure into the next life.

In *The Aeneid*, we find that the situation in the realm of the dead has become more complex since Homer's time. Not all are admitted. There is a realm for punishment, Tartarus, and a realm for reward, Elysium. Aeneas has come to see his father, guided by the Cumaean Sibyl. He arrives at the entrance, where dwell creatures like Fear and Diseases and Hunger, and encounters the shades of those falsely accused and condemned to die, and those of dead babies, crying piteously, consigned to remain forever just outside the gates. Aeneas crosses the river Acheron, where the grim boatman Charon rejects the shades of the unburied, leaving them to float and roam around for a hundred years. Once in the realm of the dead, he visits the Field of Mourning for those unhappy in love, such as his abandoned Dido, and the most remote fields where dwell the shades of fallen warriors.

Aeneas then takes the road to Tartarus, a huge fortress surrounded by a violent river, from which he hears dreadful sounds of suffering. The Sibyl instructs Aeneas on sin and its punishments, which are so numerous that she cannot recount them all. They come at last to Elysium, a brilliantly sunlit, verdant land much like Virgil's native Italian countryside. There dwell soldiers, priests, and learned men who had contributed greatly to Roman society.

Here Aeneas meets his father, Anchises, and embraces him. But Anchises, like Odysseus's mother, slips through his arms. Anchises does not want his son to be mystified about life after death, so he reveals to him its great mysteries. He speaks of the soul being contaminated by its imprisonment in its earthly body, and its necessary purification by wind, water, and fire. He tells of the soul's release to Elysium where all evil is purged, leaving only the spirit's essential flame. This is accomplished after a thousand-year cycle has been completed. At the end of the cycle crowds of souls destined for another life on earth gather to drink of the river Lethe. Freed from fretful memories, they are ready to be born again.

When we consider Plato's and Virgil's notions of the afterlife, we must acknowledge that we don't know the extent to which they reflect, or had any effect on, popular belief in their own day. Such literature would have been accessible only to educated elites. We do know that their development of ideas about the individual, the soul, and the afterlife came to have a powerful influence on future belief.

Part III

JUDAISM

SEVEN

The Eternal Covenant

He set knowledge before them.
He endowed them with the law of life.
He established an eternal covenant with them,
and revealed his judgments to them.

• BOOK OF ECCLESIASTICUS

The history of the Hebrew people is the history of their relationship with their God. It began in Genesis, when Yahweh created humans in his own image, and was formalized in the everlasting sacred covenant he made with Abraham. Their relationship has been dynamic, for Yahweh is not a remote, disinterested God but a God of love.

I once had a student who was having trouble conceiving of God; no image or symbol worked for him. But he said that when he did something kind for someone, opening a door or cleaning up a mess or maybe just listening, he felt something stirring. He said, *God happens.* The Hebrews must have had such a sense—God happened to them in the covenant and through his ongoing revelation, when he reached out to his people and they turned toward him in what Rabbi Abraham Joshua Heschel calls radical amazement.

YAHWEH'S REVELATIONS WERE CLEAR about laws for living in this world here and now but not about what happens after death. Thus the early Hebrews focused on reward or punishment for the whole nation, with earthly life under Yahweh being its own reward. Ideas about the afterlife among the Hebrews emerged as early as the seventh century BCE, but they were not very encouraging. The dead perished entirely or went to Sheol, a gloomy Hades-like place where they were separated on the basis of their faithfulness to the covenant, indicating an evolving sense of good and bad fates postmortem. One region of Sheol was called Gehenna, referring to the ever-burning garbage dump outside Jerusalem: those who had not kept the covenant would burn forever. People whose moral comportment had been average would be in a shadowy part of Sheol; the faithful in a more restful, comfortable area. But as time went on, the afterlife came to be seen as a transformed world created by God, as told by Isaiah: "For behold! I am creating a new heaven and a new earth; The former things shall not be remembered, They shall never come to mind. Be glad, then, and rejoice forever in what I am creating."

IN THE HISTORY OF JUDAISM, the First Temple period refers to the time of Solomon's Temple in Jerusalem, which stood for four hundred years before being destroyed in the sixth century BCE. In the oldest sections of the Hebrew Bible, much of which was written down during that time, there is no concrete narrative of an afterlife. But there are two notable exceptions to the idea that we must all eventually retreat to the shadows after death. Enoch did not seem to end up with the rest of the dead: "Enoch walked with God; then he was no more, for God took him." Immortality was offered to Elijah, and he was assumed into the heavenly host: a fiery chariot drawn by fiery horses swept him up to heaven in a whirlwind.

The stories of Enoch and Elijah provide a glimpse of a beatific afterlife that was not available to others in early times. They would become significant during the Second Temple period that extended from its construction in the late sixth century BCE to its destruction by the Romans in 70 CE.

During that time, the increased communication and stability under the domination of large empires made for a productive cultural mix. The Hebrews, or Jews as they came to be known after the Babylonian captivity, came into contact with Greek culture, whose philosophers advised a moral and abstemious life, and Zoroastrianism, whose founder preached staying away from evil and emulating the good in order to attain salvation. There were psychological forces at work here, too. The Hebrews were beleaguered: invaded, exiled, and oppressed by Egyptians, Babylonians, Greeks. Faith in collective salvation here on earth was waning; it did not seem that they would ever be free in this life. The focus on blessedness on earth gradually shifted to blessedness in another life.

In the meantime, Ecclesiastes, written under the domination of Hellenistic Greeks, took a stoic view: both man and beast have the same fate: "As the one dies so dies the other. . . . Both go to the same place; both came from dust and both return to dust." We cannot count on reward for our earthly struggles, so it is wise to attend to the present: "Whatever it is in your power to do, do with all your might. For there is no reasoning, no learning, no wisdom in Sheol where you are going." The author of Ecclesiastes had no hope for a life beyond this one; though he did not despair, his indifference has a rather melancholy tone. But the very fact that he brings up the afterlife is an indication that such notions had taken hold in his culture.

THE SEEDS FOR A VISION of the afterlife had been sown in the book of Ezekiel, which dates to the Babylonian exile in the sixth century BCE. As a Hebrew faithful to Yahweh, the author of Ezekiel would have expected deliverance in history, but the extravagant imagery in his visions reaches far beyond it. Ezekiel beholds wondrous things: four living creatures with human faces (man, ox, lion, eagle) and a dazzling enthroned figure above the firmament: "Like the appearance of the bow which shines in the clouds on a day of

The Vision of Ezekiel, **engraving by an unknown artist**

rain, such was the appearance of the surrounding radiance. That was the appearance of the semblance of the Presence of the Lord." Ezekiel also sees the chariot of God, in a vision that for centuries inspired Jewish mysticism and its adherents' quest to rise like Ezekiel into God's realm.

THE BOOK OF DANIEL, written in the mid-second century BCE, contains the Hebrew Bible's first explicit reference to resurrection as a passage to an afterlife. It was written during the reign of the Hellenistic Greeks, yet another time of terrible persecution, and is full of stories and visions in which the Jews could see their own plight and take heart. Surely their just God would wreak vengeance on their oppressors and look kindly on those of his people who remained faithful.

In the first part of the book, Daniel and his three comrades undergo terrible trials, thrown into both a furnace and a lion's den, but are finally saved from martyrdom through divine intervention. Thereafter comes the vision of the end times, starting with the beasts that represent empires: a lion with eagle's wings (Babylon), a bear with three tusks (Media), a winged leopard with four heads (Persia), and a fourth with iron teeth and ten horns that sprouted new ones with eyes and loud mouths (Greece).

The Ancient of Days takes his throne: "His garment was like white snow, and the hair on His head was like lamb's wool. His throne was tongues of flame; its wheels were blazing fire." The court is convened, sacred books recording future events are opened, and the beasts are stripped of power. The Ancient of Days rules in favor of the holy ones, although Greece has defeated them. Greece would become a malignant kingdom on earth, denouncing the Most High, devouring and crushing all. But justice would be done in the end: Greece would be destroyed, and "the kingship and dominion and grandeur of all the kingdoms under Heaven will be given to the people of the holy ones of the Most High."

The second part of Daniel describes the coming of the archangel Michael in a time of unprecedented distress that would continue for 1,335 days, after which the power of the destroyer would finally end. Not everyone would be saved: some of those who awoke from the dust of the earth would do so only to face "everlasting abhorrence." But Michael promises that all those who are written in the book shall be saved—those, like Daniel, with understanding and insight. They "will be radiant like the bright expanse of sky, and . . . will be like the stars forever and ever."

Daniel 12 reflects several evolving ideas about the afterlife. There is a clear reference to resurrection, and the beatific afterlife he describes has moved from below the earth up into the heavens. Whereas in the past only prophets had the capacity to encounter God, Daniel opens up the possibility for others to do so after judgment. At the end of days, accounts will be settled: those who are wise, or become martyrs in combat or captivity, will not only be resurrected but will forever shine like stars. Evildoers will also live on, to be punished. What Daniel does not say, however, is that *all* shall be raised—evidently, many Jews would simply die.

THE NOTIONS OF RESURRECTION DESCRIBED in the book of Daniel had a deep influence on Jewish eschatology (doctrine about the last things). By the first century BCE, the Pharisees, the dominant rabbinical group at the time, had come to believe that the human body would rise from the dead in glory and remain with Yahweh forever. These ideas influenced the Essenes, a group that flourished in the Qumran desert from the second century BCE into the first century CE. They awaited a messiah who would usher in a new, mystical Jewish state. On the other hand, the priestly caste of the Sadducees resisted notions of resurrection: a fierce argument with the Pharisees even made it into the Acts of the Apostles. Paul has been put on trial for "hope in the resurrection of the dead," but "a dispute broke out between the Pharisees and Sadducees. . . . For the Sadducees say that there is no resurrection or angels or spirits, while the Pharisees acknowledge all three." A great uproar occurred, and the dispute became so serious that Paul had to be rescued by troops lest he be torn to pieces.

There were several versions of the afterlife among Jews of that time. Some feature a temple in a paradisal setting. In a lengthy vision, the book of Ezekiel describes in exquisite detail the layout and dimensions of a magnificent structure on a high mountain, each gate named for one of the twelve tribes of Israel. From it flows a life-giving river teeming with every kind of creature. Along its banks grow every kind of fruit tree; they bear fresh fruit each month because the refreshing waters flow from the sanctuary.

Another version was that of the heavenly Jerusalem, whose earthly counterpart had been established as the dwelling of God when David brought the Ark of the Covenant there. Jerusalem was central to the Hebrews' identity, and "Next year in Jerusalem" is a Passover promise, for it is there that both judgment and resurrection will take place. Finally, the Jews did not necessarily think of being released from this earth up to the heavens, although the Hebrew word for sky, *shama'im*, was used as a metaphor for the abode of God and the angels. Rather, the kingdom of God, as it had been in the earliest days, was here on earth, and they "would enjoy the goodness of the Lord in the land of the living."

VISIONS OF THE END TIMES, and the world to come, also appear in Jewish "pseudepigrapha," works written in the name of an ancient figure to give them authority. The book of Enoch, an apocalyptic text told in the voice of Enoch, who walked with God in Genesis, emerged in many versions and languages between the third century BCE and the second century CE. Enoch elaborates on the fallen angels in Genesis who went on to cohabit with women, an abomination considered to be the origin of evil. The fallen angels were the source of all corruption on earth, including political and economic exploitation. Enoch's emphasis on social justice and its bearing on the end times follow the powerful tradition among Hebrew prophets. It also reflects a new vision for the afterlife in Judaism and Christianity, the ascent to heaven that demonstrates the reward for the righteous in the next life.

Enoch's account of the heavenly world is the celestial manifestation of the Temple of Jerusalem: a great house of white marble with burning gates, mosaic inner walls, floors of crystal, and a ceiling like a path of stars. His journey there, recorded in the Book of Watchers, starts with a dream in which Enoch is called by clouds and mist, blown by winds along a path of stars up to heaven. He comes to a wall built of hailstones and surrounded by a tongue of fire, and faints in fear. But then a vision within his vision brings him to an immense house of burning marble where he sees God face-to-face.

Archangels then escort Enoch through the cosmos. He sees storehouses of stars, storms, winds, and the pillars of heaven; he witnesses the punishment of rebel angels in an abyss. When Enoch arrives in a mountainous place, he hears voices and asks Raphael, his angel guide, whose voices they are. Raphael tells him that the souls of the dead reside there until the day of the great judgment—even the soul of Abel, whose spirit will pursue Cain until Cain's seed is exterminated. There are separate groups of souls: some are waiting to be judged, and some are righteous. Some souls will suffer forever, while some are not good enough to be resurrected or bad enough to be punished forever.

The book of Enoch does not give us a vision of the heavenly reward for the righteous, just a description of the tree of life. Nor does it explore new concepts of the soul: the dead exist in a disembodied intermediate state, while maintaining the moral identity on which their eternal fate depends. But unlike the pure immortal souls of Plato, Enoch's righteous are bound for bodily resurrection.

THE TWO CURRENTS OF BELIEF about the afterlife, the Greek notion of the immortality of the soul and the Jewish notion of the resurrection of the body, were debated for centuries. An early effort to reconcile the two was made by the first-century CE philosopher Philo, who lived in Alexandria in a Diaspora community of Jews that admired Greek intellectual achievement. They were interested in Plato's notions of the soul and in an afterlife for individuals rather than for the Jews as a whole.

Philo considered Hebrew scripture to be compatible with the insights of Greek philosophy and envisioned an afterlife that drew on both. Souls, he believed, are engaged in mystical and philosophical ascent, ultimately to be transported to the skies to join the heavenly host. As in Plato, earthly existence is a brief interlude; our bodies are but dust animated by the divine spirit that breathes into us an immortal soul. Death restores the soul to its original state in the spiritual world, where it truly belongs. Although many souls lose their way during their time here, a philosophical soul goes on to an existence after death. In the higher, immaterial realm, a soul can advance to live in a world of ideas—this is where Enoch can be found. In the highest world, where Moses resides, the soul can live with the deity.

Philo emphasized the Jewish idea that immortality came about through martyrdom, and his ideas are deeply imbued with biblical ethics, the most important and transcendent value being moral behavior. He also echoed Plato's reverence for philosophy and moral education: "The souls of those who have given themselves to genuine philosophy . . . study to die to the life in the body, that a higher existence immortal and incorporeal in the presence of Him who is himself immortal and uncreated, may be their portion." Those who sin lose their soul and their immortality. As for what resurrection might look like, Philo believed that God's kingdom would be perfected here on earth and that souls would have perfected bodies, made of the stuff of stars.

EIGHT

No Eye Has Seen It

All the prophets prophesied only about the days
of the Messiah; but of the world to come,
no eye has seen it.

• YOHANAN BAR NAPPAHA

I n 70 CE, the Romans destroyed the Second Temple in Jerusalem and
expelled the Jews from their land. These cataclysmic events resulted in
a radical change in Judaism, as rituals of sanctification had always taken
place in the holy Temple. The rabbis, who were teachers, sages, and legal
experts, faced the awesome challenge of sustaining hope that the Temple,
and the Jewish state, would someday be restored, while maintaining the
locus of holiness in the people themselves. A body of literature emerged
based on two ideals: the sanctification of everyday life in the here and now
and the salvation of all Israel in the age to come. By the sixth century, rabbinic Judaism had become its dominant form and the foundation for its
future; the Third Temple has yet to be built.

The Talmud is the sacred compendium of law and legend written to
preserve the memory of the Temple and its rituals, and studying these rituals became equivalent to performing them. The Talmud teaches fundamental beliefs about the next life: it will either be a time of peace when the
bodies of the righteous will be restored through resurrection or the reward
immediately after death for the individual, in company with other righ-

teous souls. In both cases, the Talmud requires repentance for sins and attests to God's ultimate judgment.

Lively debates about these teachings are to be found in the Mishnah, the earliest book of rabbinic Judaism. The idea of resurrection was particularly compelling and useful. It involves atonement, reward, and punishment; revival of the Jewish community in the Promised Land; and the integration of body and soul not only here but also hereafter. There were also persistent debates about who would be saved. The book of Daniel promised resurrection for some, in particular martyrs, while implying that most would simply die. (Although over time the comforting belief that we are all martyrs because we all die gradually took hold.) Distinguished rabbis who lived in the years just after the destruction of the Temple put forth different theories. Rabbi Eliezer said that only Israel would be saved, while Rabbi Joshua ben Hananiah took the more generous position that both Jews and Gentiles could attain salvation: "Everyone who walks in blamelessness before his Creator in this world will escape the judgment of hell in the world to come."

Still, there was some discussion of crimes that would prevent one from being resurrected. They include healing by spells; denying that the Torah is divine revelation; uttering God's name; following the teachings of Epicurus; and not believing that the dead could be brought back to life. The rabbis never even considered the possibility of a place of permanent punishment for evildoers: the "benevolence of the eternal God would not allow most souls to be permanently condemned."

Questions remained about the belief that all the dead would ultimately be revived in their own bodies and live again on earth, as scripture had not presented it as doctrine. Isaiah, chapters 60–66, describes the reclamation and glorious future of the land of Israel, and Mishnah Sanhedrin 10, another sacred text, introduces it as an eternal reward: "they will all live in the land of Israel forever." But would it be on earth, or a transformed earth, or perhaps a heavenly realm? The rabbis came to see the land described in

Isaiah as not in this world but in Olam Ha-ba, the world to come. This interpretation may have come about in response to the disasters they had recently experienced. Indeed, they may have regarded their suffering under the Romans as the martyrdom of Israel itself.

The promise of a land implied there would be bodies—souls may be immortal, but they do not require land. The rabbis reconciled the immortality of the soul and the resurrection of the body through the use of the term "vivification of the dead" instead of "raising of corpses." They did not want to define resurrection in terms of flesh, wisely preferring a less specific term that would allow God to work in his own ways.

THE SECOND SOURCE OF IDEAS about the afterlife in rabbinic literature is the Midrash, which contains comments from many rabbis over many centuries, so there is no systematic treatment of the afterlife. Early rabbis such as Yohanan bar Nappaha, a Palestinian writing in the third century, were reticent to discuss details. He quotes Isaiah to make his point: "All the prophets prophesied only about the days of the Messiah; but of the world to come, no eye has seen it." It may well be that such reticence was in reaction to the vivid depictions of the afterlife in Zoroastrianism, Christianity, and later in Islam.

There were a few rabbis who could not resist the topic, however. Rav Abba, writing in third-century Babylon, dreamed of a world where there would be no eating or drinking, procreation or business transactions, envy or hatred or rivalry. The blessed would sit around on thrones with crowns on their heads enjoying the vision of God. Others saw the afterlife as a "Rabbinic Academy on High," where the righteous, who might not have had the chance to study Torah on earth, spend eternity doing so. This is a gracious vision that makes it possible for everyone to become a rabbi. And rabbis perform the highest form of divine service, which is to advise God. The midrash Eleh Ezkerah describes rabbis sitting on golden thrones listening to a noted rabbi expound. There is much debate, but even God's opinion is not necessarily accepted right away. It is said that when a wise rabbi dies, he has been called up from earth to settle an argument: if he agrees with God, the legitimacy of God's opinion is proven.

THERE ARE VISIONS in the Midrash of another world to come, visions that began as a parallel to apocalyptic belief pointing to the destruction of this world. The idea of a paradise on a reconstituted land of Israel had become a postmortem realm, a perfected world free of earthly demands. "In this world, one has the trouble to harvest grapes and press them; but in the world to come a person will bring a single grape in a wagon or a ship, store it in the corner of his house, and draw from it enough wine to fill a large flagon." Some writers held that the world to come would commence immediately after we die. One interpreted Psalm 31:20 to mean that when the righteous leave this world, they are with the Lord: "How great is the goodness, O Lord, which you have in store for those who fear you."

And then there is the delightful solution to the problem of Jews living in Diaspora. The dead buried outside the land of Israel will come home to Israel at the time of the resurrection, literally rolling their way along subterranean paths. According to the third-century Rabbi Simai, "The Holy One . . . will burrow the earth before them, and their bodies will roll through the excavation like bottles, and when they arrive at the land of Israel, their souls will be reunited with them." In a later passage Rabbi Simai suggests that their souls will be reclothed in a body, one that is constructed from a single vertebra—an echo of Zoroastrian belief that God can reassemble a body from virtually nothing.

THE RABBIS AGREED that the Torah is "not in heaven." Its meaning was to be discerned through their interpretations, not through prophecy or miracles. They were cautious of mysticism or claims of secret knowledge. Indeed, Mishnah Hagigah 2:1 forbade discussion of two topics: the creation of the cosmos and Ezekiel's vision of the celestial chariot believed to be God's throne.

But the desire to encounter God, and to wonder about his dwelling place and how one might get there, could not be suppressed. A strain of active mysticism involving visions, dreams, and ecstatic trances began to emerge as early as the first century BCE. Mystics sought to journey to heaven, to verify God's promises to those who had gone there before.

In his vision, Ezekiel had witnessed seven subterranean chambers, the primordial waters and seven firmaments, and encountered the Power: angels, seraphim, and sparkling-winged beings joined to the great chariot in which God would descend to judge all the nations. But these secrets of creation and of the divine realm could be dangerous. There is a famous parable about four sages who enter *pardes*, a royal garden: one dies, the second goes insane, the third becomes a heretic, and only Rabbi Akiva both goes in and comes out in peace. Entering the divine realm and meeting God were potentially both perilous and transformational.

Despite these warnings, mysticism flowered in literature having to do with celestial palaces or temples (*hekhalot*) and with the chariot or throne (*merkavah*). These works deal with the process of creation and God's rule of the universe, with magic and with descriptions of the chariot. There is even a procedure whereby one could ascend to the divine realm to gaze on the figure on the throne. This figure appears in many guises—the Glory of the Lord, the Angel of the Lord—all expressions of the ways God manifests himself to us. The essential message in these writings is that while humans can look forward to going to heaven at the end of their earthly lives, some can go there before they die. Thus the common person is invited to follow legendary otherworld travelers such as Enoch and Ezekiel.

There was another incentive for such travelers. Some not only tour heaven but are transformed into angels in the process of their ascension. In 3 Enoch, or the Book of Palaces, Enoch becomes a powerful new angel—perhaps even a new star. "This Enoch, whose flesh was turned to flame, his veins to fire, his eyelashes to flashes of lightning, his eyeballs to flaming torches, and whom God placed on a throne next to the throne of glory, received after this heavenly transformation the name Metatron." As Metatron, Enoch receives heavenly secrets and a new name—YHWH Hakaton (Lord Jr.)—suggesting that such a transformed human might actually share in God's divinity. He becomes the leader of innocent souls who died studying Torah, shown as children playing under the throne of glory. Enoch/Metatron leads us on a tour of the heavenly family of angels, including the Watchers from Daniel 4, and gives an account of various fates of souls. The good souls fly around the throne of glory, while bad souls are permanently stained black like the bottom of pots, incapable of being cleansed and damned for eternity.

The mysteries in 3 Enoch pale in comparison to those in Shiur Komah, "The Measurement of the Height." Shiur Komah provides a list of God's limbs, beard, forehead, eyes, and irises, each given an unpronounceable name along with measurements in miles, feet, and fingers. In this system, the basic measurement is the length of the universe, and each of God's limbs is trillions of times longer. There are passwords and incantations calling on the Angel of the Countenance of God, and the tongue-twister of all time, an oath to be repeated 112 times in the name of *"Tutruseah Tsortak Totarkhiel Tofgar Ashruleah Zevudiel and Seharariel Tandiel Shokel Huzeah Dahivurun and Adiroron YHVH, Lord of Israel."* These mystical texts open up new possibilities for the living, giving us the chance to achieve martyrdom through rites and ecstatic experiences by dying a spiritual rather than a physical death.

NOTWITHSTANDING THESE INTRIGUING CURRENTS of Jewish mysticism, rabbinic Judaism was, from the seventh to the eighteenth centuries CE, the dominant practice for the majority of Jews, with a body of literature characterized by internal debate and a proliferation of forms: exegesis, poetry, history, philosophy. Thus, despite ongoing political and social upheaval—forced migration, persecution, religious schism—it is possible to trace Jewish thought about the soul and the afterlife through the works of Jewish philosophers. The tenth-century Egyptian Saadia Gaon was the first to put his name to books since the first century. His masterwork *Book of Beliefs and Opinions* contains a chapter titled "The Resurrection of the Dead in the Present World," in which Saadia sets forth Jewish belief about the resurrection of the dead. It would take place in the Future World of Reward, at the time of the messianic redemption, and is possible because God, having created ex nihilo, could revive the dead.

Saadia's views on the soul foreshadow those of medieval Jewish philosophers and mystics: "Soul requires the good acts of the body to perfect its peculiarly immaterial, celestial-like substance, even as the body needs the faculties of sensation and reason that the soul provides." The body and the soul are thus interdependent, and the soul matures through the contest of rival forces, as in discernment and determination versus lust. The fruits of this struggle can result in greater self-awareness, enhanced aspirations, and inner harmony.

MAIMONIDES, a twelfth-century Sephardic Jew from Spain and the leading rabbinic authority of his time, engaged in ongoing controversies about resurrection and the Messianic Age. Accused of heresy for not affirming his belief in the resurrection of the body, he responded with *The Epistle on the Resurrection of the Dead*, arguing that reward in the afterlife would be a purely spiritual state of complete joy. However, he also attested to God's power to restore their bodies to the dead. This would occur in a messianic era so that souls could grow even closer to God through moral discernment and intellectual comprehension. The resurrected body would be left behind as the soul moved into God's presence. The philosopher Nahmanides, another Sephardic Jew, responded with the more popular view of resurrection in *The Gate of Reward*. Soul and body would be reunited in the world to come, and humanity would exist throughout eternity. However, the body would be different: it would be united with the soul, in a microcosm of the whole universe.

Maimonides's ideas had lasting influence: centuries later, they would inspire Zionism. The Messianic Age would differ from the present life only insofar as the Jews would be delivered "from servitude to foreign powers." There would be no miracles, no wonders; the messiah would restore the land of Israel to the Jews, rebuild the Temple, and resume Temple sacrifice. Understandably, Maimonides faced opposition from Christians, who believed that the messiah had already come. This time he was defended by Nahmanides, who argued that the messiah would be a human being and that Jesus had not fulfilled the tasks that Jewish tradition assigned to the messiah. In *The Book of Redemption* (c. 1263), Nahmanides also questioned whether the Messianic Age would require Israel's full repentance. He argued that God uses exile to punish Israel for its sins, in preparation for messianic times, but also that it is "the nations that cause us to sin." Divided by exile and surrounded by evil opponents, Israel could never overcome its sinful state except through God's miraculous intervention. However, in the messianic time, the evil impulse would be annulled, and primordial harmony would be reestablished. Such a conception of the universe was to reach fruition in Kabbalah.

NINE

The Gates of
the Imagination

God can only be known and grasped to the
degree that one opens the gates of imagination.

· DANIEL CHANAN MATT

K abbalah" means "receiving" revelation through the tradition going all the way back to our original nature, which was illuminated by unbounded awareness. This was lost through Adam's sin, and kabbalists sought "to recover the tradition, to regain cosmic consciousness, to see from one end of the world to the other." This may seem hopelessly otherworldly and wildly ambitious. But given the persecution and social upheavals that the Jews faced throughout the centuries, a turn to mysticism was perhaps inevitable. It was certainly in keeping with the everlasting covenant with their God and the relationship that came about as a result. That relationship, while inspiring hopes for eternal life, had always been played out in the vicissitudes of earthly existence. So it was that the kabbalists reached out for God, constructing a new cosmos, a new interpretation of their struggle in this world, and a new version of ultimate salvation in which Jews would play an essential role.

The kabbalists imbued ancient religious texts with secret layers of meaning that could be discerned only by scholars steeped in the tradition. An early source, the tenth-century Sefer Yezira, or Book of Creation, presents an astonishing vision of creation coming about through divine speech, through the power of letters of the alphabet. It describes the system that maintains the harmony of the universe, which involves three levels of existence: the cosmos, time, and humanity. The Book of Creation sets up patterns of correspondence whereby, for example, twelve simple letters govern the twelve zodiac signs, the twelve months, and so forth. This system of correspondences inspired the kabbalist conception of the human as a microcosm of the cosmos.

Characteristic beliefs of Kabbalah are to be found in the twelfth-century Book Bahir. It describes a divine world made up of ten powers, conceived as a tree with ten branches. In a departure from earlier Jewish sources, there is also a hellish realm in which the powers of evil are the fingers of God's left hand. Another striking innovation is its positive view of the transmigration of souls, drawing on a passage from Ecclesiastes: "One generation goes, another comes." According to the Book Bahir, reincarnation solves the question of why the just may suffer in this world while the wicked prosper: just people may have been wicked in their former lives, while the wicked may have been righteous.

THE ESSENTIAL WORK OF KABBALAH is the Zohar, or *The Book of Enlightenment*, first printed in 1558–1560. Modern Orthodox Jews consider the Zohar to be one of the three pillars of faith and tradition, along with the Bible and the Talmud, and attribute it to the second-century rabbi Shimon bar Yochai. But its authorship has been contested, and scholars now agree that it was written by a thirteenth-century Spaniard named Moses de León. (For his part, Moses de León claimed to have copied it from an ancient manuscript, but when a wealthy follower wanted to buy it after his death, his widow said he had "written it from his own mind.")

Kabbalists insisted that they were traditionalists, transmitting ancient knowledge, although they kept their writings secret and used obscure references. Accordingly, Moses de León disguised his identity, wrote in an artificial Aramaic, attributed his work to Rabbi Shimon, and claimed sources such as Elijah and the Academy on High. Those sympathetic to Moses de León see him as a mystic who gave himself over to sources of ancient wisdom who used him as a conduit for essential, eternal truth. He was liberated from the constraints of time, place, even identity. And he seemed to be sincere, declaring that "God knows that my intention is good: that many may become wise and strengthen their faith in God."

DESPITE ALL THE CONTROVERSY, the Zohar will intrigue anyone who reads it. There are commentaries on everything from the mystical aspects of the Torah to the origin and structure of the universe, stories of wandering in heaven, meetings with heavenly personages, and visions of what took place there. In "Threshing Out the Secrets," we encounter a stunning manifestation of God, a kind of early version of the Big Bang:

> When the desire arose in the Will of the White Head to manifest Its Glory, It arrayed, prepared, and generated from the Blinding Flash one spark, radiating in 370 directions. [It then "congeals" into a hard skull.]
>
> Inside this skull lie ninety million worlds, moving with it, relying on it. [They eventually emanate through the skull to His face.]
>
> That is why He is called the Impatient One. When necessary, His face expands and becomes long-suffering, for then He is gazing into the face of the Ancient or Ancients and He feels compassion for the world.

Four rabbis witness this terrifying sight, and only Rabbi Shimon survives. God congratulates him, and he goes on to become a revealer of secrets. And they are wondrous secrets. The Zohar tells us that if we close an eye and rotate the eyeball we can envision the *sefirot*, aspects of God such as Wisdom, Love, and Judgment that became manifest in creation. The last of the *sefirot* is Shekhinah, whose union with Tif'eret (Beauty and Compassion) produced the human soul. The human path to God is not one of overcoming our innate sinfulness but of purification so that we may become vessels for the *sefirot*.

BIBLICAL AND RABBINIC JUDAISM ATTEMPTED to suppress discussion of the nature of God, and medieval Jewish philosophy attempted to purify the concept of God through reason. Direct contact with God was discouraged; God was to be sought through the interpretation of ancient texts and through prayer and its spiritual intention. A delightful exception was a process, akin to the Academy on High, whereby rabbis engaged in "questions from heaven." They asked God questions before they went to sleep, and then interpreted their ensuing dreams as his response. In contrast, the kabbalists transformed the teachings of Judaism through their mystic tradition whose hidden meaning was nothing less than the inner life of God.

One of their great questions reflects the paradox at the heart of their relationship with a timeless God: How could he be reconciled with the *sefirot*, which exist in time? One solution had roots growing from the *sefirot* into God; another had divine light pouring forth from him, bestowing the power of existence in heaven and earth. Interpretations and images of the *sefirot* proliferated: they were represented as emanations from God that sustain and nourish creation, sometimes in anthropomorphic form. The figure of Shekhinah was particularly important, with deep historical roots—indeed the term had been used in rabbinic literature to refer to God's ongoing life with his people. Shekhinah, who first appeared in feminine form in the Book Bahir, is a compelling figure, both gracious and mighty. She accompanies the mystical community of Israel in exile, and the righteous dwell with her after death. But Shekhinah is also the weakest of the *sefirot*, and evil can separate her from Tif'eret and cause disruption in the divine realm. Alas, it is woman's weak, incomplete nature and vulnerability to evil that threatens the cosmic order.

Many kabbalistic rituals concerned the perpetual struggle to save Shekhinah from the suffering and exile she endures with her people and to restore her to Tif'eret. Indeed, Shekhinah relies on the Jews to restore the cosmos to order. The kabbalists could not wait for the afterlife to participate in the apocalypse: it required their intervention in the present. Thus they had to address the phenomenon of evil. In *Treatise on the Emanations on the Left* (c. 1265), Rabbi Isaac ben Jacob ha-Cohen sets forth a system of seven divine powers of evil, which he ascribes to a distorted emanation from one of the *sefirot*, Understanding. The struggle between good and evil is ongoing—as in the Shekhinah story—and will end in an apocalyptic battle between Samael (a figure associated with Satan) with his demons and the messiah with his angels, who will triumph. This is the first appearance of a dualistic cosmos in Kabbalah, and also the first to describe redemption through a messiah, a theme that would later become essential.

IN THE LATE FIFTEENTH CENTURY, Jewish intellectuals gathered in Galilee, where they believed Rabbi Shimon of the Zohar was buried. They were actively preparing for redemption as a community through scrupulous observation of ritualistic commandments and repentance for sin. A visionary named Isaac Luria became the center of a group of disciples, some of whom believed that he was the messiah. Luria's visions took him to a celestial academy where he studied great secrets, and his teachings revealed the conclusion of the cosmic story of Kabbalah.

For Luria, existence did not begin with a perfect God creating an imperfect universe, a situation that has required incessant explanation throughout history. He taught that God's first attempt to set up the *sefirot*, the system of emanated divine powers, had been a disaster, resulting in a crisis in the divine realm. Luria represented the *sefirot* as vessels made of coarse divine light that gave shape and function to the finer divine light they contain. During their creation, they were unable to contain the flow of divine light, and the seven lower ones broke. As shards of the vessels fell downward, most of their light returned to the divine source. But some sparks of light remained caught in the shards and fed the evil forces that kept them captive, thereby becoming instruments of evil and evidence of the fracture of God.

Luria took the rare position that the origin and the potential for evil both derive from an eternal divinity and that God is imperfect. His dualism is not based on opposing forces of good and evil, or the struggle of humans with our corrupted bodies, but on God's own dualism that he emanated in a failed attempt to bring about divine unity. The story of Adam is another failed attempt. The lower realms and the *sefirot* were created; then Adam (who himself contained both good and evil) unleashed their powers on the world. If he had obeyed God, good would have vanquished evil and the cosmic and divine dualism would have come to an end. Instead, Adam disobeyed God, and the powers of evil grew more powerful.

Luria's universe is the result of a crisis in the infinite Godhead. The purpose of creation is to remedy this situation and, in doing so, restore primordial harmony. But what can we bit players in this cosmic drama hope for? Luria held out the promise of the *tikkun*: the mending of the broken vessels, when the essence trapped in evil will be freed and returned to its divine source. The *tikkun* is the reason for all creation, for human existence, for the people of Israel: to face the challenge of the original catastrophe, ultimately to bring about perfection and harmony in God and God's creation. The only weapons we have against the powers of evil are the commandments and our own ethical behavior: each small victory over evil furthers the process of *tikkun*, while each small sin delays it. The achievement of *tikkun* is deeply rooted in the Jewish tradition: scrupulous observation of the mitzvot, the God-given precepts; dedication to the norms of ethical conduct; and wholehearted pursuit of religious perfection.

Kabbalah may seem fantastical, but its practical message is profoundly orthodox. It shares the goals of traditional Judaism, pursued with enhanced dedication springing from the awareness of the cosmic consequences of deeds, both good and evil. One will never know if the deed one is performing will be the one that will free the last spark of trapped light—or prevent its release—so every action is conceivably of definitive consequence.

Each of us is responsible, and we are responsible together. The fate of creation is at stake.

ISAAC LURIA FURTHER INFLUENCED Jewish thought by placing *gilgul*, reincarnation, at the center of Kabbalah. There had been a brief mention in the Book Bahir, and the philosopher Nahmanides had affirmed reincarnation, arguing that Job's tragic fate was punishment for evil done in a previous life. The Zohar stated the doctrine in explicit terms: "Truly, all souls must undergo transmigration . . . the revolving scale is set up and men are judged every day at all times . . . they are brought up before the Tribunal, both before they enter into this world and after they leave it."

Luria believed that every person receives a soul spark from Adam, infecting him or her with evil. Reincarnation provides a chance for the soul to move up a rung on the ladder of purification, an elevation that has physical, emotional, and intellectual dimensions. Each soul has five strata, and each stratum has its own history and wanders on its own from body to body, generation to generation. Thus each soul is a composite of parts that have their own history and experiences. Rabbi Hayyim Vital told the history of his own soul, which was in fact the soul of the messiah. It had come from the body of Cain, and its strata had been reunited in Vital's body. Rabbi Vital claimed that Luria had revealed all this to him and that Luria knew the history of every soul. Whether or not he was indeed capable of such insight, Luria's ideas spread widely, although reincarnation remains controversial among Jews.

LURIA'S TEACHINGS put the fate of God, the universe, and the Jewish people in human hands. Understandably, such an obligation was hard to sustain, and people looked again to a messiah, a divine figure who could take responsibility. Shabbatai Zevi, a kabbalist born in Smyrna, took on that role, although his strange, provocative behavior got him banished from various communities.

But he found an ardent disciple in Nathan of Gaza, who already considered himself a prophet. It was a good match. Nathan began to preach that the *tikkun* was complete and the messiah had come, and word spread quickly throughout the Jewish world.

Nathan introduced the role of the messiah into the process of *tikkun*, along with the idea of a core of evil that humans alone could not overcome on their own. A divine messenger—Shabbatai Zevi—was required who would collect the spiritual power of a whole people and use it to overcome that evil. Unfortunately, Shabbatai was accused of sedition by the Grand Vizier and, to save his skin, took on the Muslim faith.

Nathan, loyal prophet that he was, explained away the shame of Shabbatai's conversion by declaring that the *tikkun* had been completed and the age of redemption had begun. The messiah had pretended to convert so he could enter the realm of evil powers and vanquish them. Some of Shabbatai Zevi's followers even converted to Islam, living as pretend members of orthodox Jewish communities in an underground network that secretly worshipped their messiah and celebrated their redemption.

Kabbalistic belief persisted, primarily in Hasidic communities, and in the late eighteenth century, there was a resurgence of belief in a messiah, by now a quite humble figure. It was held that one's approach to God had to be mediated by a "rebbe," a messenger of God responsible for the souls of his followers, as well as their worldly well-being. Hasidic communities were each led by such a mystical leader, a local rather than a universal messiah. In our time, Rabbi Menachem Mendel Schneerson came to be regarded as the last leader of Habad (Lubavitch) Hasidism. The legend of his Lubavitcher lineage was that the seventh leader would be childless, as Schneerson indeed was, and would be the messiah. Schneerson died in 1994 but is revered still, and by some awaited.

TEN

Today

A Promised Land

Where is our Kingdom of Israel? Where is the
House of God?

• RABBI ABRAHAM ISAAC KOOK

Traditional Jewish belief has held that death is not the end of our existence, but instead of formal dogma there have been many creative proposals about the afterlife. It may be a perfected, paradisal version of this world where the resurrected righteous of all nations will live. There may be a place for punishment of sinners, but it will be temporary. Souls may be reincarnated, or wait for a messiah to bring about resurrection. The restoration of primordial harmony sought by Kabbalah mystics is deeply rooted in Jewish tradition, and so is the hope to someday enter a Promised Land flowing with milk and honey.

But the vision of Zionism, founded by Theodor Herzl in the late nineteenth century, was decidedly this-worldly. The Zionists looked not to a messiah or another world for deliverance from oppression; rather, they took matters into their own hands. Theirs was a political organization (albeit with a utopian vision), and its adherents conceived of the Jews not in terms of a religion but as a people who deserved its homeland. This horrified the Orthodox, who held that if God had wanted their ancestors to settle Palestine they would have done so. But the Zionists sought freedom from rabbinical objections. There was to be no messiah, and redemption was to be material rather than spiritual. Eventually, Rabbi Abraham Isaac Kook reconciled the two factions by recognizing the legitimacy of secular Zionism but also considered its mission to be sacred, bringing about the Messianic Age.

In 1920, Jews living in Palestine established the Labor Brigade to acquire more land for their Zionist project. One of its efforts was Ein Harod, an early kibbutz, home to exuberantly hopeful young Jewish pioneers. One wrote, "I cannot but think of the sons of Israel in their tents in the desert. But this is our last stop. Here our wandering ends." There was a palpable sense that what they were doing was of biblical (if not particularly religious) significance. This sense of fulfilling history is also evident in the efforts of Shmaryahu Gutman, who in 1942 led an expedition of young settlers on a grueling pilgrimage from Jerusalem to Masada. He wanted to revive the significance of the ancient site and its tragic story as inspiration for the future of his people—a future that was in grave doubt at that time.

David Ben-Gurion declared that the Bible was the deed of the Jewish people to the land of Israel, and in 1948 the state was established. In 1967, during the Six-Day War, the Temple Mount was liberated by the Israeli army from Jordanian occupation, and thus the Jews secured the site of the First and Second Temples. However, given its significance to Muslims, Jews refrain from worship there, and the Third Temple will not be established. This is one of the profound ironies of modern Israel; another is the continuing challenge of sharing the land with people who lived there long before the Zionists arrived. The utopia—one might say the heaven on earth—envisioned by the early Zionists was to be a land without strife governed by enlightened policies, but that has not come to pass.

It is impossible to untangle the threads of religious and secular belief in modern Israel, but not in a form of Zionism that has arisen among some contemporary Christians. They believe in the special status of the Jews and their claim on the Holy Land, regard modern Israelis as an extension of biblical Israelites, and look forward to the reestablishment of the Temple.

Indeed, they believe that, starting in 1948, Old Testament prophecies are being fulfilled and that the strife and struggle in Israel are evidence that God's plans for the end times are being played out. It seems clear to others that much of Christian Zionist teaching contradicts that of Jesus Christ himself. Oppression of the Palestinians is tolerated, and peace efforts are the work of the Antichrist, as they thwart God's plans. What sort of heaven might come about as the result of such conviction, and what sort of god is responsible, is impossible to imagine, much less to hope for.

Everyday Mysticism

And in my going out to meet you,
I found you coming toward me.

• YEHUDAH HALEVI

Christians of the nonmystical kind think of the afterlife in terms of heaven (and to varying degrees, hell). They believe it is where we will be with God, but it lies in the future, beyond the chasm of death and the limits of time. We describe it in terms of lush earthly beauty and bliss, although we are wisely leery of describing what God might turn out to be like.

Rabbi Abraham Joshua Heschel gives us a distinctly Jewish version, one that is firmly rooted in the present. For him, the weekly Sabbath is a family day with God, a time of peace and repose, of freedom, of the restoration of our human dignity. And it is when we "embrace the presence of an eternal moment." And when we feel our souls stir, or are graced with an unexpected insight or a holy encounter, eternity is suddenly fulfilled. These moments constitute ongoing salvation, the chance to gather our scattered lives, to heal wounds and soothe strife, to come into harmony and clarity with God. This is all part of a great ritual of history wherein the ultimate meaning of our deeds extends far beyond our individual lives and our time, toward, perhaps, *tikkun*.

This intimation of eternity being fulfilled lies at the heart of every Jewish conception of life beyond. The experience of God as a real, conscious, loving presence implies that death will not separate us from him, although our future life with God is not a matter of much speculation. There are of course stories—the early rabbis told of the Academy on High with its ongoing conversation. And it is said that the afterlife will be a great banquet. A table will be set with the most marvelous food, but we will not have hinges in our elbows, so we cannot feed ourselves. Those of us who are loving and generous will quickly figure out that we can feed each other across the table: that's heaven. Those of us who are selfish and greedy will starve: that's hell.

My favorite story is the tradition of drinking four cups of wine at the seder feast, while leaving another full for Elijah. He will accompany the messiah and (presumably fortified by the wine) will resolve all disputes and uncertainties. Still, I suspect Elijah will not put an end to the lively debate that characterizes Judaism. Debate is not just a way to understand the faith; it is the way Jews live their faith and carry it forward to successive generations. Perhaps the Jewish sense of being chosen by God, and being in an ongoing, dynamic relationship with him, gives them a sense that the faith can be constantly refreshed with no risk to its essential truth.

NOT SURPRISINGLY, the Jews I spoke with had lots of different ideas about the afterlife. Rabbi Patricia Karlin-Neumann of Stanford University told me that she hadn't even heard of a world to come until she was in rabbinic school—her Reform congregation focused on the here and now, on accompanying the dying and remembering the dead. Indeed, the Hebrew word for "funeral" is *levaya*, which means escorting, being present for one another as we cross the border. As Rabbi Patricia put it, "We escort, and God willing, we will be escorted." And it is Jewish custom to reminisce about times shared with those gone ahead, to tell their stories and invoke their names during celebrations. In this way loved ones live on in our memories, guiding and inspiring us.

Rabbi Patricia is full of stories of making the passage with loved ones and keeping them alive in memory. When her mother died, a bird hovered over her friends and family gathered at the graveside and then flew off. Rabbi Patricia saw it as transporting her mother's soul—who knows where?—and it gave her great comfort.

The days surrounding her father's passing were remarkable as well. She was very pregnant; he had just visited her, and was to return for the birth, but died on his way to the airport. He was buried on a Friday, but since you cannot sit shiva on the Sabbath, many of her friends came to her house Saturday night after sundown. Rabbi Patricia felt out of sorts, and a woman friend convinced her that she was going into labor. Sure enough, she gave birth in short order. People calling or stopping by with condolences were told, "It's a girl!" Rabbi Patricia knows her father would have loved it: buried on Friday, he spent the Sabbath with his little granddaughter, and then she was born on earth. To this day the two have a very close bond across lives, through the stories the family tells, noting the flashes of presence they feel now and then.

RABBI PATRICIA'S STUDENT SIMONE belongs to Reconstructionist Judaism, a movement aimed at combining the rigor of Conservative Judaism with the open-mindedness of Reform. As she put it, "It's where some really creative Jewishness is happening." In her community, there is a prayer for those who mourn, who remember, but it doesn't mention death. They say the name of their lost one in their hearts, and see it as a chance to use their mouths as a vessel for the words of the departed, which are "Blessed be the glory of God." On Yom Kippur, the Day of Atonement, they refrain from food, sex, and bathing, and everybody wears white, shroud-like garments. They spend the day praying in the synagogue in a rehearsal for death, although once again there is no vision of what comes afterward.

Death came for her grandmother when Simone was fifteen, and the family kept an account of their conversation with her as she slipped away. She was afraid of the unknown, of being alone, but realistic—"When you die, you go through seven planets, or you just acquiesce to the situation. You can't go looking for something you don't know." But she told of a dream she'd just had, in which she was a little spirit floating around, watching Simone dance. Her mother said she hoped that's what was coming, and then her grandmother slipped away. But Simone was filled with hope for some future encounter and feels inexplicable moments of connection (indeed, she speaks of her grandmother in the present tense). Once she opened one of her grandmother's books of poems and found one about what the poet wanted on the day she will die. Scrawled in her grandmother's hand across the poem was "I will bake a peanut-butter cheesecake and give the first taste to Simone for her approval." As Simone tells it, "The next day, for the first time, they had cheesecake in the dining hall. Hello! Such a sweet thing."

But she knows these feelings are just intimations, and she spoke Rabbi Heschel's words to describe the limits of our nature: "Citizens of two realms, we all must sustain a dual allegiance: we sense the ineffable in one realm, we name and exploit reality in another. Between the two we set up a system of references, but we can never fill the gap. They are as far and as close to each other as time and calendar, as violin and melody, as life and what lies beyond the last breath."

Part IV

CHRISTIANITY

ELEVEN

Jesus on Earth

Behold, I am sending My messenger to clear the
way before Me, and the Lord whom you seek
shall come to His Temple suddenly. As for the
angel of the covenant that you desire, he is
already coming.

· BOOK OF MALACHI

As a believing Christian, I cannot set aside entirely my ways of thinking and feeling about Jesus, whose faithful presence sustains me. But
Jesus did live in a particular time and place, with family and friends,
and his fate is one of the turning points in human history. Understanding the
context of his earthly life, his words and actions, is essential to understanding
his teaching about eternal life in heaven.

In Jesus's day, Jewish thought on the afterlife was divided, even conten-
tious. The Sadducees would hear no talk of resurrection, unlike the Pharisees, who also embraced apocalyptic ideas. The Essenes were a separatist
community whose beliefs and way of life were revealed in the Dead Sea
Scrolls discovered in the mid-twentieth century. They left Jerusalem at
least one hundred years before the time of Jesus, protesting the worldliness
of the Temple, and regarded themselves as the faithful remnant of their
time, indeed of all time. The Essenes believed that their evil age was coming to an end and that the Lord would revisit the world in power. There
would be a cataclysmic struggle between good and evil, involving people

and cosmic forces. The Messiah of David, a kingly figure, would lead the war and bring God's Kingdom into being. The Messiah of Aaron, a high-priest figure, would purify the Temple and reveal the significance of the Scriptures to the Messianic Age.

The Essenes believed that their community was sustained by grace and knowledge flowing from God. Each initiate was required to swear that he had been chosen by God from all eternity to become one of the elect and that he had been loved by God from before creation. Their remarkable provenance presumably prepared the Essenes for their sweeping mission of revealing the mysteries of the nature of spirits, the heavenly world, and God's plan for humankind.

The Essenes led the kind of monastic life later associated with Christianity—they swore obedience and renounced private property and held that rigorous separation from the wicked world and meticulous personal holiness enabled them to withstand evil. They were the Sons of Light, in fellowship with those in heaven even during this life. Everybody else—other Jews, Gentiles, priests, and most likely all women—were lumped together as Sons of Darkness. In the end, the Sons of Light would fight alongside angels to triumph over the Sons of Darkness and the forces of evil and would help bring about a golden age.

These beliefs were enacted in two ceremonial dramas central to the life of the Essene community: the angelic liturgy and the great banquet. The first was based on a series of thirteen songs that described persons singing praise in angelic tongues around an elaborate throne. The community likely chanted the songs in unison to create mystical union with angels, enacting a transformation from human to angelic being. At the climax of the liturgy, God would appear in anthropomorphic form with human saints, resurrected and transformed. But how would "angelification" come about—as the result of martyrdom, or at the end times, or both? Would it be an individual reward, or one for the community, whose members were celibate in anticipation of a future angelic existence? The Scrolls give us no answers.

The great banquet was held in anticipation of the triumphal feast of the

Priest and King Messiahs, foretold in Isaiah: "The Lord of Hosts will make on this mount for all the peoples a banquet of rich viands, a banquet of choice wines." Later, Jesus would promise his apostles that he would not drink wine again "until the day I drink the new wine with you in the kingdom of my Father," and thereafter Christians would make such a banquet the center of their worship. While it is tempting to see in Essene belief and practice the seeds of early Christianity, there is no proof that either John the Baptist or his cousin Jesus of Nazareth were Essenes. But they lived in a cultural context rich with notions about the afterlife: controversy about resurrection, fear of the apocalypse, but also hope for a sacred community in the afterlife.

WHILE THE ESSENES WERE RADICAL SEPARATISTS, Jesus walked among the people. His references to resurrection and judgment are rooted in Jewish scripture, as are his ethical teachings, which reach beyond a system of reward and punishment to God's absolute love and mercy. He both taught and lived out the covenant imperative that worship of God requires justice among people. And in the way of the biblical prophets, he carried on a dialogue with an unseen order, withdrawing regularly to speak with Abba, his father.

Jesus proclaimed that God's power was breaking into the present day and that he had been sent to deliver God's people from oppression. But he did not refer to himself as the Messiah, and he did not fit the description— certainly not like the glorious Essene personages. The Jews, ground under the heel of the Romans, were looking for a messiah in the line of David who would restore their earthly kingdom. Jesus spoke instead of the kingdom of God, through symbols and parables. The now-familiar images he used—the treasure hidden in the field, the net set out to catch fish— encouraged his audience to find God here and now, while still looking beyond. But to live in the kingdom of God, conversion and action were required. One must seek first God's kingdom and God's justice, which always carries with it mercy and surprising loving-kindness.

In religious traditions that anticipate a final judgment, there are moral codes that serve as blueprints for an upright life. For Jesus, what was really important was not so much observance of the law—he left no detailed instructions—but love and mercy. In the parable of the Good Samaritan, Jesus tells the story of a member of a despised sect who alone among a series of passersby rescued a man who had been robbed and beaten half to death. When Jesus asks which one was truly a neighbor to the victim, a Pharisee answers, "The one who treated him with mercy." Whereupon Jesus says to him, "Go and do likewise." He was telling us to spot the rhyme between what the Samaritan did and what we might do; to be faithful to the story but creative in the ways it might play out in our own lives.

The final judgment preached by Jesus is found in Matthew 25 when the Son of Man comes in glory and separates the righteous from the accursed. The terms are stark: those who turn away from the poor, who do not feed the hungry or welcome the stranger, will be damned. Those who embrace the poor, who clothe the naked and visit the sick, will be saved. In serving the poor they have served the Lord himself: "Whatsoever you do for the least of these, you do for me." The most straightforward of teachings reveals a profound mystery. Jesus lives on in the poor, and if we truly see the poor, we see him. Every act of loving-kindness is a direct encounter with Jesus.

Jesus not only preached the kingdom, he embodied it, and in doing so gave us a glimpse of God's eternal order. He cleansed the Temple in protest against its corruption. He showed mercy to all manner of sinners and shared meals with them. He gathered disciples of all kinds: Galileans, Pharisees, women, a Zealot, inviting them to be a new people of God. But much of what Jesus did lies outside our customary ways of knowing. He worked wondrous deeds, miracles that intervened in the laws of his Father's creation. He walked on water and calmed the storm; healed lepers and raised the dead. He had a way of imbuing even simple actions, like feeding people or making wine flow, with a power that enabled his followers to glimpse the hidden reality of God.

Jesus proclaimed that the kingdom was at hand, and yet its full manifestation has not yet come to pass. Living in the kingdom is a great paradox, a fundamental tension at the heart of our religion, for the kingdom is already here, and not yet here. Christians keep faith in an unseen God and strive to live in such a way that we bring about the fulfillment of our faith and our good works; then we will see God: "For now we see through a glass, darkly; but then face to face."

DANIEL HAD WRITTEN that those with insight would shine like stars forever, and Jesus spoke of the fate of the righteous, who would shine like the sun in the kingdom of their Father. When the Sadducees challenged him about resurrection, Jesus astonished the crowds with his audacious reply: the Sadducees did not know the scriptures or the power of God. "And concerning the resurrection of the dead, have you never read what God himself said to you. . . . God is God, not of the dead but of the living." He knew he was going to that God, and told his disciples that after suffering greatly and being put to death, he would on the third day be raised. His earthly life indeed came to a brutal, ignominious end on a cross outside Jerusalem, and what happened next may only be understood through faith.

The first account of Jesus's resurrection was written by Paul in the middle of the first century CE and was based on his own conversion experience. As both a Jew and a Roman citizen, Paul had been an enthusiastic persecutor of Christians, and he set out for Damascus to bring prisoners back to Jerusalem. On the way a great light shone around him, and he heard Jesus's voice asking why he was persecuting him. The light blinded Paul, and he asked the voice what he should do. Jesus told him to go to Damascus where he would find out what his mission was to be. There a devout Jew named Ananias restored Paul's sight and said: "The God of our ancestors has chosen you to know his will, to see the Just One and hear his own voice speaking, because you are to be his witness before all mankind, testifying to what you have seen and heard."

In doing so, Paul drew from scripture and delivered his message in apocalyptic terms. For believers, the coming end times would bring a new kind of heaven—resurrection and transformation, a dramatic change in their very nature. In the meantime, there would be a new kind of community, one that would embody radical change through its worship, its missionary efforts, and heroic suffering.

It was Paul who developed the concept of the divinity of Jesus the Christ and set forth the virtues of faith, hope, and love as the essence of new life in him. He did not envision a heaven where the resurrected would dwell with God; rather, he wrote of the transformation he had experienced: "Through the Law I am dead to the Law, so that now I can live for God." Those who converted would be transformed through their belief; their natural bodies would be raised as spiritual bodies. And the veil that obscured the thoughts of believers reading the old covenant would be removed on turning to the Spirit of the Lord. Freed, they would gaze on him, and all would "grow brighter and brighter as we are turned into the image we reflect."

Resurrection of the individual was a stretch for contemporary Jews, who were accustomed to thinking of resurrection as a large-scale event that would happen to all of God's people, perhaps even the whole human race, at the coming of God's kingdom to earth. And resurrection meant coming to bodily life again after bodily death, not some glorious transformation. But Paul's message was clear: Jesus had brought resurrection to humanity. "Death came through one man [Adam] and in the same way the resurrection of the dead has come through one man." Our resurrected bodies would be imperishable; powerful, not weak; spiritual, not physical. The resurrection that had begun with Jesus would be completed in the great final resurrection at the end, when death would be destroyed.

PAUL WAS THE ONLY NEW TESTAMENT WRITER to have direct experience of the risen Christ. The Gospel accounts are at best secondhand, derived from

the tradition originating with those who learned from Jesus. The cast of characters varies, but all versions tell of an empty tomb and encounters with the
risen Jesus. He speaks to his disciples and comforts a weeping Mary Magdalene, emboldening her. When Thomas comes seeking proof of the claims that
his fellow disciples have seen Jesus, Jesus invites him to "give me your hand;
put it into my side. Doubt no longer but believe." Thomas does not touch him;
instead he exclaims, "My Lord and my God!" As two of his followers journey
to the village of Emmaus, Jesus accompanies them to an inn where he breaks
bread, blesses it, and shares it with them. Their eyes are opened and they
recognize him—but he disappears from their sight.

She who mourns, he who doubts, they who are unknowing are transformed through their encounters with the risen Jesus. They are newly
made, the first inhabitants of a new creation that extends from this life into
eternity. Jesus charged his followers to bring this Good News to the whole
world, assuring them that "I am with you always; yes, to the end of time."

TWELVE

Staying Alert

"So stay awake, because you do not know either
the day nor the hour."

• GOSPEL OF MATTHEW

Forty days after his resurrection from the dead, Jesus, having blessed his disciples, was carried up to heaven. His followers affirmed that Jesus was the Messiah, and as news of his resurrection spread, they came to see it as the definitive saving act of God. The Second Coming was at hand, and they would soon join Jesus in glory. But time went on, and Jesus did not return. Early traditions—Paul's imminent end times, the coming of the kingdom—had to be reinterpreted.

In the meantime, Jesus's followers needed to stay alert. They were not to wait passively for the end of time; they were to keep watch and take action in the present. The new community was to be an earthly manifestation of the kingdom of God, open to all: women and children, slaves, and all manner of foreigners.

But as the Second Coming withdrew into the future, questions arose: Would there be an interim period between individual death and final judgment? And who would be eligible for resurrection, and thus for an afterlife? Surely it would not be limited, as in Daniel, to martyrs. Indeed, the gates of heaven were opening up to welcome people like the thief crucified with Jesus and wretched Lazarus at wealthy Dives's gate. Even evildoers would attain immortality, but in complete isolation. When Dives asks to warn his brothers about his fate in hell, Abraham reveals that "between us and you a great gulf has been fixed, to stop anyone, if he wanted to, crossing from our side to yours, and to stop any crossing from your side to ours." Finally, the new religion needed to reconcile Jewish notions of bodily resurrection and Greek notions of immortality of the soul.

EARLY CHRISTIAN DEBATES about heaven and hell took place in a culture and a historical moment saturated with apocalyptic fear and trembling. In the Gospel of Matthew, the final judgment occurs when the Son of Man comes in glory and sits on his glorious throne. All the nations are gathered before him, and he separates the righteous from the evildoers: some will proceed to eternal salvation, some to eternal damnation. But the passage was oriented toward the present: Matthew was instructing Jesus's disciples on how to live their lives in preparation for the Second Coming. The book of Revelation is a full-blown apocalyptic vision. Its author, John the Revelator, was writing in a time when the Temple in Jerusalem had fallen, the "Lord and God" Emperor Domitian was in power, and Christian communities established in Asia Minor (and elsewhere) were facing waves of persecution.

John the Revelator was most likely Jewish, as Revelation is written in the poorest Greek in the New Testament. He may have been a member of a prophetic movement in the churches of Asia Minor and exiled to the rocky island of Patmos. John knew well the series of communities he addresses: their geography, their commercial situations, and their particular failings. He was clearly in a position of influence, warning the communities against specific threats such as pagans and Jews, and general threats of false teaching, persecution, and complacency. In Revelation, John presents a vision of the coming end times, in keeping with first-century Christian thought.

John describes being possessed by the Spirit and greeted by "one like a son of man" whose appearance is astonishing: his hair white as snow, his eyes burning, with a voice like the sound of the ocean. This personage declares that he was once dead but is now alive forever and has the keys to death and the netherworld. He orders John to write down things he sees in the present and things that are still to come.

John is granted visions of heaven and of what is to come in the future. In the first vision, God appears in human form on a jewel-encrusted throne, guarded by spirits with six wings and many eyes. Beside them on each side are twelve lesser thrones with twenty-four elders in white garments and golden crowns. They throw themselves down, worshipping with lightning, thunder, and the unceasing song: "Holy, holy, holy is the Lord God Almighty; he was, he is, and he is to come."

John then spies in the hands of God a scroll with seven seals and a figure near the throne, "a Lamb that seemed to have been sacrificed; it had seven horns and it had seven eyes, which are the seven Spirits God has sent out all over the world." The Lamb receives the scrolls from God, breaks the seals one by one, and four horses emerge: they are power, war, famine, and death itself. When the fifth seal is broken, a multitude of martyred souls appears, crying out to be avenged, but they are given white robes and told to be patient. Then the cosmos goes haywire: there's an earthquake, the sky appears as a torn scroll, the moon turns to blood, and all the inhabitants of earth cower under rocks, crying out to be spared the wrath of the Lamb. John then encounters the 144,000 humans sealed as servants of God, and a multitude from all nations who have survived great distress and who join the animal spirits and elders and angels at the throne of God.

When the Lamb breaks the seventh seal, "there was silence in heaven for about half an hour."

After that intermission, the blowing of trumpets by angels produces a series of terrifying phenomena, such as a third of a sea turning into blood, an eagle flying overhead crying *Woe! Woe!* and plagues of locusts, fire, sulfur, and smoke. Unfortunately, the third of the human race that is not killed in all this mayhem still does not repent of their evil deeds and demon worship; they will be dealt with later. Revelation proceeds with more thunder and earthquakes, angels, beasts, plagues, and wild scenes of destruction. In one scene, John encounters a woman clothed with the sun who is giving birth to a male child. An enormous scarlet dragon with seven heads and seven horns arrives to eat the child, but he is swept up to heaven as the woman escapes to the desert. He later comes upon the whore of Babylon—Mother of Harlots and Abominations of the Earth—after which an angel flies down from heaven, proclaiming that Babylon has fallen, all her riches and power gone in the space of an hour. A great warrior with a sword emerging from his mouth arrives and vanquishes the kings of the earth. An angel seizes Satan and ties him up. A thousand-year reign begins: the souls of holy martyrs come to life to be priests of God and Christ, while all other souls have to wait until the reign is over. At that time, Satan is unleashed to gather all the evil ones; they attempt, unsuccessfully, to invade the land of the blessed.

Finally, John beholds a great white throne upon which one sits whose presence causes the earth and sky to vanish. This is the final judgment scene: the dead stand before the throne, the book of life is opened, and the dead are judged according to their deeds. Death and Hades are thrown into a burning lake and those whose names are not in the book of life are thrown in with them. A new heaven and earth come to pass, and a new Jerusalem is sent from heaven by God: pure gold, fifteen hundred miles in length and width and height, surrounded by jasper walls encrusted with jewels, with twelve gates guarded by twelve angels, one for each of the tribes of Israel. A river of life-giving water flows from the throne of God down the middle of its street, lined on either side by the tree of life whose leaves are the medicine for the nations. The Lord himself would serve as its temple and its light, and only those in the Lamb's book of life would be allowed to enter.

John's revelations come to a close: the angel attests that what has been revealed is true. John falls down at his feet, but the angel declares that he is a fellow servant, that John is to worship God and not to seal up the prophetic words in the book. Then comes the voice of Jesus: "Very soon now, I shall be with you again, bringing the reward to be given to every man according to what he deserves. I am the Alpha and Omega, the First and the Last, the Beginning and the End."

The Woman and the Beast from the Silos Apocalypse in the British Library

The elaborate imagery in Revelation—symbols, numerology, proclamations—is familiar from the vision of Ezekiel, where he encounters the divine in the form of a man, surrounded by winged animal spirits. But John has a fuller vision. He includes humans—the elders; 144,000 people from all the tribes of Israel; people from every nation, race, tribe, and language. And his images of the Lamb, and the letters to specific, real-life communities, are both new elements in an apocalyptic work.

Sometimes the images are clear: the beasts and the whore of Babylon refer to specific world powers such as Rome. Sometimes they have many meanings, such as the woman clothed with the sun crying out in labor. She may be Israel giving birth to the Messiah; she could also be the church and her children in the wilderness under Satanic attack after the Messiah has been taken up to heaven. And she could be the same figure as the bride of the Lamb, the New Jerusalem, who comes down from heaven at the end.

The book of Revelation has been subject to all manner of interpretation through the centuries. On the intriguing matter of the seventh seal, Catholic scripture scholar Raymond Brown saw it as simply the unveiling of the next set of sevens: angels with trumpets. But filmmaker Ingmar Bergman considered the seventh seal to be the silence of God. The passage is certainly both mysterious and thrilling. The breaking of the seal imparts a revelation laden with meaning so powerful that the entire realm of heaven is reduced to silence. But is the meaning inspiring or terrifying? Life-giving or death-dealing? And why did it quiet things down for specifically half an hour, in a realm usually considered outside of time? We have no answers to these questions; we can describe the afterlife only in terms of our limited reality. Fortunately, this has not deterred us from continually reenvisioning what lies beyond.

THERE WAS A STRONG TENDENCY, from Zoroaster to Jewish apocalyptic writers to John the Revelator, to understand this world against the background of a spiritual world of good and evil powers in conflict, with an afterlife based on the resolution of this conflict. Gnosticism was an important strain of apocalyptic Christian belief, unknown for centuries until Gnostic scrolls (possibly banned by Christian authorities who considered them heretical) were unearthed in upper Egypt in 1945.

The Gnostic version of cosmic history was one of struggle between spirit and matter. Before the material world was created, there had been only the good realm of the spirit, inhabited by the one, true, all-powerful, and incomprehensible God. This God did not create our world, as an all-good God could not have been the source of such a corrupt realm, nor was he involved with it. He populated his realm with spirit couples and their offspring, but a spirit named Sophia attempted to understand the divine realm and, as a result, fell away from the other spirits.

The emotions Sophia felt—anger, terror—became persons on their own and created the world in order to capture her, to divide her into myr-iad pieces and trap her in matter. Bits of Sophia, tiny slivers of light, were imprisoned in an elect people who felt alienated from the world and des-tined for somewhere else. These bits were hidden within odious material human bodies but released at death, opening the way to a better, more godly existence. However, only those who had been saved by gnosis, secret knowledge known only to the elect, could achieve such an afterlife.

It is not clear exactly what this secret knowledge entailed, although there were myths about how spiritual bondage had come about and how to escape it, as well as maps and secret passwords for the spirit on its journey to God. Jesus had no role in liberating souls but was an important spiritual guide. There was also a version of the divine realm, one composed of heav-ens through which the spirit would pass. These were sometimes associated with angels—Uriel with the moon, Gabriel with the sun, Michael with Jupiter (although these associations vary). Metatron (formerly Enoch) dwelt in Saturn, the final heaven where God himself resides. To accomplish the liberation of their souls from matter, Gnostics aspired to an ascetic life, eschewing gluttony, drunkenness, and sexual activity—although those who wished to discredit them claimed they engaged in all these vices.

Some Gnostics believed that as the elect they would be drawn back to their heavenly home and equipped with the knowledge to achieve salvation. Orthodox Christians could achieve a form of not-quite-so-glorious salva-tion through faith and good works. Finally, there was everybody else: they had no spark of the divine within them and were bound for destruction along with the rest of the material world.

THE PROFUSION OF CONFLICTING IDEAS among Christians required the Church Fathers to clarify and consolidate theology and authority as well. Ire-naeus, Tertullian, and others writing in the first and second centuries consid-ered themselves to be in the direct line of authority: they had either known the Apostles or had been significantly influenced by them.

Irenaeus's teachings on the afterlife followed existing tradition. God would restore the cosmos to himself; the blessed would witness the renewal of the world, see Christ, join in the communion of saints, and live in peace and comfort in their true home. There were to be three successive periods in human history. The first was Irenaeus's own time, a time of persecution, when the inherent goodness of the world, its potential for peace and prosperity, was prevented from fulfillment by powerful worldly pagans. That fulfillment would come in the next period, the Kingdom of the Messiah, in accordance with Revelation and other biblical sources. The righteous would be resurrected; a full material life, reflecting that of (largely urban) Christians, would be restored on earth; and a glorious thousand-year reign would ensue. There would be no original sin, no old age or death. Martyrs would reclaim their place in the world; women would be endlessly fertile (and presumably enjoy it). There would be no sickness, no work, and wine would flow freely.

The final period would be the Kingdom of God the Father, the ultimate destination for believers, but Irenaeus did not describe it in the lush detail of the earthly kingdom. No wonder, for there God would bestow in a paternal manner "those things which neither eye has seen, nor the ear has heard, nor has thought concerning them arisen within the heart of man." The blessed would enjoy life with God not as purely spiritual entities freed from their corrupt bodies, as the Gnostics had it. Instead, the Holy Spirit would breathe eternal life into the bodies of the saved, transforming them into spiritual bodies.

Tertullian went further in describing what would happen. Because Jesus Christ had risen bodily from the grave, so would his followers: "What is raised is this flesh, suffused with blood, built up with bones, interwoven with nerves, entwined with veins, (a flesh) which was . . . born, and . . . dies, undoubtedly human." And he declared that while this was a shocking idea, "it must be believed, because it is absurd!"

It is indeed absurd, and Christians still fall into Platonic, even Gnostic patterns of thought—the demise of the created order, a purely spiritual existence in the afterlife. These notions contradict orthodox belief that Jesus's Resurrection will lead to the resurrection of the whole world. In Romans 8, Paul refers to creation as a prison of decay but also to creation being liberated. In the end, he attests to the mystery of it all, how we hope despite not being able to know, and wait patiently.

THIRTEEN

Augustine's Visions

With so many witnesses in a great cloud on
every side of us, we too, then, should throw off
everything that hinders us, especially the sin that
clings so easily, and keep running steadily in the
race we have started.

• SAINT PAUL

D uring the first two centuries after Jesus died, his followers went
out into the world, established communities, withstood persecution, and formulated a coherent, distinctive theology to ground
their mission. By the third century, what had been a Jewish cult had grown
to be an international institution with a clerical hierarchy. The formal Christian creed was formulated in 325 at the Council of Nicaea, including belief in
Jesus's resurrection and Christian anticipation of the resurrection of the dead.
The body of orthodox Christian scripture—the New Testament—was completed around 404, early heretical belief having been effectively erased.

In 380, Christianity was adopted as the official religion of the Roman
Empire, and for a short while the relationship between the orthodox Christian church and the Roman state was a fruitful one. The mission of the
church to convert the heathen was supported and enabled by Roman rule.
The state was able to demand enhanced allegiance from its subjects through
the new official faith. But the empire declined, and in 410 the Goths sacked
Rome. For many Christians, this was a sign of the end of history. Eternal
life felt very close.

CHRISTIAN VIEWS OF HEAVEN emerging during this time were dominated by two ideas. The first was that heaven would be theocentric, oriented toward God and a direct experience of the divine. The second was that ordinary society, built on kinship, marriage, and family, must be rejected. This attitude was rooted in the New Testament: when Peter tells Jesus that the disciples have given up everything to follow him, Jesus replies that those who give up family and land for his sake will receive a hundred times more. There was also a strong aversion to sexuality. In 1 Corinthians Paul wished that all men were unmarried like he was, as "it is a good thing for a man not to touch a woman." Fortunately, marriage was an option, if a lesser one: "it is better to be married than to be tortured."

This was a popular theme among the early Church Fathers. Origen castrated himself out of loathing for his body, and Ambrose of Milan declared that "he who has preserved [chastity] is an angel; he who has lost it is a devil." The church was reacting against Greco-Roman licentiousness, but that presented problems in developing notions of heaven: In a place of bliss, where all suffering was to be banished, how is it that one of life's great pleasures would be taken away as well? Would heaven be essentially spiritual, and if so, what would resurrection of the body entail? Would heaven be an individual encounter with God or a communion with God and others?

The writings of Augustine of Hippo reveal a remarkable evolution in his conception of heaven. His early works were written under the influence of Christian asceticism, which took many forms: fasting, celibacy, monasticism. Its worldview was informed by the familiar dualism: the spiritual was far superior to the material, which was considered degraded. Christian ascetics rejected material rewards and sought a heaven that would be the continuation of their way of life. Its benefits were considerable—physical health and moral education—and its aspirations noble: communication with the divine and visionary experiences. Such a life was considered fitting preparation for a purely spiritual heaven.

Augustine also came under the influence of the founder of Neoplatonism, Plotinus. His philosophy was aimed at loosening the soul from the body and strengthening its spiritual power. On the death of the body, the soul would rise to the transcendent world of eternal, immaterial ideas to contemplate true beauty. Finally, Augustine's faith was shaped by Manichaeism, founded in Persia in the late third century by the prophet Mani, who proclaimed it to be a synthesis of all religions up to that time.

Mani's was the most elaborately apocalyptic vision yet, profoundly dualistic and full of loathing for physical matter. A primal battle resulted in a sinister earthly creation, including Adam, who was captive to the powers of evil. In an echo of Gnostic belief, his body harbored germs of light, and Jesus saved him, revealing himself to be the personification of the Cosmic Light imprisoned in all matter. The aim of the Manichaean elect was to set their light free from the pollution of matter by leading a strict, ascetic life: no meat, property, wine, magic, or commerce. Most significantly, sex was prohibited, as it led to the reproduction of the human vessels that kept light imprisoned. At the end of the world, the light particles would be gathered together, and a great fire would burn for 1,486 years while the righteous enjoyed the torments of the wicked. Light and darkness would be separated, angels of light would return to heaven and the dark realm would sink away forever. Thereafter, eternal tranquility would prevail in the realm of light, with three fates available to humans. The elect would be crowned in glory, and their light particles set free. Others would enjoy the same reward, but only after a long period of purgation. Sinners, however, would wander in torment surrounded by demons and eventually be thrown into hell.

For almost a decade, Augustine studied the teachings of Mani's followers and defended their positions ardently, horrifying his friends and his saintly mother, Monica, with his heresy. He was involved with a Manichaean monastic community in Rome in 373 CE, but on returning to Carthage he repudiated its philosophy, declaring that it was depraved and led to nothing. By the eighth century, Manichaeism had died out.

THERE WAS YET ANOTHER, very deep influence on the young Augustine, an experience he had in 387, shortly after he had been baptized a Christian. He and Monica were enjoying their garden in Ostia and wondering about life in heaven. In Augustine's words, they climbed together "beyond all corporeal objects and the heaven itself, where sun, moon, and stars shed light on the earth." They ascended into internal reflection: "We entered our own minds." But having traveled so far together, they experienced the beatific vision alone; it was purely God-centered. Monica died shortly thereafter, as though her mystical experience had freed her soul from her body.

Between 397 and 400, Augustine wrote his *Confessions*, in which he recounted his wild youth and his conversion to Christianity. Of the vision at Ostia, he wrote: "At that moment we extended our reach and in a flash of mental energy attained the eternal wisdom which abides beyond all things." But Augustine struggled to attain mystical experience, due, he believed, to lack of moral strength and purity. Indeed, he recalls begging God, "Grant me chastity and continence, but not yet." Eventually he came to understand, despite his failings, that it was through love that he could experience God. "I was astonished to find that I already loved you . . . caught up to you by your beauty."

At this point in Augustine's life, this marvelous love was a taste of a purely spiritual heaven: immaterial souls in communion with God. Ascetic Christianity, Plotinus, and the Manichaeans had made of his flesh a heavy burden. Even the joy and solace of human relationships, so comforting in this world, would be irrelevant in the next, as the human pursuit of happiness could be satisfied only by God. But Augustine's vision of heaven changed as he grew older, embracing the whole community of the blessed, who would see and praise God together.

AUGUSTINE'S VISIONS

AUGUSTINE BECAME BISHOP OF HIPPO in 395, and remained there until his death in 430. In those years, he wrote *The City of God*, incorporating most Christian thought up to that time and setting forth a vision of salvation that is based on human history and society. Part II gives an account of a city where good and evil are intermingled, actually comprising two underlying cities: the City of God and the Earthly City. The City of God, reminiscent of the Jewish New Jerusalem, seeks glory from God, the Witness of our conscience. The Earthly City, reminiscent of Rome, seeks glory for itself from men. The heavenly city is imbued with love of God: all serve each other in charity, seeking their "reward in the fellowship not only of holy men, but of angels, so "that God may be all in all." The Earthly City is imbued with love of self, to the point of contempt for God. Those in power are mastered by it, while those who consider themselves wise become fools.

The progress of the two cities is traced from their origins in the separation of the good and bad angels, Adam's sin, Hebrew history, and the coming of Jesus. In the end times, the Jews will recognize Jesus as the Messiah. The righteous will be persecuted by the Antichrist, who will then be defeated. The dead will rise and be judged and the world renewed. The book concludes with eternal punishment for the Earthly City and eternal happiness for saints. The Christian community will dwell in a renewed heaven, their corrupted bodies having been "transmuted" into immortal bodies, renewed in their flesh "to some better thing."

AS HIS IDEAS ABOUT HEAVEN DEVELOPED, Augustine extended the idea of a redeemed community to the community of all believers in Christ. He included angels as well, with eternal communication among all. He was not alone in envisioning heaven through this "ecclesiastical" model. Cyprian of Carthage wrote of the great pleasure we would take in meeting the fathers, apostles, prophets, and martyrs in heaven. Heaven would be an eternally

Christ sitting on a throne, Basilica of Santa Pudenziana, Rome

happy home shared with friends, family—all those who love God. Ambrose described heaven as a new Jerusalem where joy would be found in union with Christ, in a community that would include not only the saved but also the church on earth, where bishops and sacraments act as conduits of grace.

Notions of heaven were not restricted to the writings of learned theologians. In one of the oldest sites for Christian worship in Rome, the Basilica of Santa Pudenziana, an early-fifth-century apse mosaic shows a heavenly gathering with Christ in the center. He is seated on a bejeweled throne and wears the golden toga signifying imperial authority, with apostles in senatorial togas on either side. Above Peter and Paul are women holding wreaths, symbolizing church and synagogue, and above them are the domes of heavenly Jerusalem. The sky above Jesus holds a brilliant cross and the icons of the four evangelists: angel (Matthew), lion (Mark), ox (Luke), and eagle (John). It is a dignified, even regal gathering, but interestingly the apostles, who have individualized faces, gaze outward toward us, as though from a porch above the altar. A worshipper might feel included in their sacred space, in their sacred company.

Another view of heaven is offered in *The Vision of Paul*, a document in wide circulation as early as the third century, supposedly discovered in Paul's house in Tarsus along with a pair of shoes in a marble box. It was purported to be the original account of Paul's vision of heaven. The writer declares: "I must boast. . . . I know a man in Christ who fourteen years ago was caught up into the third heaven—whether in the body or out of the body I do not know, God knows. And I know that this man was caught up into Paradise . . . and he heard things that cannot be told, which man may not utter." Nevertheless, the story got out. Older versions put Paul in the line of Enoch and Elijah who had bodily visited heaven and hell, and the version that comes down to us is a vivid account of a crowded, busy after-life. It's full of angelic activity, descriptions of the City of Christ and Regions of Hell, encounters with Enoch as well as Abraham, Job, and other dignitaries. Augustine took a dim view of this work, refusing to believe that Paul would have revealed an experience that Paul himself considered unlawful to utter.

But there are echoes in Augustine's later writings of this kind of heaven, populated by distinct individuals and angels. Those who are saved will live there in a holy community of all saints that spans past, present, and future. Mary will be a central figure: devotion to her had grown steadily in early church tradition, and the idea of her bodily assumption enabled believers to look forward to meeting her there. The Council of Chalcedon (451), which settled the doctrine that Jesus is fully divine and fully human, gave Mary the designation of Theotokos: she was not just Mother of Jesus, but also the Mother of God. And she was becoming the Queen of Heaven.

In the heavenly community, one's individual identity will be retained, and heavenly experience anything but uniform. All will be equally blessed, equally fulfilled, according to their capacity for fulfillment, and thus some will shine more brightly than others. In heaven, though, our tendency toward envy will be long gone. This is the definitive Christian community: companions sharing faith and joy in a cloud of witnesses to which those still in their earthly passage also belong, carrying out the work of God on earth with guidance and inspiration from their companions in heaven. They are the work of Wisdom: "In each generation she passes into holy souls, she makes them friends of God and prophets."

Baptized Christians who lived upright lives were eligible for admission to heaven, but what about those who led righteous lives before the coming of Christ? Augustine's solution to this thorny issue was that there were "natural" Christians before the Incarnation who needed no posthumous salvation since they had lived properly during their lifetime. As for babies who died before baptism, Augustine seemed not to trust sufficiently in the mercy of God: he taught that they bore the mark of original sin, thus, along with all other unbaptized people, they would go to hell. He rejected a benevolent practice that had some currency at the time: baptism of the dead so that they might go to heaven.

AUGUSTINE VIEWED THE SPAN of human history through the lens of theology. The Fall perverted the human will, directing it toward evil inclinations, which can be healed only through the intervention of God. Christ is the new Adam, and heaven is a return to a transformed, eternal earthly paradise where there can be no further fall. The end of the world, of this age, is not just an event in space and time but also the end of the corrupted state of humanity, whose redemption began with God's covenant with the Jews and extends to the second coming of Christ and the resurrection of the dead. But heaven is God within us as well as God above us, and persons and communities are being saved in an unfolding process.

The mature Augustine taught that at the Second Coming the living will be transformed and the faithful resurrected, their souls clothed once again in their bodies. He did not repudiate his earlier rejection of the flesh but acknowledged that once it was redeemed and led by the spirit, it could participate in the glory of God. A glorified body would not just be spiritual. It would be beautiful, fleshly, and communicative. In *The City of God*, he addressed all-too-human questions: we'll rise with the bodies we had at thirty; thin and fat will become just right; deformities will disappear (with the exception of wounds caused by martyrdom), and baptized babies will take the form they would have grown into as adults. But there will be no eating, drinking, marriage, or sex. In *Retractions*, written near the end of his life, Augustine went so far as to say that our bodies will be like the resurrected body of Christ—made of flesh and bone, and touchable by others.

Augustine describes how this will come about. "Both sexes will rise. For there will be no lust here, which is the cause of shame. . . . All defects will be taken away from those bodies, but their natural state will be preserved. The female sex is not a defect, but a natural state, which will then know no intercourse or childbirth. There will be female parts, not suited to their old use, but to a new beauty. . . . It will inspire praise of the wisdom and goodness of God, who . . . freed from corruption what he had made." Whereas Adam and Eve could enjoy themselves before the Fall, the resurrected will not do so in their new paradise. But this won't be a problem, for the Spirit will dominate the flesh, which will no longer be rebellious, and all human relationships will be oriented toward God.

Augustine had come to see the spirit operating from within, rather than above and beyond, the material. The new body emerges from and transforms the old body in a process of conversion from baptism to the Last Judgment to the eternity of heaven. Indeed, the soul yearns for the body to complete its evolution, accomplished through Christ. But immortality is not an attribute of the soul alone—it is a gift, breathed into resurrected bodies by the Holy Spirit.

The heaven that these resurrected bodies will inhabit is one of blessedness and bliss, utter fulfillment of mind, will, and, above all, love. But it is a universalized form of love with no exclusive relationships: those forged on earth will be replaced by the society of angels and the heavenly community of the saved. This love is a Christian combination of the Platonic idea of *eros*—affective love—and knowledge. It is through this form of love, a gift of grace, that we are able to see and know God and to find our true selves in God. As Augustine wrote: "Late have I loved Thee, beauty so old and so new. . . . I tasted Thee, and feel but hunger and thirst for you."

FOURTEEN

Many Heavens

The dull spirit rises up through the material
to the truth.

• ABBOT SUGER

A ugustine's blessed community of saints united in love and knowledge of God became the established view of heaven in Christianity. But medieval Christians continued to explore variations—a
theocentric heaven focused on God; an anthropocentric heaven oriented
toward human experience there, and all the ways in which we might earn
heavenly reward. In any case, heaven continued to be the antidote to a miserable life on earth, drawing people to the faith—with hell as the alternative, of course.

IN THE SIXTH CENTURY, Benedict of Nursia established a rule for monastic
life that was promoted by church authorities, and monastic centers spread
rapidly throughout Europe, bringing order to a scattered church and establishing it at the center of people's lives. In keeping with the Benedictine mission to take on whatever work was necessary in their particular circumstances
(teaching, farming, ministry), Benedict's teachings about heaven were concerned with human behavior on earth and its consequences in the afterlife.
He used the image of Jacob's Ladder: "By our ascending actions we must set
up that ladder on which Jacob in a dream saw angels descending and

ascending. . . . We descend by exaltation and ascend by humility. . . . The ladder erected is our life on earth, and if we humble our hearts the Lord will raise it to heaven." Each rung of the ladder represents the achievement of a virtue such as selflessness and obedience, with the tenth rung being (lamentably) the absence of mirth, for "Only a fool raises his voice in laughter."

A contemporary but strikingly different vision of heaven is that of Pseudo-Dionysius the Areopagite, who wrote in the name of a first-century CE Athenian saint. Nothing is known about him except that he was a Syrian monk, but his works were highly influential. In *On the Celestial Hierarchy*, Pseudo-Dionysius does not describe heaven itself but its heavenly inhabitants: the variety of angelic beings and what they symbolize. There are three sacred hierarchies of angels, all mentioned in scripture: seraphim (Fire), cherubim (Wisdom), and thrones (Seats of God), all of whom have six wings extending up, down, and outward to fly. Through their presence, knowledge, and order they are closest to God. Then come dominions, virtues, and powers, representing Justice, Courage, and Harmony. These angels are charged with spreading God's light to the worldly realm. Finally, principalities, archangels, and angels—Authority, Unity, and Revelation—are close to humanity and thus can guide us away from evil and toward God.

FROM EARLY CHRISTIAN INTO MEDIEVAL TIMES, stories abound of travelers to realms beyond earthly existence. Most of these stories are not visions of a marvelous afterlife, nor do they feature a famous protagonist. The travelers are humble individual souls on the journey from a body into what lies beyond death, which they see in terms of the world from which they embark. We recognize ourselves in them, and perhaps come to understand the path we are on, ineffable as our destination may be.

Pope Gregory the Great was not an original thinker like Augustine, but he was a brilliant administrator. As Roman imperial power declined, he worked to make the church a stable, independent entity and instructed

Christian leaders to provide good example and preaching to the faithful, who in a time of great social upheaval were in an apocalyptic frame of mind. The final book of Gregory's *Dialogues* presents proofs of the soul's immortality based on deathbed visions and eyewitness accounts. One concerns a soldier who comes upon a bridge over a foul, smoking river that leads to a pleasant land of sweet-smelling flowers. The bridge becomes wide to let the righteous pass and narrow to pitch the evil into the river, pulled down by hideous creatures. It is intriguing to find Gregory describing a bridge like the one Zoroastrians (and, later, Muslims) encountered: Could Gregory have known such stories? Or is it an archetypal image, a human insight appearing in many traditions over hundreds of years?

Gregory's heaven has to be earned, but it will compensate for the woes of this world. The saved will know past, present, and future, and understand the cosmos to the extent they are able. They will be equal to angels, happy in their potential for love and joy, living together in a perfected community. The good will recognize friends and family—indeed, everyone. And they will enjoy the beatific vision of God, which is inexhaustible because humans can never really fully comprehend God. Gregory offset this promise of heaven with the threat of hell, where demons lurk in bushes—in one scene, a gluttonous nun eats a lettuce that turns out to be a demon who proceeds to torment her. Interestingly, those residing in heaven will see the punishment of those in hell, but the heavenly inhabitants will not be disturbed because they desire only God's will.

Gregory's accounts represent a turning point in otherworld traveler stories: they focus on the interim period between death and resurrection rather than on the apocalyptic scenes that still dominated people's view of the afterlife. Gregory suggests that otherworldly visions are on the rise because the world to come is drawing near and mixing its light with the darkness of the present age. In the *Dialogues*, however, Gregory is more concerned with what begins at the hour of death than with predictions about the end times.

Until the twelfth century, the locations for Christian afterlife were heaven and hell. There was no distinct place called purgatory. The almost-good might have to wait outside heaven, and the almost-bad outside hell. There is a slight suggestion of a separate place in the story of a seventh-century traveler named Drythelm who dies temporarily and is taken on a tour by an angel. He views heaven from the top of a high wall, and the area nearest him is pleasant-looking, with people clothed in white seated together, rejoicing. This turns out to be the assembly of people destined to enter the full experience of heaven.

By the time *The Vision of Thurkill* was written by Ralph of Coggleshall around 1206, this waiting room had become a very different kind of place. As in Drythelm's vision, it is behind high walls, but it is a dreadful scene. Black-spotted souls are detained there for as long as it takes to purify them. They start in a fiery corridor, then proceed to an icy salt lake where they are repeatedly immersed. Finally, they have to cross a bridge with thorns in their feet, moving at different speeds depending on the gravity of their offenses—and the number of Masses said on their behalf back on earth.

By the late twelfth century, pilgrims were visiting Saint Patrick's Purgatory in County Donegal. Attended by Augustinian monks, they entered a door into a narrow cave with steps descending into a cramped niche. They believed the cave to be a site for spiritual healing, exempting them from suffering in purgatory after death. Tales of the visions they had there spread all over Europe. The *Treatise of the Purgatory of Saint Patrick* by H. of Saltry tells of Knight Owen returning from the Crusades to his birthplace in Ireland, filled with remorse that he has devoted himself to violence and plundering, and, what he regretted more, the desecration of churches and theft of ecclesiastical property. In the normal course of events, Owen would have been considered a menace to be banished from his people and sent by his bishop on a pilgrimage. But he insists on descending into the Purgatory of Saint Patrick. After a fifteen-day retreat, he steps into another world and follows a long, dark passageway toward a glint of light. At the end he meets twelve monk-like figures who warn of perils to come and instruct him to call upon the name of Jesus for protection.

They disappear; an earthquake ensues, and Owen is off on his journey with demons for guides. He tours four fields where sinners are being tortured in horrendous ways: baked in furnaces, plagued by serpents. When they come to the mouth of hell, a well where bodies shoot up and down in flames, the demons throw him in, and he becomes oblivious as he falls and falls in this bottomless pit of lost souls. Owen is saved when he remembers to call on Jesus. He is then taken to a river of fire and forced to cross a bridge that is impossibly slippery, narrow, and high; but as he goes, it widens, for he has been cleansed of his sins. He comes upon a bejeweled gate and is greeted and guided by two archbishops through a dazzling pastoral land. This is the intermediate world where, as in Drythelm's vision, the purified await God's call to heaven. As Owen witnesses a flame from on high illuminate each person, he is filled with a great sweetness and the desire to stay forever.

Alas, he cannot: he must go back to the world he came from to live a good life so as to be able to return. Owen's way home is easy, as he has been purified and demons flee from him. He is given absolution and sent on his way through the doorway of the cave into the light of dawn.

Owen's story is a classic example of the genre: as a pilgrim, his journey is identified with the final passage of death. The trials he encounters—the bridge ordeal, the cleansing fires—not only prepare him for the punishment he will face after judgment but also enable him to work it off. The presence of guides provides continuity between worlds, and they enable the pilgrim to progress toward the ultimate destination. But the tale is remarkable in that the protagonist does not fall into a deep sleep or temporarily die so that he can have a visionary experience: it tells of Owen literally stepping through a physical doorway into another world.

Church authorities made good use of the idea of purgatory, encouraging prayer and other pious activities on behalf of the dead that were an important source of revenue. As a place for unquiet spirits, purgatory also served to replace the persistent belief in ghosts and hauntings. But the authorities did not directly control Saint Patrick's Purgatory and came to regard it as a scandal. It was demolished on orders of the pope in the later twelfth century, then was reestablished and thrived until 1632, when the monastery was closed. But the flow of pilgrims never abated, and the site is visited by pilgrims to this day.

THE MONASTIC COMMUNITIES under which Christianity flourished gave rise to a pastoral version of heaven, described in *The Elucidation*, a widely disseminated theological work written around 1100. After the Last Judgment, God would reverse the effects of the Fall and restore the original Garden of Paradise. The earth, in whose bosom the body of Jesus lay, had been nourished with the blood of the saints and would be a mass of flowers. The blessed would be restored to nakedness, a state of natural simplicity, and would no more blush about parts of their bodies than they would now about their beautiful eyes. But with the urban revival in Europe during the twelfth and thirteenth centuries, urban culture took prominence over nature in notions of heaven.

During that time, a reclusive nun from Pisa named Gerardesca had a vision of a city-state in the midst of an immense park with three places to live, in order of spiritual merit. The city, the heavenly Jerusalem, paved with gold and jewels, was the home of the Trinity, Mary, angels, and the holiest saints. The distinguished blessed lived in seven castles on mountains around the city and were visited three times yearly by the city folk. Other fortresses were the abode of everyone else, the not-so-distinguished blessed. But all souls had access to the Holy City, for medieval cities and castles were places of security as well as power and privilege. In Gerardesca's heaven, festivities went on eternally: there were processions and rituals and rich clothing—certainly not sacred nakedness.

The architecture of the time reflected such images of heaven, in the richly stained glass and soaring vaulted ceilings of cathedrals such as Saint-Denis, the early Gothic masterpiece of Abbot Suger, who presided over its reconstruction. He conceived of God as the Father of Lights; Jesus as the "first radiance," and people as the "smaller lights." The west façade of Saint-Denis embodies Suger's desire to reach God: it shows the way toward the light of God, toward heaven. Abbot Suger's original inscription on the west façade includes this passage: "The work which shines here so nobly should lighten the hearts so that, through true lights they can reach the one true light, where Christ is the true door. . . . The dull spirit rises up through the material to the truth."

THOMAS AQUINAS WAS a towering intellect of this time, indeed of all time. A Dominican friar, he was not a contemplative but engaged in life as a teacher and writer. He saw individual life and the collective experience of humanity on earth as a journey that begins with God, is dominated by the desire to return to God, and ends with the promise of that return. In *Treatise on the Last Things*, part of his (unfinished) masterpiece *Summa Theologica*, Aquinas does not describe heaven through the rich imagery found in Gregory or Gerardesca, except for the quality of light. The glorified bodies of the blessed will shine seven times brighter than the sun, and that which lies beneath the empyrean will become a house of light, as it had been before the Fall. Glorified bodies will be dominated by the spirit, with no need to eat or drink, or to engage in odious elimination. The blessed will form a communion in which the good of each is communicated to the others.

On the intriguing question of whether the blessed would see the sufferings of the damned, Aquinas argues against the understandable objection that such an experience would indicate a "deformity of their perfected sight." Far from it—"Wherefore in order that the happiness of the saints may be more delightful to them and that they may render more copious thanks to God for it, they are allowed to see perfectly the sufferings of the damned." Needless to say, the scene of saints peering down into hell to enhance their blessed reward is difficult to reconcile with the notion of a loving and forgiving God and the loving and forgiving lives the faithful must have led to be admitted to heaven.

Aquinas draws from biblical tradition and from Augustine the idea that sight is the noblest, most spiritual sense and makes human bliss possible. Thus life in heaven will consist of the beatific vision: perfect contemplation that yielded knowledge of God through an enhanced and illuminated intellect. But there will be gradations to the intensity of this vision. Aquinas devised a system linking degrees of merit, love of God, and worthiness to eternal beatific knowledge. "The more love of God someone will have in heaven, the more perfectly one will see God, and the more blessed one will be," with the lowest rank being unbaptized children, who will be happy in an animal kind of way.

On the matter of what happens to the soul upon death, Aquinas proposes an eternal moment in which both individual judgment and the Second Coming happen all at once, although, paradoxically, not in a strictly simultaneous way. The righteous will be granted the beatific vision at death, but only as purely spiritual beings, as they would not yet have their bodies back. But according to the *Supplement*, which was compiled from Aquinas's notes after he died, this stage in the progression of the soul might involve a place where the least bit of pain is more than the greatest pain one can ever endure in this world. It is not a formal purgatory but a place where everybody except Jesus and Mary waits for the Last Judgment. God will be reigning and visible, but this is not the final state of fulfillment and bliss.

This interim period continued to be hotly debated: what happens to our bodies and whether we achieve beatitude at death or have to wait until the Last Judgment. Most early Church Fathers held that the soul had to wait for the end times, but others argued for the moment of death. The controversy became part of the political struggles of that time, with various entities such as the University of Paris, King Charles VI, and the Spiritual Franciscans attacking Pope John XXII, who asserted that souls had to wait, but recanted shortly before he died. In 1336, Benedict XII declared that it was perpetual truth that the blessed dead will be in heaven without their bodies before the Last Judgment and will see God face-to-face. To this day however, the Eastern churches continue to espouse the necessity to wait until after the Last Judgment.

FIFTEEN

They Had Love Always

Theologians may quarrel, but the mystics of the
world speak the same language.

• MEISTER ECKHART

Mystics do not wait for heaven; they seek union with the divine in their earthly lives. They are receptive to God in their hearts and minds in ways that transcend reality and transform their souls. Such openness requires abandonment of worldly things that are but an illusion to be broken through to find the reality of God's love.

The great medieval mystics taught different pathways to union with God in this life, and some had visions of the next. For Dominican monk Meister Eckhart, one needed to become poor in spirit to the point of self-annihilation; indeed, he denied any distinction between God and self. The Franciscan Bonaventure taught that our ultimate destiny and happiness lie in the encounter with God through love. The English monk Aelred believed that friendship rooted in Jesus's love inspires friends to love God.

Julian of Norwich had visions, recorded in her *Revelations of Divine Love*, wherein she was infused with a "graced wisdom that enabled her spirit to expand within an inner sky of boundless awareness." God revealed to Julian his own love-longing: he desires that we come to know and love him so that he can bring us to heaven and at the Last Judgment endow us with bliss. Julian witnesses God in heaven as a lord in his own house who has invited all his dear friends to a solemn feast. He fills his house "with joy and cheer. Utterly at home, and with perfect courtesy, himself was the eternal happiness and comfort of his beloved friends, the marvelous music of his unending love showing in the beauty of his blessed face." Julian is shown three forms of heavenly bliss: the thanks God would give the soul for suffering and service, the way all heaven's inhabitants would be aware of this thanks, and the freshness and pleasure of God's thanks that one would enjoy forever. To bring all this about, the Trinity would perform a Great Deed by which "all shall be well, all shall be well, and all manner of things shall be well."

MANY MEDIEVAL MYSTICS WENT beyond friendship and God's graciousness to express their religious experience in terms of erotic love. Belgian poet Hadewijch described the intense spiritual love in which the loved one and the Beloved "abide in one another in fruition, mouth in mouth, heart in heart, body in body, and soul in soul, while one sweet divine Nature flows through them both, and they are both one thing through each other, but at the same time remain two different selves—yes, and to remain so forever."

The Flowing Light of the Godhead is an account of a heavenly journey that is steeped in eroticism. It was written by Mechthild of Magdeburg, a noble, well-educated German woman who lived simply and chastely in a small, independent religious community. Mechthild's vision takes her through three different realms of heaven. The first is an earthly paradisal garden inhabited by souls who have not been sent to purgatory nor deemed worthy of entering heaven. As in other chronicles of heavenly visitors, Mechthild walks in the garden with Enoch and Elijah. The second heaven is a great dome of ten levels, or choirs, that grow smaller as they extend upward. This area was once full of angels, but there are vacant spaces where Lucifer and his followers dwelled. Mechthild learns that after the final judgment, the blessed will take their places according to merit, with the lowest spaces given to small children who die before they can earn heavenly reward. The three highest levels of this region of heaven are for martyrs, apostles, and holy women rewarded with eternal life like Mechthild and Mary, the Mother of God.

She goes on to the third heaven, where God lives, and is admitted to Christ's bridal chamber, where holy women from the highest realm of the second heaven have intimate union with him. When Mechthild visits this chamber, she kneels, thanks Christ for receiving her, takes off her crown, and puts it into the scars of his feet. Then "he took her into his divine arms, placed his paternal hand unto her breast and beheld her face. And in a kiss she was elevated above all the angelic choirs." In another visit, Mechthild is in the guise of a noble lady who yields to Christ, who appears as a beautiful youth. "Thus comes to pass what both of them desire: he gives himself to her, and she herself to him."

In Mechthild's heaven, the beatific vision was for all the blessed, but the beatific union with Christ was reserved for only the purest of virgins. It was the consummation of the soul's desire, not illicit erotic contact—pure love, in the medieval courtly tradition. The meaning of *virgin* was transformed to mean a spiritual lover. This type of vision never became part of official church teaching, as Augustine's and Aquinas's ideas did. But the two approaches coexisted peacefully: the theological, abstract heaven in the university and the pulpit, the mystical heaven in private.

MARY, THE MOTHER OF JESUS, was available to everybody. Visions of heaven often include a glimpse or an encounter with her: it was not necessary to be an ascetic mystic or a brilliant philosopher or to lead a formal religious life to appeal to her. She came to be seen as a loving mother to all. Devotions such as the practice of the rosary developed during this time, with its meditations on the mysteries of Jesus and its repetition of prayers, in particular the Hail Mary. French cathedrals such as those in Paris and Amiens were dedicated to her, as were English Lady chapels. Mary was widely depicted in European art, in very human ways that made her far more accessible than the remote figure

Mary, Queen of Heaven **by the Master of the Saint Lucy Legend
in the National Gallery of Art**

in Byzantine icons. Just compare Antonello da Messina's Benson Madonna
from the fifteenth century, in which a sweet girl cuddles her baby son whose
hand is tucked cozily into her bodice, with the thirteenth-century Byzantine
Enthroned Madonna and Child and its regal throne and grave, stylized physiog-
nomies.

Miraculous stories about the Virgin began to spread in the twelfth century in many forms and languages. They reflect a significant theological

development, told through tender tales of Mary's intercession in obtaining God's mercy for those facing his justice. The medieval fathers attested wholeheartedly to Mary's power. Aquinas declared that "God has entrusted the keys and treasures of Heaven to Mary," and Bonaventure saw her as our guide on the way and the very gate to heaven. We see this Mary in Sandro Botticelli's ravishing *Madonna of the Magnificat* being crowned by courtly angels bearing a gossamer gold crown lit from above by a divine sun. In *Mary, Queen of Heaven* (by the Master of the Saint Lucy Legend, c. 1500), she prays surrounded by angels, afloat over the earth, with the Trinity enthroned in heaven above.

THE DIVINELY INFUSED COSMOS, the yearning toward union with God, God's light and love drawing us to him, the ecstatic union with God and the beatific vision that surpasses expression—these characteristics of medieval Christian mysticism culminated in *The Divine Comedy*, written over the course of twelve years by the Florentine poet, politician, and philosopher Dante Alighieri.

Dante did not model his work on the New Testament or other Christian works. Instead, he revived the classic model of Virgil's story of Aeneas's travels for his own journey to hell, purgatory, and heaven. The universe in which he travels is that of Ptolemy, wherein the sphere of the earth is located at the center of several concentric spheres. The first is air, the next ether, and then the sun, moon, and planets. Beyond them is the firmament filled with stars, and finally the primum mobile, the outer sphere that moves all the inner spheres around the earth every twenty-four hours. Beyond the firmament is God's world, with two levels: the first is the spiritual heaven or empyrean, where the blessed and angels live with God in his visible form. In the final heaven of heavens resides the Godhead itself. In the ancient universe, each sphere sounds a distinctive note in a celestial harmony that reflects the perfect order and glory of the cosmos—indeed, it is said that the cosmos is "what God sings."

THE DIVINE COMEDY consists of three books: *Inferno*, *Purgatorio*, and *Paradiso*. It was studied by Dante's contemporaries as though it were sacred scripture, although church leaders had declared Christian revelation complete by the fourth century. Christian tradition holds, however, that works can be inspired, even if they are not revealed. Dante himself believed that human language was incapable of manifesting God but that God's Word could come to life in human words. He aimed "to reverse the ancient exile of our language from its source, to bring our fallen words through hell and purgation so that in the context of heaven they may rejoin the divine syntax." Indeed, the form of *The Divine Comedy* reflects the Trinity: three parts, composed of thirty-three cantos in vernacular Italian, written in verse triplets.

The Divine Comedy is both a vision and a journey to heaven and back to this life. Dante set it in 1300 and reported it in spatial and temporal terms. He makes it clear in the beginning that he is both poet and pilgrim—an everyman figure—and that the purpose of the poem is to write of the good he finds on his travels. Though he must include pain and suffering, he tells the reader, he will also find love, "God's love that in the beginning set all the beauty of the universe in motion."

The narrative begins with the *Inferno*, on Holy Thursday through Good Friday. Dante is rescued from moral wandering by his long-departed childhood love Beatrice, whose love will free him to seek union with God. She sends Virgil to guide him, and the two descend through the circles of hell: limbo, lust, gluttony, greed, wrath, heresy, violence, fraud, and treachery, arriving at the dead center. There Satan is fixed in a frozen lake, the very opposite of God's being and truth, gnawing on Brutus and Cassius, who betrayed Caesar, and Judas, who betrayed Jesus.

The travelers emerge back on earth on Easter Sunday morning and proceed to Purgatorio, a mountain in the southern sea, opposite Mount Zion. There they encounter on the lower slopes souls who have been excommunicated or have been late in repenting their sins. Passing into Purgatorio, they explore seven terraces, where those who are guilty of one of the seven deadly sins (pride, envy, wrath, sloth, avarice, gluttony, and lust) are suffering appropriate punishments. As a falconer would hood his falcon to train it, for example, the eyes of the envious are sewn shut with iron wire. The travelers encounter notable people: Pope Adrian V on the avarice terrace; and on that of lust, the poets Guido Guinizelli and Arnaut Daniel. For each sin, Dante presents its virtuous opposite: humility for pride, zeal for sloth.

Virgil leaves him at the top of the Purgatory terraces—he cannot travel further, as he was born before Christ and is not saved. Dante goes on to a lush earthly paradise, an eternal springtime. He is cleansed of his sins in the river Lethe and restored to the memory of virtues in the river Eunoe. Beatrice arrives to guide him for the rest of his journey, although she reproaches him for his failings. Because Dante has been cleansed of his sins, he recognizes his beloved as the splendor of eternal living light and glory of the human race. They then leap up to the stars. The cosmos is suffused with the ultimate Light of God and the cosmic harmony of the spheres, the ultimate reconciliation of all dissonance. Beatrice and Dante together are love, drawn toward its source.

Beatrice and Dante travel through the spheres, and the light from God increases in keeping with the worthiness of each heavenly body. On the moon, they encounter pale shades whose bodies will be restored at the Last Judgment. This is the sphere of faithfulness marred by inconstancy, as the moon waxes and wanes. Next is Mercury, home of those whose service was marred by ambition, and Venus, love marred by wantonness. Dante converses with historical figures: on Venus, the troubadour Folquet de Marseille gives a discourse on the temptations of love. There seems to be a hierarchy of souls in different spheres, but Dante learns that all souls are in the presence of God, fully blessed according to their own potential for love and joy.

Beyond the earth's shadow, moving more swiftly, Dante and Beatrice come to the Sun, the ravishing realm of wisdom and home to the wise. They are surrounded by twelve dancing lights: the souls of King Solomon,

Aquinas, and others who have illuminated the world with their intellects. Aquinas tells Dante that love has grown within him so that he can continue his travels and that God lovingly gives birth to all things seen and unseen, mortal and immortal.

Mars is next, the place of courage, eternal home to warriors such as Joshua and Charlemagne; then Jupiter, where dwell just rulers such as David. Saturn is a place of temperance, inhabited by contemplatives: there they encounter Saint Benedict, who has in place of a face a blazing light. Indeed, the beauty and intensity of Saturn is such that it might prove hazardous to the pilgrim, so God has muted both its sights and sounds. Dante beholds a golden ladder and exclaims that he thought all the stars in heaven were pouring down there. The ladder stretches upward so that these uniquely insightful souls can ascend to contemplate God more closely. Dante follows them but pauses to look back, to reflect that worldly ambition, seen from there, is as nothing.

Ascending to the Fixed Stars, the heavenly realm of the Church Triumphant, Dante finds that Beatrice's brilliant light has become that of Christ, although his eyesight is too weak to bear it. When Christ and Mary descend from the empyrean to welcome him, words fail him: "In order to represent or image the highest heavens, the sacred poem must leap a gap, like the one who finds the road washed out before him." Dante is tested by Peter, James, and John on faith, hope, and love, for he must learn all he can to teach those back on earth. Faith and hope will have been fulfilled, but love will endure in heaven. Having been approved by Peter and inspired by the Holy Spirit, Dante declares that his sacred poem has been wrought by both heaven and earth.

Dante is by now blinded by light and love and realizes that God is love. Beatrice restores his sight and they make their last ascent to the primum mobile, the final sphere of the universe, which is moved directly by God. There dwell nine choirs of angels: seraphim, cherubim, thrones, dominations, virtues, powers, principalities, archangels, and angels, each of which acts as the intelligence controlling one of the heavenly spheres. The primum

Illustration for Dante's *Paradiso* by Gustave Doré

mobile is enclosed not by something physical but by Light and Love, and from there Dante can look to the otherworld, the empyrean, which has no time, space, or physical being.

When he finally reaches the empyrean, the highest sphere of heaven, Dante encounters a river of light, of divine grace, alive with angelic sparks, flowing between banks blooming with faithful souls. Bathing his eyes in its water, his sight is transformed and he cries, "I saw . . . I saw . . . I saw," entreating God for the power to convey what he has seen: a circle of light emanating from God. Circular rows of seats for the blessed arise in the shape of a heavenly Rose formed by a ray of light from the primum mobile, gold as the angels and white as the blessed. Dante turns to Beatrice, only to find Bernard of Clairvaux, his final guide. He cries out for Beatrice, but she has taken her place in the third tier of heaven, just below Adam and Moses and Peter. He prays to her, and she smiles on him before turning back to the Light.

Bernard invites Dante to look up through the Rose to Mary, on her throne high above all the ranks of heaven, encircled by angels singing her praises. Gabriel sings "Hail Mary" as he did at the Annunciation, and all heaven replies in a song of serenity. Bernard gazes so lovingly at Mary that Dante's own love catches fire. Bernard then invites him to look at God, "so far as the divine glory permits," and prays to Mary to help him do so. The sight and under-standing Dante has earned enable him to enter into the Light: "Ah, overflow-ing grace through which I could presume to fix my gaze on the Eternal Light so fully that I used up all my sight." He speaks directly to the Trinity—"O eternal Light, you who alone dwell within yourself, you alone understand yourself, and, loving, smile upon yourself"—and beholds the shape of a human form within the Light, a vision of the Incarnation. Dante has been swept beyond human limitations: "At this point high imagination failed / But already my desire and my will / Were being turned like a wheel, all at one speed / By the love which moves the sun and other stars."

Dante, the pilgrim poet, returns from his visionary journey to tell a story for the ages. Seven hundred years on, its images reappear and its mes-sage of hope resonates again and again. T. S. Eliot was guided by Dante when he wrote the *Four Quartets*, concluding with Julian of Norwich's as-surance that "all shall be well and all manner of thing shall be well" in Dante's heaven, where:

> the tongues of flames are in-folded
> Into the crowned knot of fire
> And the fire and the rose are one.

VISIONS OF HEAVEN in medieval Christian Europe were otherworld oriented, but by the fifteenth century, in the culture that grew up in Italian cities, renunciation of the world and the practice of contemplation were no longer celebrated so much as life here on earth. Pleasure and happiness were recognized as legitimate goals, with virtue as a path to happiness, not an end in itself. It was through active participation and enjoyment of the world that love of God could be expressed. The Renaissance heaven was also more anthropocentric than previous versions. The philosopher's knowledge of God and the mystic's love had not sufficiently addressed the common longing for human love and companionship in heaven. Now we could encounter family, friends, perhaps even erotic love. A more human conception of heaven had emerged.

Renaissance depictions of heaven drew from Byzantine art, in which heaven was not only a place for the blessed to contemplate and praise God but also a place where they enjoyed an independent existence. Glorious heavenly cities appear together with lush paradisal gardens. Although such gardens had been described in the *Elucidation* and the vision of Mechthild, it wasn't until the Renaissance that they became an essential element in the heavenly scene, along with the beatific vision. Aquinas and Bonaventure had both denied the possibility that there might be plants and animals in heaven. But the Dominican Savonarola's *Compendium of Revelations* testified to a broad field of delicious flowers with crystalline streams and animals whiter than snow (ermines, rabbits, and the like) playing in the grass and multicolored birds singing sweet songs.

Renaissance images of heaven are full of people interacting with each other, and in this they were influenced by the classics. Petrarch wrote that Cicero "believed in the immortality of the soul and that some celestial abode awaits the honorable souls after this life." Indeed, in his writings *On Old Age* and *Scipio's Dream*, Cicero presents not ascetics or mystics but statesmen and public benefactors as moral exemplars destined for heaven.

This classical influence is evident in Raphael's *School of Athens*, painted on a wall in the Apostolic Palace in the Vatican opposite his *Disputation over the Most Holy Sacrament.* The *Disputation* shows a Christian version of heaven: notable personages such as Jerome, various popes, and Dante gathered on a terrace overlooking a dreamy landscape, above which Jesus appears on a cloud full of cherubs bearing aloft the dove of the Holy Spirit, accompanied by more august personages: Moses, John the Baptist, Mary. He is framed by a golden aureole crowned by an image of God the Father attended by higher ranks of angels.

The School of Athens is another kind of heaven, a perfectly symmetrical classical temple with statues of Apollo and Athena above Plato and Aristotle, who are framed in the central doorway. Plato points to the heavens and Aristotle to the earth, reflecting the ways in which they interpreted reality. They are surrounded by philosophers such as Epicurus, mathematicians such as Euclid, prophets such as Zoroaster, and other figures, one of whom might be Raphael himself. The atmosphere is one of supreme calm, although each figure is engaged in work or conversation. It is a gathering of the greats, in a place of exquisite beauty, a celebration of human knowledge. But to Raphael, Christian theology was supreme, and his *Disputation* was his testimony.

THE POETRY OF THE ROMAN Tibullus was another influence on Renaissance notions of heaven. He described the personal pleasures it would bring: "They had love always wherever they were . . . to those on whom Love's God breathed kindly did gentle Venus bring open pleasures in the shady vales. No watchers were there, nor doors to close against the vanquished."

This notion of a kind and companionable heaven is evident in *On Pleasure*, in which theologian Lorenzo Valla describes the traveler Antonio in search of his mother, father, brother, and sister, and his children—all of whom have gone before. When he reaches heaven, he is greeted with the greatest warmth not only by his relatives and friends but also by Mary, who clasps him to her breast and kisses him. All bodies are suffused with a great sweetness; one can play with angels and pursue all manner of learning "without error,

Disputation over the Most Holy Sacrament by Raphael in the Vatican Museums

The School of Athens by Raphael in the Vatican Museums

doubt, or ambiguity." In such a heaven, one would surely find the scene in Fra Angelico's *Last Judgment* wherein an angel embraces a man.

Pleasing Explanation of the Sensuous Pleasures of Paradise, written by the monk Celso Maffei, celebrates a very tender version of heaven. Here, Maffei describes the senses of the blessed as deliciously enhanced, and they all will be able to show affection to family members. Indeed, the saints will embrace Christ as he embraced the little children on earth. There will be kissing among all, even across great distances in paradise. There is a hierarchy, albeit a whimsical one: "According to a rough estimate, the body of the lowest saint will taste fifty times better than honey, sugar, or some natural food and drink of their world; another saint will taste a hundred times sweeter . . . and so on."

Aquinas had argued that the distance between the soul and the divine would be determined by spirituality, knowledge of God, and merit for doing good on earth. Mechthild had envisioned female virgins on the top rung; Dante placed Beatrice along with Mary, Moses, and Peter. In Giotto's *Last Judgment* the blessed are ranked, fixed on the beatific vision of God. In contrast, Renaissance paintings, with their active, engaged inhabitants, do not emphasize rank according to merit earned on earth. If saints are depicted, so are other blessed people like widows and martyrs, all free to mingle. And while they may enter God's place to praise him, they have their own in which to live.

SIXTEEN

Predestination for Glory

In my Father's house are many mansions. . . .
I go to prepare a place for you.

• GOSPEL OF JOHN

The lush, earthly Renaissance vision of heaven flourished for only a short time. Over the course of the sixteenth century, great social changes swept across Europe, and inadequate reform in the Catholic Church and the advent of mass publication led to intense popular interest in religious matters. These changes together brought about the Protestant Reformation and the Catholic Counter-Reformation. Where once different forms of spirituality had coexisted peacefully, wars of religion broke out across Europe.

By the time Michelangelo was painting *The Last Judgment* above the altar in the Sistine Chapel in 1534–1541, the vibrant humanism that informed his earlier work there had given way to a moralizing pessimism. Twenty years before, he had celebrated the prospect of fallen mankind being exalted through a redeemer; he now painted that redeemer as a terrifying judge. Christ is the massive central figure, his powerful right arm smashing down the evil on the left, driving them into hell, while on the right the dead rise up from their graves and the good ascend toward Christ. Mary huddles at Christ's side; she has no power of intercession, no role in this drama. In the throngs of people there are biblical figures—Abel, Noah,

The Last Judgment **by Michelangelo in the Sistine Chapel in the Vatican**

Rachel—as well as historical figures such as the traitorous Ugolino and Ruggieri from Dante's *Inferno*. The living are represented as well: Pope Paul III's aide Biagio da Cesena, who had objected that so much nudity was not fitting for a papal chapel, is depicted as Minos among a bunch of devils, with a great serpent curled around his body. It seems as though all humankind is here, and Michelangelo is foretelling a harsh judgment. In a world fraught with betrayal, confusion, and violent discord, it may have felt too late for mercy.

———

THE SIXTEENTH-CENTURY PROTESTANT REFORMERS called for a return to the early Christianity of the New Testament, which they considered more egalitarian than the hierarchical (and corrupt) Catholic Church. They regarded members of the clergy as spiritual guides, not privileged authority figures. Their theology was profoundly God-centered: humans were no longer free to approach God as a friend or intimate, and souls were unworthy even in eternity. Christianity was divided not about the existence of heaven but about how one earned it, and disputes arose over the issues of justification by faith, free will, and predestination.

Martin Luther and John Calvin emphasized openness to the secular world as well as total faith in God. Luther, a German theologian who had left the Augustinian order to marry a former nun, taught, "We are not made for fleeing human company but for living in society and sharing good and evil." Calvin, a French theologian based in Geneva, Switzerland, emphasized the duty to sanctify the world through struggle and labor and held that the materially successful received on earth some portion of their ultimate reward, proving their status as the elect. The poor and luckless seemed abandoned by God and thus not worth considering. This attitude seems very far from Matthew 25, where Jesus sitting in judgment made very clear who would be rewarded and why: those who side with the poor, who care for the downtrodden. But reformers argued that the Catholic belief in the efficacy of good works was in error, as were indulgences. People could not save themselves by their own efforts or by membership in the church. Indeed, such beliefs distracted one from complete faith in God.

Luther had a profound sense of man's fallen nature and believed that one must have a receptive, humbled will to receive the saving grace through which God would control both intellect and will to do good—indeed, Luther denied free will. Salvation could come about only through faith, which is a gift of God through grace. Luther did not endorse predestination, as Calvin did, stating, "It is plainly owing to the mere pleasure of God that salvation is spontaneously offered to some, while others have no access to it." Calvin admitted (wisely) that this concept "is attended with considerable difficulty, rendered very perplexed and hence perilous by human curiosity." But in confronting such a severe and incomprehensible doctrine, Christians can be confident in God's infinite justice and compassion.

In Luther's vision of the afterlife, there was no provision for the soul to go through progressive stages. He famously objected to the teachings of the Church on penance, the sale of indulgences, and purgatory, in his 95 Theses. "There is no divine authority for preaching that the soul flies out of purgatory immediately the money clinks in the bottom of the chest." Instead, "Any Christian whatsoever, who is truly repentant, enjoys plenary remission from penalty and guilt and that is given him without letters of indulgence."

Luther taught that the soul would go either to hell or to heaven, and its body would sleep until they were reunited at the final judgment. There would be no purgatory—why would there be, he argued, if one's admission to heaven was through grace alone? As for heaven, Luther's ideas reflected his view of the cosmos. The earth was still the center of the universe, but the regions extending outward were increasingly impure. At the Last Judgment, God would purify the earth and force all unclean matter to the bottom, to hell. Animals and plants would continue in their perfected state: fish, sheep, even "ants, bugs, and all unpleasant, stinking creatures will be most delightful and have a wonderful fragrance." Apparently, this purification did not extend to the elimination of human waste: to avoid that, there simply would be no food or drink.

For Luther, heaven would be home to a community of the blessed (the one holdover from the Renaissance heaven) in which gender would be retained but not rank or profession. No princes, no preachers, no hierarchical organization of society: God would be the only authority. Union with God had begun on earth, with Christ dwelling in us—what was incomplete on earth would be fully realized in heaven. Like Luther, Calvin foresaw the end of hierarchy. The "ministries and superiorities of the Church," even the angels would have to give up their official standing. And since family units were based on authority (interestingly, not love), there would be none; indeed there would be no community: "To be in Paradise and live with God is not to speak to each other, and to be heard by each other, but is only to enjoy God, to feel his good will, and rest in him."

THE CATHOLIC COUNTER-REFORMATION SHARED a great deal with the Protestant Reformation: efforts to renew the church, strong emphasis on God rather than humans, and emphasis on leading a Christian life. In reaction to Luther's teaching, however, the Council of Trent (1545–1563) stressed that heaven was earned not just through faith—it required good works and acts of piety, along with the sacraments. The Council also declared that heaven would be "the vision of God and enjoyment of His beauty who is the source and principle of all goodness and perfection," a view similar to that of the Reformers. But Mary was also a central figure, as intercessor and as queen: "the greatest enhancement of the glory of paradise by way of her bodily beauty and her divine presence," reigning over heaven and sharing in the royal magnificence and power of Christ.

The Council rejected notions of equality among the inhabitants of heaven, which instead would be a lot like the church on earth: beginning with a hierarchy of lowly laity, moving up to priests and so on up to saints; and with separate communities for men and women. Indeed, Dominican theologian Antonino Polti identified a dizzyingly specific list of fifty-eight examples of celibates, martyrs, theologians, and founders of religious orders so that we mortals on earth could emulate and ultimately join them. Heaven had become an instrument of moral discipline through its promise to the good and the threat of hell to the evil. Indeed, a painting of the Last Judgment by Peter Paul Rubens in a church in Neuberg, Bavaria, that featured a great chain of gorgeous naked bodies was removed for fear it would lead the faithful astray.

THE COUNTER-REFORMATION FOCUSED ON the individual's path to a heavenly life rather than grand visions of the end times or pastoral visions of heaven. El Greco's *Burial of Count Orgaz* depicts the moment when the soul makes its final passage from this world to the next. Set above the sarcophagus in which the count is buried, the bottom half of the painting shows Saints Stephen and Augustine come from heaven, cradling the count's lifeless body. This scene is depicted in realistic terms—the grandees are recognizable powers in Toledo and the saints are clothed in richly embroidered gold vestments. The count's body, however, is rendered in the cool gray light that permeates the upper half of the painting. In between the two realms we see an angel bearing the count's soul—a childlike wraith—up to heaven. There Mary and John the Baptist appear on either side, leading to Jesus on high. He is the source of the light that pervades heaven—a light that does not suggest day or night, as it is beyond time. For El Greco, the two realms are equally real; the limits of the temporal, natural world and the eternal, supernatural world are transcended through mystical devotion.

Such devotion was encouraged by contemporary saints such as Francis de Sales, Teresa of Ávila, and Ignatius of Loyola. In the first broadly popular book for lay Christians, *Introduction to the Devout Life*, Francis de Sales espoused "devout humanism," wherein everyone is called to union with God. Everyone can lead a deeply spiritual life even in the midst of a busy world, centered not in the mind but in the heart. It is love that "quickens us to the attentiveness of contemplation, and that attentiveness gives rise to a greater, more fervent love." Francis's view of the soul reflects his loving regard of others: rather than being doomed by its fallen nature, the soul is meant for heaven, in "predestination for glory." In his gentle, intimate view, souls will engage there in an eternal loving conversation with God, and Jesus will allow us to meet friends. God will reveal all divine mysteries so that the blessed can comprehend the incarnation and participate in its sacred mystery.

The Burial of Count Orgaz by El Greco in the
Church of Santo Tomé, Toledo

Both Teresa and Ignatius sought surrender to God through meditative prayer and ridding themselves of distractions from within and without, and both left guides for others to follow their practices. Teresa of Ávila described the journey to God in *The Interior Castle*, inspired by a passage in the Gospel of John: "In my Father's house are many mansions. . . . I go to prepare a place for you." This is no tale of a hero and his otherworldly adventures; rather, it is the journey of a soul toward God through the "many mansions." Outside the castle, "thought remains in the outskirts . . . suffering the assaults of a thousand wild and venomous creatures." Inside, in the first rooms, the soul is converted and begins to pray. The second rooms contain discouragement; the third pose the risk of the soul being stuck, neither experiencing nor demonstrating God's love.

It is at this point that the soul must let God take over, and the fourth set of rooms holds the beginnings of contemplative prayer. The soul becomes closer to God in the fifth rooms, made evident in love of neighbor. In the sixth rooms, joy, the soul comes to understand that following Christ necessitates both pain and joy. In the seventh, the soul finds peace and stability. A "spiritual marriage" has taken place: the soul has achieved unity with God. There need be no mention of heaven here—for Teresa, the boundary between life and death had been breached, and *"sólo Dios basta"*—God alone suffices.

Ignatius's *Spiritual Exercises* is a manual for a course of reflection, self-examination, and prayer, aimed at transforming both mind and heart. The person doing the Exercises seeks present experience through her imagination, locating herself in a concrete way in a scene—for example, imagining herself to be the woman touching the hem of Jesus's cloak, and being healed. This in turn informs her discernment of good and evil and leads her to detachment from anything that stands in the way of union with God. This is the way of the mystic, who understands that such union is not something to be relegated to the future but to be sought with one's God-given faculties now.

Ignatius's legacy includes not only his guide to mystical experience but also the Society of Jesus, the Jesuits who became missionaries all over the world. The nave ceiling in the church of Sant'Ignazio in Rome was painted by Jesuit brother Andrea Pozzo during the 1690s to celebrate their work and Ignatius's triumphant reception in heaven. A marble disk embedded in the floor marks the place from which the viewer engages in a spiritual exercise, contemplating the vision. In a feat of trompe l'oeil she is swept up through the church ceiling, passing beyond a marble temple swirling with saints and angels and allegorical figures (including the four known continents), on up to Ignatius being borne on a cloud of angels toward Jesus and

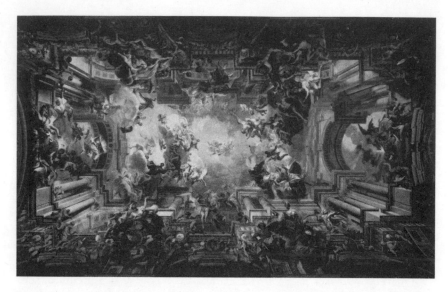

The Triumph of Saint Ignatius by Andrea Pozzo in the Church of Sant'Ignazio, Rome

Mary. The boundaries of earthly reality have burst open, and all are invited to ascend with Ignatius as he enters a heaven of light.

THE LATE SIXTEENTH TO MID-SEVENTEENTH CENTURIES were volatile times in religious thought. Along with the encouraging spirituality of Francis de Sales, and Ignatius's and Teresa's guides to mystical experience, there emerged strains of asceticism in both Protestantism and Catholicism, such as Puritanism and Jansenism. These movements involved a fatalistic sense of life, and there emerged, perhaps in reaction, more popular views that heartened the faithful in a world of suffering. *The Pilgrim's Progress* by John Bunyan is a variation on the theme of a journey in the afterlife. It is a story not about heaven but about getting there, with weak, flawed souls making their way along a perilous path.

Everyman Christian leaves his reluctant family behind in the City of Destruction, where sin flourishes and hell is imminent. He takes the "straight and narrow path," in search of the Celestial City. His adventures, enemies, and friends are all designated in the most straightforward way. Christian has to make his way beyond Vanity Fair and the Slough of Despond; he must withstand the predations of Sloth, Hypocrisy, and Giant Despair; but he is accompanied and encouraged by his guides Evangelist, Faithful, and Hopeful.

Christian makes his way with Hopeful through the dangerous Enchanted Ground, where the air can make one fatally sleepy, and crosses the River of Death, which only Enoch and Elijah have been able to avoid. Accompanied by Two Shining Ones, they come to Mount Zion and the Celestial City, entering through a gate inscribed: "Blessed are they that do his commandments, that they may have the right to the Tree of Life and may enter through the Gates into the City." The Celestial City is a familiar heaven: it shines like the sun; the streets are paved with gold; men are walking around with crowns and palms and golden harps, and angels chant continuous praise to God.

With Christian safe in heaven, his wife, Christiana, makes the same journey with their sons and their neighbor Mercy. They are guided by Great-Heart who slays monsters and giants, and cared for in a refuge for pilgrims run by personified virtues such as Charity and Prudence. Their journey takes much longer than Christian's, with more challenges such as finding wives for the young men and welcoming children. Christiana's band is a more feeble lot than Christian's, and they are accompanied by the likes of Mr. Ready-to-Halt, Mr. Despondency, and Mr. Despondency's daughter Much-afraid.

At last, a messenger arrives with a note for Christiana that reads: "Hail, good woman, I bring thee tidings that the Master calleth for thee and expecteth that thou shouldest stand in his presence, in clothes of immortality, within this ten days." She crosses the Dark River and takes off in a chariot. Others are summoned and transported, but the story ends without even a glimpse of the heaven beyond. Still, what earthly traveler cannot appreciate the progress of these pilgrims? With our own bumbling companions, we confront challenges on our way to the afterlife; and though we are bolstered by our hopes, our homecoming lies ever beyond us.

IN *PARADISE LOST*, the poet John Milton describes two perfect realms: God's heaven and the Eden of Adam and Eve. God's heaven has no saints, as there are no humans there—it is oriented toward God, with angels in attendance. Eden is a lush garden, a warmer and more intimate place oriented toward humans. But in both realms angels sing and dance, eat and drink, and go camping among the Trees of Life. They even make love—in a heavenly way. Raphael tells Adam that whatever he and Eve enjoy in the body, the angels enjoy without the obstacles of joints and limbs. They embrace air with air, a union of pure spirit in pure desiring.

Milton presents sex as an essential part of life before the Fall and deals with it in an unembarrassed way. Indeed, Milton (who was unhappily married) considered sex and companionship to be essential to human happiness and celebrates married human love as both a symbol of God's love and the source of life. Unfortunately Eve eats the fruit of the Tree of Knowledge, and Adam follows out of love for her, putting his natural affinity for Eve before his obligation to submit to God. They think their love of each other is fuller than the love of God, and it is this sin, along with their desire for the knowledge of good and evil, that causes their downfall.

But all is not lost: God shows Adam his plan for his children's future, and Adam realizes that each of us must have our fill of knowledge but not aspire to be gods. His sin and expulsion from the Garden have been transformed by God's benevolence. And thus our parents depart, hand in hand with slow and wandering steps, taking their solitary way.

MILTON'S VISION OF HEAVEN is by far the most well known of his time, but there was a broad range of opinion among his contemporaries. The Anglican bishop Joseph Hall was blunt in his description of a thoroughly God-oriented heaven, which would be free of gardens, friends and family, and presumably food and drink: "Nature has no place in glory; here is no respect of blood;

none of marriage: this grosser acquaintance and pleasure is for the paradise of the Turks, not the heaven of Christians."

Others looked forward to more fulsome human relations in heaven. After his wife's death in 1698, John Dunton, editor of the *Athenian Gazette*, wrote "An Essay Proving We Shall Know Our Friends in Heaven." He fervently believed that he and his wife would be united in heaven, although without any physical love involved. Otherwise, according to his unique theology, "the angels . . . would certainly be seduced from their innocence and fall as Adam did."

The Puritan Richard Baxter was more reserved in his view of heavenly company—there would be a communion of saints, but they wouldn't be interested in each other: "All the glory of the blessed is comprised in their enjoyment of God." Baxter believed that heavenly life itself would be eternal praise of God, particularly through song, and offered a path toward such a heaven. Through singing (as a spiritual, not a carnal, pastime) in this life, God "tunes up our dull and drooping souls to such joyful praises, as may prepare us for his everlasting praise in heaven." Singing not only prepares us for heaven, it gives us a taste of it. "The liveliest emblem of heaven upon earth is when the people of God . . . join together both heart and voice in the cheerful and melodious singing of his praises."

This sense that singing together is not only worship but also an emotional experience that brings one closer to God inspired Charles Wesley's remarkable body of some eight thousand hymns, the best known of which may be "Love Divine, All Loves Excelling." It celebrates God as Love coming down to earth in compassion, in Jesus, and asks to have our power of sinning taken away so that we might be worthy of receiving his life. Its final stanza is a leap in faith to heaven:

> Finish then thy New Creation,
> Pure and spotless let us be;
> Let us see thy great salvation
> Perfectly restored in thee,
> Changed from glory into glory

Till in heaven we take our place,
Till we cast our crowns before thee,
Lost in wonder, love, and praise!

The words to such hymns give us a way of envisioning heaven, as they do in George Frideric Handel's stirring oratorio *Messiah*. Its lyrics were compiled from the King James Bible by Charles Jennens, who used verses to tell the story of Jesus Christ. From the prophecies of Isaiah, we hear good tidings of an exalted world to come and the revelation of the glory of the Lord, Emmanuel himself. We hear the story of his birth and his suffering and death and resurrection. And then come the end times, when the trumpet shall sound and the dead shall be raised incorruptible, and we all shall be changed: we mortals will put on immortality and death will be swallowed up. The Kingdom of this world has become the Kingdom of our Lord, and of His Christ, and he shall reign forever and ever.

The oratorio concludes with a mighty hymn of praise to Jesus reigning in heaven:

Worthy is the Lamb that was slain,
and hath redeemed us to God by His blood,
to receive power, and riches, and wisdom, and strength,
and honour, and glory, and blessing.
Blessing and honour, glory and power to be unto Him
that sitteth upon the throne
and unto the Lamb, for ever and ever. Amen.

A glimpse of heaven is also found in the *Requiem* by Johannes Brahms. The traditional requiem, originating in the fifteenth century as the Catholic Mass for the Dead, concerned the repose of the soul of the departed, replacing joyful elements of the mass such as the *Gloria* with hymns about the Dies Irae (Day of Wrath) and prayers such as Requiescant in Pace (Rest in Peace). Brahms's *Requiem* has a much different orientation. Its libretto, derived from Luther's translation of the Bible, contains no dogma or talk of judgment. Rather, it concentrates on the comfort to the living—to those who mourn—promised by the Lord. Its central piece, "How Lovely Is Thy Dwelling Place," is a hymn of longing for the presence of God in the courts of heaven where burnt offerings are made at the blessed incense altar. It tells of those who through their trust in God inspired "highways to Zion in their hearts." They will meet together with the Lord, whose gracious and glorious presence will satisfy all need:

> Not one good thing wilt Thou withhold
> From those who walk in uprightness;
> Bless'd is the man that trusts in Thee
> With grace and glory measureless.

SEVENTEEN

Eternal Progress

That's what eternities are for.

• RUSSELL HANCOCK

For all the dogma promulgated, all the artistic visions and intriguing stories of otherworldly journeys, none of us has ever met anybody who has returned from heaven with a verifiable report. And yet so many descriptions of heaven are delivered as though they were definitive. There comes a point—right about now for this pilgrim—when one realizes that self-appointed holy men have been declaring very different theories down through the centuries, each adamant that he has the truth and that the rest of us had better accept it or else. The visions of our next otherworld traveler are a timely antidote.

Emanuel Swedenborg was an eighteenth-century polymath: a scientist, philosopher, theologian, and, in his own way, a mystic. Once a member of the Swedish Board of Mines, he had a spiritual crisis in his fifties and later declared that churchmen knew nothing of heaven, hell, or his own life after death. Thus, "to prevent so negative an attitude . . . it has been made possible for me to be right with angels and to talk with them person to person." Swedenborg meticulously documented his dreams and inner experiences in his *Dream Diary*. He followed meditation practices that he could not have known were those of Hindus and Buddhists. They were at first intensely intellectual but eventually opened up to the "hypnogogic" state experienced by people going in and out of sleep. Swedenborg trained himself to go into a trance wherein his body felt paralyzed but his consciousness was intensified.

Swedenborg believed the next phase of life to be very close, in line with the Protestant view that the soul went immediately to heaven or hell. And many of Milton's ideas are elaborated in Swedenborg's heaven. Two perfect worlds are combined into one heavenly realm, with angels who are actually former humans. Heaven is a continuation and fulfillment of earthly life, with all its sensual pleasures, and is busy and progressive, for spiritual maturation is eternal. Human love is essential to heavenly life, and not in conflict with the love of God. As Swedenborg testifies: "All my experience in heaven bears witness to the fact that the divine nature that comes from the Lord, affects angels, and constitutes heaven, is love." But in touring Swedenborg's heaven, one does get the sense that the beatific vision might be starting to fade.

In Swedenborg's afterlife, spirits ready for heaven become angels, and they teach other spirits to look inward to examine the lives they have led. Those who refuse to do so are unable to discern the path to heaven, condemned by their own limitations to see only the path to hell. This notion of self-judgment appears in Zoroastrianism and in Islam, but Swedenborg's theory is a distinct departure from traditional Christian belief that God decides a spirit's eternal fate at death and the Last Judgment. He considered this belief to be a radical underestimation of God's goodness and of the capacities of humans to choose our own path, even after death.

In Swedenborg's heaven, the sources of truth and beauty are found in nature, and matter is a manifestation of the spirit. Further, "heaven is yoked with earth by means of correspondences." For example, immature spirits may appear as animals: cats are those who listened to sermons but did not heed them. Houses in heaven represent the virtue of their inhabitants, and their contents "correspond to the goods and truths they have from the Lord." Not only are there houses, but cities and mountains, food and games, friendship and love. Heaven is welcoming, familiar, material in such a way that we still enjoy bodily pleasures. People live with others who have similar characters and move to higher levels of being as they grow spiritually. This happens to everybody: Swedenborg recounts being summoned by Luther, enthroned among his students seated according to their fidelity to his teachings. Luther is put out that Swedenborg has experienced new revelations, but after speaking with him he realizes his own errors and laughs at them.

Swedenborg's heaven is a busy one, in motion as the earth is in motion. In order to grow spiritually, one must engage in charity and service to others. The spirits of women take care of babies in heaven; angels are sent to guard the living or are involved in heavenly civic affairs. All are manifesting God's love. An angel who refuses, or is unable, to fulfill his obligations is manifesting a "different nature" and is thrown out of heaven. The others progress spiritually through three levels. At the first, natural level are angels whose understanding has been raised a bit above that which they achieved on earth. At the next level, the spiritual kingdom, angels show their mutual love through Christian charity. They have churches and clergy to preach to them, and now and then hypocrites visit, but they feel tortured and "turn blue in the face, almost to die." Finally, angels in the celestial kingdom no longer need clergy. They are naked—in Swedenborgian correspondence to their innocence—and concentrate solely on God. They are at the highest level of spiritual maturation, but they continue to progress forever toward greater and greater innocence.

SWEDENBORG, LIKE MILTON, believed that friendship and sexual relations are intrinsic to our nature and essential to our happiness. True earthly marriages endure in the afterlife; otherwise new partners better suited to heavenly progress are found. Celibates who wish to remain so are quarantined on the side of heaven so as not to "infest the sphere of married love." Spirits make pure and holy love with a pleasure that is divine. There can be spiritual offspring, but procreation is not the point of heavenly marriage. Women who so wish are given children who have died to raise with the knowledge of the good and true, so that they, too, can progress. Those who were unmarried on earth, like Swedenborg himself, will form spiritual marriages in heaven. In fact, Swedenborg had a wife picked out already: the Countess Elizabeth Gyllenborg-Stjerncrona.

Swedenborg's version of heavenly companionship is thoroughly romantic and central to heavenly activity. Spirits are able to experience the love of God through true marriage, not solely in contemplation of the beatific vision or in sacred conversation with other heavenly beings.

Swedenborg's account of heaven certainly gives us much to look forward to. One does wonder, however, how he could have gained knowledge of states achieved by other people only after they have gone through progressive stages of spiritual development. Was he so privileged as to be able to just drop in? How could he, a mortal, have understood what was going on in these upper reaches? I suppose these are questions we might use to challenge all our otherworld travelers—but then who would be our guides? In any case, Swedenborg proposed visions of heavenly life that have persisted into the twenty-first century: they are human-oriented and dynamic, full of variety and change, for constant growth in knowledge and joy are essential to human happiness. He himself is largely forgotten.

For the poet and mystic William Blake, there was "no birth and no death . . . only the perpetual pilgrimage within time towards eternity." He believed in the superiority of subjective experience, with the imagination as the path to understanding. Boundaries between worlds seem not to have existed for him; the imagination existed simultaneously here and beyond. Indeed, Blake believed that his sources for his portrayal of heaven—in his poetry, etchings, and paintings—were actually heavenly: his dead brother, Voltaire, the angel Gabriel. "I am under the direction of Messengers from Heaven, daily and nightly."

Blake wrote *The Marriage of Heaven and Hell* as a parody of Swedenborg's ideas. In a text interwoven with his illustrations, he inverts good and bad and celebrates the tension between such "contraries." Blake pokes his thumb in the eye of a timid, pale piety, celebrating instead an energetic, robust embrace of life and the power of imagination. Walking along the fires of hell, he delights in the enjoyments of Genius that to Angels look like torment and insanity. His version of the book of Proverbs is the Proverbs of Hell: "The road of excess leads to the palace of wisdom," and "Prudence is a rich, ugly old maid courted by Incapacity." At dinner with Isaiah and Ezekiel, he grills the latter on why he ate dung and lay so long on his right and left sides. He claims that Angels "have the vanity to speak of themselves as the only wise; this they do with a confident insolence sprouting from systemic reasoning."

Blake charges Swedenborg with writing no new truth, just all the old falsehoods. But he eventually came to appreciate Swedenborg: "The works of this visionary are well worthy of the attention of Painters and Poets; they are foundations for grand things." He agreed with Swedenborg that the Last Judgment was not a single, terrifying event but was ongoing: "Whenever any Individual Rejects Error & Embraces Truth a Last Judgment passes upon that Individual." His version of heavenly love was certainly influenced by Swedenborg and Milton. The love humans experience on earth is the highest ideal for Blake and continues in the next, as can be seen in his many depictions of families reunited and humans lovingly embracing after death. Such scenes are not allegorical: for Blake, their literal meaning reflects eternal truth, the mystical union of "primordial man and woman, body and soul, lover and beloved." Human love reflects the eternal in the human character, not communion with the divine.

FOR NINETEENTH-CENTURY BELIEVERS, heaven was closer than ever. A departing soul did not make a radical break from this world, and her heavenly destination was full of familiar activities aimed at eternal spiritual progress. The worship and union with God that had been the sole or primary purpose of heavenly existence was giving way to education, service, and raising families. "Heavenly rest" was not necessarily rest but activity without fatigue or frustration, and there were many mansions in which to keep the soul busy.

In theological reflection and mainstream church teaching, heaven continued to be theocentric, but a strong emphasis on the family was emerging among both Protestants and Catholics. The Holy Family was celebrated, along with the chastity of Mary and Joseph—a far cry from Blake's mystical human love. Pope Leo XIII hoped that "each family would truly present a likeness of the heavenly home." These ideas flourished in the popular imagination, fed by essays, stories, and novels such as *The Gates Ajar*, the 1888 bestseller by Elizabeth Stuart Phelps. Mary, a young woman who has lost her brother in the Civil War, keeps a diary of conversations with various people about what she can hope for in heaven. Her minister, Dr. Bland, offers a dry, traditional focus on union with God; her aunt Winifred— intelligent, loving, well versed in scripture—believes otherwise: very few people would be happy eternally just "studying the character of God." Love of God, on earth and in heaven, is expressed through one's human relationships. How could it be otherwise? It is miserable to be separated from loved ones, and heaven promises joy.

What heaven is like is Phelps's own notion of joy, of course—Aunt Winifred's "beautiful home, and my husband and [child] as I had them here; with many differences and great ones, but mine just the same." Phelps's heaven does not feature blissfully self-absorbed couples as in Swedenborg or Blake but rather a large extended family. It also provides the opportunity for good people from all ages to mingle, and Civil War soldiers are shown meeting with Abraham Lincoln.

Mark Twain was scornful of Phelps's "mean little ten-cent heaven about the size of Rhode Island—a heaven large enough to accommodate about a tenth of one percent of the Christian billions who have died in the past nineteen centuries." Historian Jeffrey Burton Russell has a more serious critique, cautioning that this kind of "feel-good" religion is as deceptive as it is attractive, its beliefs not rooted in reason, tradition, or scripture but through new and personal revelation.

PERSONAL REVELATION WAS the wellspring of the Church of Jesus Christ of Latter-day Saints. Its founder, Joseph Smith, grew up in the "Burned-over District" of New York State, so called because there were no souls left to convert due to successive waves of religious fervor during the early nineteenth century. Young Smith was visited by God the Father and Jesus Christ, who told him not to join a religion. Instead, he founded one that would embrace every truth without limitation, without prohibition "by the creeds or superstitious notions" of others. He received revelations over the course of ten years and was eventually called to restore the true church of Christ. By the time he died, he had dictated over a hundred revelations and written epistles and sermons.

But Smith was seldom dogmatic and acknowledged that his efforts were flawed by his own "crooked, broken, scattered, and imperfect language," as well as human weakness. Smith's efforts were just the beginning of Mormon doctrine, which is regarded as a living tradition. The Mormon story unfolds in a still-evolving universe, with an embodied God and an eternal human spirit. Revelation, both public and personal, is continuous, and scripture is expanding, including anything spoken by Mormon prophets when inspired by the Holy Spirit.

A former bishop of a California congregation, Russell Hancock, described for me the Mormon history of the cosmos, which has existed and will exist eternally. God and Jesus created our universe (one of many) fully comprehending the laws of science, which are part of eternal truth that continually unfolds in human understanding. Hancock told of a great council where all God's children were gathered to plan for their life on earth. Lucifer presented a plan whereby everybody would be saved. Jesus had a more challenging idea: that humans would have a conscience and be free to make moral choices. There ensued "the war in heaven," after which Lucifer and his hosts were cast into hell. As for humans, we would fail again and again, but this would enable us to repent and make spiritual progress. Still, our sins would require atonement, and Jesus took on that "bitter cup." Hancock moves seamlessly from his reading of science to what I understand as metaphor but which he accepts as literal truth. He frankly acknowledges his own limitations, however, rooted as he is in this time and place, with knowledge that is incomplete.

OUR STORIES OF OTHERWORLD TRAVELERS, and of mystical transport, have told of humans reaching beyond their natural boundaries to encounter the divine and the world beyond. While there are accounts of appearances to mortals by Jesus, Mary, and various saints, nobody has been granted as many prolonged and elaborate visitations as Joseph Smith. He did not go to heaven to meet God, the saints, and the prophets. They came to him: Abraham, Noah, Adam, and apostles who had lived on the American and Asiatic continents. Even Enoch, that inveterate traveler, visited Smith.

All these apparitions were possible because for Mormons, heaven and earth exist in the same material universe—spirit is simply a finer and purer form of matter. God does not exist outside time and space but is a real person with a tangible body of flesh and bone and a heart that feels our joy and suffering. God is the supreme intelligence, with the power to unite and elevate the human family in heaven—although he is neither the source nor the creator of souls. Mormons have reimagined God, and humans as well. We have existed from eternity, first as "uncreated intelligence" and then fashioned into spirit form by God. Through the eons, we become knowledgeable and godly through our moral choices, and God then sends us to earth to take on mortal form. We forget everything from our pre-earthly existence but continue our development, endowed with the Light of Christ so that our conscience reflects traces of eternal realms and values, and with God-given "ordinances," sacred formal acts that promote eternal progress.

And, of course, there is continuous revelation. In a faith that is explicit and literal in its teachings, it may fulfill the same function as mysticism in other religions, a wellspring that tempers institutional dogmatism and re-freshes the spirit. Thanks to revelation, there will come a time when there will be no more mysteries; indeed, achieving complete understanding of things is part of becoming divine. When I admired his patience in waiting for that day to arrive, Hancock replied, "That's what eternities are for!"

MORMON BELIEF IN THE AFTERLIFE is clearly set forth in current doctrine and is anything but metaphorical. "Mormons have a tremendous imagination: we contemplate these things, and we talk about these things as if they are really happening, and that requires a combination of faith and hope and imag-ination," Hancock said.

At death, Mormons believe that the soul leaves the body and enters the spirit world, a new stage of life in which the soul develops until the resur-rection. This realm is separated from our world by only a thin, permeable veil: our world and that of the dead are closer than we realize, and linked by love. One Mormon described it as a waiting place before eventual return to the Heavenly Father. The righteous are in a traditional lush paradise, reunited with their families, and they are busy evangelizing those in the spirit world who have not heard Mormon revelation while on earth. Those who do not live righteous lives experience torment. As in Swedenborg's heaven, there is no judgment at death. The suffering of evil spirits and those ignorant of the truth are not eternal, and they retain their free will. Thanks to the ministrations of Mormons in the afterworld, and those on earth who research ancestors and ensure that appropriate ordinances are performed for them, evil spirits can choose to believe, and thus to progress spiritually.

Mormons believe that there will be a Second Coming and that Christ will inaugurate his reign of a thousand years beginning with a sweeping physical transformation of earth and its inhabitants. Mountains will be flattened, continents reunited; evildoers will be banished to the spirit world, and Satan rendered powerless. All those who have led virtuous lives,

Mormons and non-Mormons, will be resurrected. Their spirits will be joined with their renewed bodies, and they will live in peaceful harmony in the new Eden on earth. It will be a busy millennium, with families to establish, cities to be built, and crops to be tended. And there will be souls to be saved: indeed, such efforts will be redoubled. Mormon scholar Gordon Allred wrote, "It can well be said that the resurrection and millennium . . . will be a fine time for the genealogist and temple worker—the finale and crescendo to the whole symphony of vicarious work." All work accomplished on earth, in the spirit world, and during the millennium will give people the chance to attain perfection and thus to become gods.

When Christ's reign comes to an end, and Satan has been allowed to tempt the righteous for a short time, the Final Judgment will take place. Every soul will be reunited with its body and sent to one of three stages of glory, or to eternal hell. The highest level of heaven will be the celestial glory, wherein the renewed earth will be a sea of fire-infused glass. There will be different degrees of glory here, with the exalted at the top. Not only will they have progressed during their lives through belief, ritual, and virtue so as to attain heaven and be admitted to the presence of God; they will also have achieved personal perfection. Heaven for the exalted is not reunion with the Heavenly Father but actual participation in His divine nature. "As man expands toward divinity, more and more of the divine enters into his being, until he attains a fullness of light and truth."

Family, an essential part of God's plan, is the basic unit of life on earth and in the celestial heaven. Mormons are called on to procreate, and that requires men and women in a partnership that is eternal. (That may not sound like heaven to many, but Mormons believe that God will heal all broken relationships.) The celestial heaven has three realms. Only men who have entered into an everlasting covenant of marriage (through a temple marriage ceremony called "sealing") can reach the most exalted state, and their wives achieve godliness by participating in their husbands' eternal priesthood. The children these couples produce on earth are eternally sealed to them, so that they can continue as a family in eternity. The exalted couple reproduces for all eternity, as do women who have not had children on earth but are faithful and have received the proper ordinances. Their "spirit children" eventually enter bodies and have children of their own, and their parents continue to progress through even more reproduction. They become like God, populating and ruling over worlds where spirit children have taken on bodies. And God himself continues to grow; the increase of his dominion is his progression through eternity. The nineteenth-century notion of a snug, domestic heaven revolving around an intimate, couple-based family life has taken on cosmic proportions.

The two lower realms in the celestial heaven have not been fully explored in Mormon theology, except to say that the inhabitants are not gods but angels and that they will be single servants ministering forever. Farther down, there are two other heavens: the terrestrial and the telestial. The first is the abode of people who believed in Jesus while on earth but did not keep the principles and ordinances of the gospel. There also dwell souls from "the heathen nations" who were honorable on earth but did not accept the fullness of the gospel even in the spirit world. Those who make it to the terrestrial heaven will enjoy the presence of Jesus but not of the Father. The telestial heaven will be the home of liars, adulterers, all those who did not accept the gospel. They are not worthy of resurrection at the Second Coming but have to spend extra time in torment so they can repent and prepare themselves for heaven. They will be resurrected after the millennium, become servants of the Most High, and receive the Holy Spirit, but they cannot enter the realms of Jesus or the Father.

Almost all humans will eventually find their way to some level of heaven, based on the lives they have led on earth and in the spirit world. They will have a chance to hear the gospel and to progress, aided by Mormons in both worlds. But the "sons of perdition" who followed Satan on earth and turned against God will dwell in a heaven that is not glorious, and the sons of perdition who followed Satan in preexistence will suffer with Satan in eternity.

EIGHTEEN

God's New Creation

All the way to heaven is heaven if you have
eyes to see.

· GREG BOYLE, S.J.

Times of upheaval and change such as ours have always inspired apocalyptic forms of faith. Many contemporary religious conservatives believe these are the end times, that their people are faced with multiple threats, that their way is God's way and the only way. Indeed, roughly half of evangelical Americans are Christian Zionists, whose beliefs are based on a theological worldview known as "premillennial dispensationalism." In this view, history has been divided by God into distinct periods—called dispensations—in the unfolding of his plan for humanity. Ours is the final dispensation, just prior to Jesus's millennial kingdom described in Revelation, after which the Final Judgment will take place.

Jesus is to return right after the Temple is rebuilt and Israel is restored as an exclusively Jewish state. Because God promised in Genesis to bless those who bless Israel, Christian Zionists have a vested interest in the fate of modern Israel. One of their prominent spokespersons, the Reverend Robert Jeffress, gave the blessing at the 2018 opening of the American embassy in Jerusalem, referring to the founding of modern Israel as a re-gathering of God's people and to biblical prophecies about Christ's Second Coming. For Christian Zionists, the relocation of the United States embassy from Tel Aviv to Jerusalem—against the wishes of its allies and other countries in the region—is a key step in bringing about the end times, which they eagerly await.

There is also a notion among some evangelical Christians, based on Paul's first letter to the Thessalonians, that the "rapture" is coming, whereby Christians alone will be delivered from an earth undergoing a fiery destruction. "At the trumpet of God, the voice of the archangel will call out the command and the Lord himself will come down from heaven; those who have died in Christ will be the first to rise, and then those of us who are still alive will be taken up in the clouds, together with them, to meet the Lord in the air. So we shall stay with the Lord for ever."

THE REVEREND GLEN DAVIS, an ordained Assemblies of God minister who works with Chi Alpha Christian Fellowship at Stanford, focuses on Jesus's return. It will be an actual irruption into history, the end of this universe and the beginning of a new one in which the body will be raised imperishable. The Garden of Eden will return as a whole civilization, and this time we will steward creation as servant leaders, looking after others' interests, including angelic or other beings God may create in eternity. Reverend Davis speaks enthusiastically about what God might establish in heaven—a whole new physics, whole new ways of being. We can be sure there will be no tears, no sickness or suffering. Our bodies and our souls will be perfected, although in distinctive ways: we will be fully ourselves. Heaven will be dynamic, as God is dynamic. We will know, understand, and enjoy God, as well as other people, ourselves, and the physical world. Reverend Davis believes that our brains will remain finite, but once we fill them up, we will forget what we have learned and experienced and start all over again. We will keep growing and maturing, forever becoming wiser and more insightful.

The path to heaven involves our being perfected before we get there, as it is a perfect place. As a Protestant, Reverend Davis does not believe in a phase of purification. The sorting of souls will have been done already, based not on good works but on whether we have accepted God's free offer of grace through Jesus. He does not propose "complicated scenarios like Jesuits and rabbis" (a bit disappointing to me, as they number among my great friends). God extends his invitation to spend eternity with him in the most understandable terms possible, and we accept it. Our salvation is complete, and our names are written in the book of life.

CHRISTIAN THINKING ABOUT HEAVEN is thinking about the kingdom of God. For Reverend Davis, we on earth live in the kingdom to the extent that we recognize God as king of our souls, our family, our work. Eternity may manifest itself in the present in the form of miracles, reminders of what is to come. For Anglican bishop N. T. Wright, our hopes for a better world in the present must be considered along with our hopes for a better world in the future. Those who apprehend such things through mystical experience, like novelist Kathryn Harrison, do not make much of a distinction at all. She takes Jesus literally when he says the kingdom is upon us; she knows God and is not waiting for heaven. We can live in the kingdom right now, and the more love we have, the more there is. Others plant themselves firmly in the earthly manifestation of the kingdom, without worrying much about the next life. My dear friend Nancy Greenfield, longtime Catholic chaplain at Stanford University, confessed that she'd never been in a hurry to get to the afterlife because to get there, you had to be dead. She can't work toward a goal she can't see or understand but is nevertheless asked to accept on faith. She concentrates on creating as much of a heaven-like space for her friends and family as she can, now, so that they are all happy. It seems to me that the mystic and the pragmatist have arrived at the same understanding of the kingdom.

Even though Christians are already living in the kingdom of God, most believe that life after death will not simply be a matter of our names being written in the book of life but will require dealing with what we did in life. Many of the Christians I spoke with had an almost instinctual sense that there would be a phase in which we would be made ready for union with God in heaven. As my wise friend Janine Applegate said, "If purgatory did not exist, the heart would create it." Even people who, like Swedenborg, were agnostic about such a phase recognized its value as a progression from one world to the next. Some spoke of judgment, others of a sense of incompleteness, of not being ready for heaven, but none emphasized the necessity of suffering sufficiently to be worthy. Their view of God as merciful and loving enabled them to be optimistic. Of course, they also lead good lives.

THOSE WHO TRY TO ENVISION HEAVEN, without drawing on rare and often vague biblical descriptions, do so through a mystical lens. Dean Applegate, retired choirmaster of Portland's premier Catholic choir Cantores in Ecclesia, spoke of the consciousness we have of some ultimate reality, the sense that gathers in our lives that there must be some final resolution. It is not scripture or church doctrine that points the way for him; it is the mystics—Julian of Norwich and Meister Eckhart, who wrote in his *Sermons* that "the eye through which I see God is the same eye through which God sees me; my eye and God's eye are one eye, one seeing, one knowing, one love."

This blessed sight came up in a conversation I had with a young man who worked with gang members in Los Angeles whose lives had been rescued by the Jesuit Greg Boyle. He remembered a picnic where they had all gathered, having set aside their violence and enmity. Father Boyle welcomed them by saying that heaven would look no different from that moment, that "all the way to heaven is heaven if you have eyes to see." In such moments we glimpse the eternal fullness of things.

When we finally get to heaven, what will we find? Although many I spoke with had thought long and hard about the next life, they threw their hands up at this question: "Lord, I believe; help thou mine unbelief." Others said simply that we'd get what we want; our desires would be fulfilled. Nancy Greenfield described us sailing beyond the horizon—"I think it's going to be about each person, each ship if you will—having its own goal, its own direction, its own mission, and for us that means having our own sense of what it means to be perfectly happy. What makes us happy is unique." Some looked forward to the beatific vision, seeing God in his full-ness, whatever that might entail. Many spoke of moving encounters with others that had given them a sense of heaven's actuality, and the necessity for that blessed sight. Nobody brought up the harps-and-angels version of heaven, except for a writer who offered Orwell's mocking vision: choir practice in a jeweler's shop.

Dominican priest, theologian, and dear friend Patrick Labelle, with whom I spoke not long before he died, never stopped asking questions. But he trusted that in heaven his curiosity would be satisfied and turned to joy. His lifelong hunger for both truth and love would also be fulfilled. He de-scribed his vocation of preaching, quoting his brother Aquinas, as taking what you believe, heart and mind working together, and translating it into something that will be attractive to people, all within a loving relationship grounded in a common faith. Father Pat's ideas were grounded in the world, but uplifting: he helped people raise their minds and hearts to God. Now he's there himself.

Another elderly priest told me that he had finally figured out that heaven for Christians is pure relationship. "That's all it is. Because if God is love, by definition, it has to be relationship." All people have a capacity for love, even if it is stifled. He wasn't worried about that—God's love is infinite and all-powerful. The only way we could escape God's love is to refuse it.

I was uplifted by my friends' visions of heaven but was left wondering about those who might not share their capacities for reflection and relation-ship. What about infants who die, and people with grave mental disabilities? And what about my mother, who spent the last years of her life in the fog of Alzheimer's, her wit, her kindness, her deep prayer life—all gone? I told the priests about the Mormon notion that such people are advanced souls who do not need the challenges of earthly life to progress further; rather, they are put here to teach the rest of us how to love. The priests listened kindly but had another solution—all would be well, they said, for the prayer and common faith of the communion of saints would help these souls get to where they might not have gotten on earth, all the way to a full life in God. As Father Pat said, prayer is a partnership, and loaves get multiplied.

The communion of saints became part of most Christians' idea of heaven long ago, so powerful a reality that we couldn't help but acknowledge it. The great cloud of Christian witnesses, living and dead, who watch over us, united in prayer, is the antidote to the idea of the solitary soul making its way to the next life, and explains everything from answered prayers to uncanny feelings that a departed loved one is near to our persistent longing to join those who have gone ahead to heaven. They are not so far away after all.

Part V

ISLAM

NINETEEN

The Path to the Afterlife

O ye who believe!
Believe in Allah
and His Messenger
And the scripture which He
Hath sent to His Messenger
and the scripture which He sent
to those before him.
Any who denieth Allah,
His angels, His Books,
His Messengers, and the Day
of Judgment, hath gone
Far, far astray.

• THE HOLY QUR'AN

Muhammad ibn Abdallah was born in 570, in Mecca, a city in the west of the Arabian Peninsula. He was a member of the Quraysh clan, part of a tribal society eking out its existence in a desert with scarce resources. Clans were in regular conflict over water, food, and caravan routes; justice was accomplished through group vengeance. The clans were polytheist, with Allah in the supreme position as creator and sustainer of life, but he was remote from everyday concerns. Religious belief was fatalistic—there was no meaning or accountability beyond this life, no resurrection of the body or divine judgment, no eternal punishment or reward. Muhammad's revelations were to change all that. They led to a reformed social order and a new missionary religion with a vision of a lush, sensual paradise.

IN THE TRADITIONAL ACCOUNT of the beginning of Islam, Muhammad is fasting in a cave outside Mecca in 610. The angel Jibril (Gabriel), a messenger from Allah, visits him and commands:

"Proclaim! In the name of thy Lord and Cherisher, Who created— Created man, out of a leech-like clot of congealed blood: Proclaim! and thy Lord Is Most Bountiful—He Who taught the use of the Pen—Taught man that which he knew not."

Thus was dictated the Qur'an, verse by verse over the next two decades. Muslims believe that it comes from a perfect copy kept in al-Jannah, the garden paradise of Islam, and that the language in which it was delivered, Arabic, is the language of God. Muhammad was receiving not a personal revelation but a divine law for a whole people, with Allah as the one gracious and merciful God, Master of the Day of Judgment. Muhammad taught that Islam was the restoration of the true faith, monotheism, which he traced back to Abraham, Moses, and Jesus. But while the Israelites received the Torah from God, they worshipped the Golden Calf. And though Jesus was sent with the revelation of monotheism, recorded in the Gospels, his followers preached the Trinity. For Muslims, the Qur'an is the final wave of revealed wisdom from the one god, Allah. He is all-powerful and transcendent but also an interested god, concerned with humans, capable of acting in history with mercy and justice.

"Muslim" means "one who submits," through gratitude for life and strict observance of the law. Muslim doctrine, morality, community, and mission are based on the Qur'an, the law, and Muhammad's example. Islamic moral order is embodied in the *ummah*, the community of believers, with its model for righteous behavior expressed in the Five Pillars. *Shahadah* is the confession of faith: There is no God but Allah, and Muhammad is his Prophet. *Salat* is worship, to be performed five times a day, through prescribed ablutions, positions, movement, and timing. *Zakat* is the sharing of wealth, assuring the downtrodden that their suffering deserves alleviation, and forging a bond of humanity between the wealthy and the poor. *Siyam*, fasting, is required of Muslims for self-discipline and commiseration with the hungry. Finally, *hajj*, the pilgrimage to Mecca, is required of all capable adults at least once in their lives. It is an exercise in solidarity: Muslims on pilgrimage are not allowed to show wealth, social class, knowledge, or anything else that might set them apart.

Every Muslim is called to be a *khalifah*, a steward of God, charged to transform all the earth into paradise. As a result, all problems of humankind are their concern, and Muslims are encouraged to compete to do the better, the more noble deed. They trust that God will reward them according to their success in achieving God's plan for creation, which is the universal and highest good of all peoples and all things.

IN THE ISLAMIC VERSION of cosmic history, there is no account of a primeval battle between good and evil. The cosmos is orderly, with a heaven, earth, hell, and living beings governed by God, who is creator and judge. The world of matter, by virtue of being the work of God, is good. Nature is a blessing created for humans to enjoy and to improve through good deeds, and it provides a foretaste of paradise. It is populated by various beings, all bound to obey God. Jinns are created from fire and capable of assuming physical form. They can be good or bad and are subject to judgment, as humans are. Angels, created from light, serve as messengers and guardians. Devils are angels who refused God's order to prostrate themselves before Adam. Humans, created from earth, are born innocent and become guilty only through doing evil.

The Muslim interpretation of the Fall is that Adam is the one tempted by Satan, and though he and his consort disobey God and eat forbidden fruit, the sin is their own, not an "original" sin that curses their descendants. Their transgression does not involve the tree of knowledge—in Islam, the pursuit of knowledge is a duty. And the Fall is not about Man having a flawed nature that requires salvation—that idea, so prominent in Christianity, has no parallel in Islam. Adam repents and God grants Adam mercy and guidance, and thus the story is the origin of teachings on sin and repentance. The relationship described between God and humans is unique, for God breathed his Spirit into Adam and made humans his representatives on earth, created to carry out his will. Such responsibility has cosmic proportions, and humans will be judged according to the degree they carry out God's will on earth.

Muhammad's teaching on judgment is one of the most important Muslim beliefs, after the oneness of God. It is proclaimed in the Qur'an: "It is Allah Who Gives you life, then Gives you death: then He will gather you together for the Day of Judgment, about which there is no doubt." Resurrection of the dead is a promise but also a threat. The Qur'an's message regarding the Day of Judgment is urgent, emphasizing that earthly life is a brief, precious opportunity, a singular chance. And it is full of vivid imagery of the Garden, designed to persuade unbelievers: those who have no faith are advised to incline their hearts toward the Hereafter: "Let them Delight in it, and let them Earn from it what they may."

There is an intriguing minority view that God does not do the judging. An early Muslim scholar, Hasan al-Basri, wrote: "O son of Adam, you will die alone, and enter the tomb alone, and be resurrected alone, and it is with you alone that the reckoning will be made." This passage assumes that the individual soul carries its unique identity into eternity and also hints at self-judgment, as do some verses in the Qur'an: death burns away all self-serving defenses, and the soul experiences an absolute, objective perspective of its life lived on earth.

IN THE END TIMES, Jesus, not Muhammad, will come back to earth. Passages from the Qur'an indicate that Jesus did not die on the cross but rather "Allah raised him up Unto Himself." Hadiths, the authenticated words and deeds of

Muhammad, are rich with stories of his return. Some say it will come in the time of the Mahdi, a descendant of Muhammad, at a time when Muslims are being wiped out. The Mahdi will have reestablished the righteous Caliphate, uniting Muslims and restoring them in a global community, until the evil forces of the "deceiving Messiah" overcome the Muslims. At this point, Jesus, the True Messiah, will descend from heaven clothed in yellow garments, with his hands on the wings of two angels, and alight on top of a white minaret in Damascus. His breath will reach as far as his sight and will deal death to nonbelievers. He will join the Mahdi, leading the Muslims to victory over evil forces in the "great Battle." Thereafter he will reign in an era of peace and prosperity, and Jews, Christians, and Muslims will all call him the Messiah. He will also get to live out the rest of his life, perhaps marrying and having children, and after forty years die of old age. He will be buried by Muslims next to Muhammad in Medina, where an empty space is reserved for him.

After Jesus passes naturally from this earth, humanity will return to its wicked ways, until the Final Judgment. It will be a day of harvest, of separation and sorting out, an all-encompassing day when everything will perish but the face of God. The Qur'an gives no date for the "hour of doom," which may take 50,000 years. The angel Israfil will blow his trumpet for the Final Judgment, and souls will reunite with bodies reclothed in flesh, starting with their coccyx, the only part of the body that does not decay. (This is similar to Zoroastrian and Jewish belief.) The earth will be devastated, and natural processes reversed: sun darkened, stars falling, and mountains moving. Pregnant camels will be neglected, savage beasts mustered, and the seas will boil. Scrolls will be unrolled, heavens stripped away, and hell set ablaze.

A great gathering will take place, and good people will go to their prophets—Abraham, Moses, Jesus. Everyone will be given a record of his or her deeds, in the right hand for the righteous who are to be saved, in the left for the wicked who are to be damned, and all will contemplate their lives on earth. Scales will weigh their deeds, and souls will know their fate.

The Qur'an stresses individual responsibility and God's justice, but some verses suggest that Muhammad will be permitted to intercede for souls, and some believe that all of the great prophets will be empowered to do so.

As in so many religious traditions, dating back before Zoroastrianism, a bridge must be crossed at the final reckoning. For the righteous destined for paradise, the bridge widens, and the person—always a man—may be greeted by a beautiful maiden. But for the damned, the bridge becomes like a knife edge and the person falls into the fire, dragged down by an ugly hag. The faithful, morally upright person will regain a renewed body in a paradise, enabling him to enjoy eternally the pleasures of the body: wine, food, sex, and so forth. The damned will be separated from God forever, suffering physical and mental torment in an all-encompassing fire. If they ask for relief, water like molten brass will be poured on them to scald their faces. It will be an evil fate.

ALL FAITHS THAT PREACH a final reckoning have the same question. What happens to those who have already died? The belief that souls survive death, waiting for the Day of Judgment, developed gradually in Islam. Revelations about the afterlife in the Qur'an do not refer to the immortality of the soul; they concern resurrection of the body and eternal life as a gift from God. It was thought that souls of prophets and martyrs go right to paradise, where they are kept in the gizzards of green birds close to God's throne. Souls of common people remain in their graves, awaiting resurrection.

By some accounts, the death process begins forty days before a person is to die, when a leaf falls from a tree. An angel records this and notifies Death, often seen as the terrifying angel Izra'il. The process of death is agonizing: angels appear at the deathbed and force the dying person to give up food, drink, and finally breath. A scribe then records her life. Some sources say the soul slips from the body, and Izra'il shows it where it will go. Another view is that the soul and body are reunited so that angels can interrogate the person about his faith in a kind of preparatory judgment.

What happens then is disturbing: the body's decomposition may be experienced through the senses, the level of suffering determined by one's moral conduct in life. The grave becomes tight for some, comfortable for others. Other accounts say everybody suffers, from snakes, scorpions, and such, and that unbelievers face much worse punishment.

The interim state in Islam, *barzakh*, began as a barrier separating the dead from this life but became a separate purgatorial place where the dead atone for sins through repentance and punishment. But how can a person be lying as a corpse in her grave while also off doing penance? The solution, if it can be called that, is that the body itself remains the carrier of individual identity so it can be rewarded or punished before the Final Judgment. In Islam we see the same dedicated effort to explain the interim state as in Christianity, with similarly mystifying results.

TWENTY

Companions of the Garden

To those who do right is a goodly reward—
Yea, more than in measure! No darkness nor
shame shall cover their faces!
They are the Companions of the Garden; they
will abide therein.

• THE HOLY QUR'AN

I n Arab traditions that preceded Islam, there was some sense of a transformation after death, not necessarily leading to an afterlife or an afterworld. It was believed that the soul became a ghostly owl that hovered
over the grave of the deceased and that the screech of the she-camel Salih
would bring about the end of the world. The fate of the tribe, not the individual, was at stake, and the emphasis was on punishment for disobeying
divine commandments rather than some future existence.

A discourse by Muhammad recorded by historian Ibn Ishaq shows Muhammad having difficulty convincing people that their lives had a future
beyond earthly existence, that the Last Judgment was at hand, and that
there would be dire consequences for the faithless. He describes the paradise of the Garden as something to be worked and fought for and the Fire
as a place of punishment. Muhammad's audience contests whether his
source is divine. One person declares that Muhammad would have to climb
a ladder to the sky and have angels testify for him (a prefiguring of Muhammad's Ascension). They all want relief from their hard-pressed exis-

tence and speak of blessings that foretell those of the Garden with its verdant landscape and golden palaces. But they do not comprehend Muhammad's shift from the present to a future beyond this material world: if they are to submit to God, they want their reward in the here and now.

Muhammad's followers, in contrast, developed elaborate descriptions of the rewards believers will enjoy in paradise. References in the Qur'an are brief—there will be greetings by angels, a gourmet banquet with Allah, in a setting of deep tranquility. But later Muslim writers greatly embellish the paradise glimpsed in the Qur'an. The thirteenth-century *Liber Scalae*, or Book of the Ladder, features a paradise with ruby-encrusted walls where virgins wait to satisfy the desires of new arrivals; pavilions of pearls and emeralds; fruit trees; sumptuous food and drink.

Muslim teaching makes a distinction between the afterlife and the afterworld. The afterlife comes as part of a progression in the seasons of the soul. In the pre-life, each soul is asked by God: "Am I not your Lord?" and on giving assent, flows into a woman's womb. Earthly life leads after death to the life of the grave, and finally to the Day of Judgment and life eternal. The afterworld is the actual setting for the afterlife. Scholar al-Suyuti, writing in the fifteenth century, believed that heaven and hell are already part of the present cosmos, within time and space. The faithful dead can travel, visiting the living in dreams and visions. When the end times come, the afterworld will "be brought nigh to the Righteous—no more a thing distant." For Muslims, the afterworld is a realm where the truth and power of Islam are realized.

MUHAMMAD LED HIS FOLLOWERS toward the afterlife and afterworld through his visions; indeed, his ability to visit the unseen world was proof to them that he was truly a prophet. By insisting on the immediacy of the afterlife, he inspired dreams and visions of the Garden. Muslims could anticipate the transformation of their earthly world and locate their companions in the Garden—and their enemies in the Fire.

Muhammad entered the afterworld through different portals. Many hadiths describe "The Eclipse Prayer." On beholding a solar eclipse, Muhammad prayed and saw the Garden and the Fire. His sense of them was immediate: he reached out and touched his vision of abundant grapes, though he did not bring back the fruit. Other visions occurred during sleeping and waking states, and while he was teaching. At one point he revealed, "The Garden and the Fire were displayed in front of me on this wall just now and I have never seen a better thing and a worse thing." Muhammad also saw specific people in the afterworld and used them as models for individual behavior. One was his first wife, Khadija, who enjoys preeminent status in Islamic narratives. She was the steadfast companion to Muhammad's trials and earned a special palace in the Garden. He saw people he knew in the Fire as well: those who did not believe, including friends and members of his own family.

Some Muslim traditions present these accounts as tests of faith by God to see if Muhammad's followers could believe such things. His Eclipse Prayer is a drama set in nature and would have been easier to accept than his Night Journey (Isra) and Ascension (Mi'raj). In this cosmological drama, Muhammad crosses space and time, flying off to a faraway city in the middle of the night. As in his other visions, he has glimpses of the rewards for good behavior and punishment for bad, but this time, instead of receiving a revelation, he travels to the afterworld.

A bit of historical context is in order. The Night Journey and Ascension took place on the twenty-seventh day of the month of Rajab, around 620. The place from which Muhammad ascended came to be identified as Jerusalem, the religious capital of Judaism and Christianity and the dwelling place of the prophets. Muhammad claimed his place in their lineage, and Jerusalem became an important pilgrimage site for Muslims (who conquered it in 637), as well as for Jews and Christians. The story of the journey and ascension took root despite scant reference in the Qur'an: "Glory be to Allah Who did take His servant for a Journey by night from the Sacred Mosque to the Farthest Mosque, whose precincts We did Bless—in order that We Might show him some of Our Signs: for He is the One Who heareth and seeth all things." It appears in the hadith literature, and Muslims continue to elaborate on it in stories, poems, and miniature paintings.

In Islamic texts, there is much debate as to whether Muhammad visited the afterworld literally or metaphorically. Was the Night Journey a way of representing the hajj to Medina? Were the journey and ascension bodily events, and thus miracles, or did they take place in spirit, manifesting communication between God and humans? All accounts of experience in the beyond are subject to such challenges; their significance will always be read differently, and for different purposes. In any case, Muhammad's purpose was clear: he used his adventures to expand his teachings about the afterlife, its specific pleasures and pains, as well as its implications for the living. One's moral behavior in this life was the basis for one's fate in the next, but there were degrees of reward and punishment. It was not enough to be passably good to reach the Garden; you had to be exemplary to reach its higher realms.

THE EARLIEST RECORD of the Night Journey and Ascension is that of eighth-century historian Ibn Ishaq, in which he weaves together various versions. Muhammad is awakened three times by Gabriel and taken on the steed Buraq, "the animal whose every stride carried it as far as its eye could reach on which the prophets before him used to ride." They travel over "the wonders between heaven and earth" and arrive in Jerusalem. Muhammad meets and prays with Moses, Jesus, and Abraham. He is then given three vessels, full of milk, wine, and water, and presented with a simple choice. If he drinks water, he and his people will drown; wine, they'll go astray; milk, they will be rightly guided. So he drinks milk, and the other prophets approve. Through prayer and testing, a brotherhood of prophets has been established, with Muhammad in a superior role. The prophets acknowledge his message that there is one God and that Muhammad is God's final messenger.

Muhammad then ascends a ladder and is greeted warmly by thousands

The Night Journey of
Muhammad on His Steed,
Buraq **by the calligrapher**
Sultan Muhammad Nur
Bukhara, from a copy
of the *Bustan of Sa'di*
in the Metropolitan
Museum of Art

of angels except one, Malik, who reveals the Fire to him. Muhammad is overwhelmed—in some versions of the story, he faints away. He proceeds to the lowest heaven, where he sees Adam reviewing the spirits of his offspring, exclaiming, "A good spirit from a good body!" or, frowning, "Aff! An evil spirit from an evil body!" Muhammad next encounters a host of suffering souls and notes their sins. There are men with lips like camels who jam stones into their mouths only to excrete them and begin anew: they had devoured the wealth of orphans. There were women hanging by their breasts: they had "fathered bastards on their husbands."

Muhammad finds prophets and angels attending each successive level of heaven. Adam, Malik, and Isma'il occupy the lowest, then, in a progression through the hierarchy, Muhammad meets the biblical prophets, and John and Jesus. Joseph, Idris (who may be Enoch), Aaron, and Moses are next, and at the top is Abraham, the father of Arabs, with whom Muhammad identifies. Finally, he encounters God in the highest heaven, where God enjoins him and his followers to pray fifty times a day. Fortunately, with the help of Moses, Muhammad persuades God to reduce it to five times a day.

This story was told and retold over the course of centuries. Indeed, there were already twenty-six separate traditions included in an early collection by historian Abu Ja'far Muhammad al-Tabari. Muhammad's steed Baraq is sometimes a horse with wings or with a peacock's head, or a white donkey with a woman's head. Muhammad can be guided by the angel Mikail (Michael) as well as Jibril (Gabriel) to Jerusalem. On the way they meet people tortured for sins committed during their lives—and in some versions, he recognizes them. Muhammad is said to have tied Baraq to the Wailing Wall near a large rock from which he ascends to heaven. The ladder is sometimes represented as seven layers of silk on which he floats up through the moon and stars. His ultimate destination has been described as a lotus tree that is the throne of God, who is so brilliant that Muhammad cannot see him and communicates through Gabriel.

A lengthy Persian version in al-Tabari's collection tells of Jibril and Mikail preparing Muhammad by removing his heart, washing it three times, and filling it with various virtues. They replace his heart in the Prophet's chest and mark him with the seal of prophecy between his shoulders. Muhammad then follows Gabriel to the places of reward and punishment on Buraq, here described as a winged, human-faced ass. He tours an eight-tiered heaven, encountering prophets along his way. Reaching Allah in the highest realm, Muhammad receives his mission as messenger of revelation, as well as the eight parts of true religion: Islam (submission); hajj (pilgrimage to Mecca); jihad (sacred war); almsgiving; ritual prayer; Ramadan fasting, and commandments to perform good and avoid evil deeds. A heavenly vision thereby became a vehicle for Islamic evangelism.

The stories of Night Journey and Ascension validated Muhammad's message to his followers. By asserting that he had seen everything promised in the Qur'an, Muhammad verified the existence of the afterlife and the truth of his teachings on reform and judgment. Accounts of his experience served a powerful social function, with promises of the Garden to those who had undergone suffering in this world and threats of the Fire to those who had caused it.

The stories also unleashed Muslim imagination. Islam discourages visual representation of animate beings, out of an aversion to idolatry, but manuals about the afterlife proliferated. Whereas the hadith literature was an authorized tradition, manual writers gathered material from many sources and focused on their particular audiences, be they theologians or general readers. They were able to use whatever means they deemed effective to exhort people to make moral choices, laying out codes of behavior and punishments for sins. The power of their speculation was such that the beloved mystic Rabi'a al-Adawiyya was seen one day running with fire in one hand and a bucket of water in the other. When asked where she was going, she said she wanted to set fire to heaven and to extinguish hell so that people would love God solely for himself and not for fear of punishment or desire for reward.

WHEN ASKED WHICH GOOD DEEDS would guarantee admission to the Garden, Muhammad replied, "Prayer at its appointed hour . . . kindness to parents . . . earnest endeavor (jihad) in the cause of Allah." Judgment would be rendered accordingly, with mankind divided into three groups. The "foremost of faith" would recline on jewel-encrusted thrones surrounded by attendants with large, beautiful, lustrous eyes. The "companions of the right hand" would have similar circumstances but not quite so fancy; and the ill-fated "companions of the left hand" would drink boiling water like diseased camels raging with thirst: "Such will be their entertainment on the day of requital."

Muhammad taught that there were two hazards from which Allah must protect a man so that he might enter the Garden. "They are what is between his jaws and what is between his legs: an undisciplined tongue and unbridled sexual appetite will lead to the Fire." The Qur'an links specific behaviors with specific consequences: female infanticide will bring fire; belief in the unity of God will merit the Garden. So, too, in the Ascension stories and manuals—particular sins are punished in particular ways: the torment predicted for one who fails to give alms is to be ridden about by a bald monster who coils around the sinner's neck and sticks his tail into his nose. In general, Muslims are to stay away from anything that interferes with their worship of God.

Women were seen as facing significant obstacles to the attainment of the Garden, as they could not rise to the same ethical standards as men. They were particularly compromised by adornment and luxurious silk clothes—those things that enhanced their sexual enticement. That was not their primary failing, however. The basis of all sin was the denial of Allah's generous favors, opposition rooted in pride and ingratitude. And alas, it was women who seemed to be particularly guilty. Muhammad's revelation indicated that most of the inhabitants of the Fire were women: they were ungrateful for any good deed done to them, to their husbands, and to God: "If you have always been good to one of them and then she sees something in you not to her liking, she will say, 'I never received any good from you.'" This self-pitying lament, reported by a ninth-century scholar, does not seem to fit with the reformer who forbade the abuse and exploitation of women. And it did not bode well for women, either on earth or in heaven.

ACCORDING TO THE QUR'AN, the Garden contains all kinds of delights: fruit, carpets, exotic companions, water, and green cushions. The concept of the Garden developed between the seventh and twelfth centuries, becoming a place of beauty and perfection as well as an eternal home. Social life in the

Garden (in contrast to isolation in the Fire) would be rich and complex. Earthly trials and tribulations would be no more, and the rejoicing inhabitants could enjoy not only their family and friends but also their ancestors and descendants who had been faithful. The bodies of the saved would be transformed: they would be in perfect health, forever young or ageless. They would have the hearts of birds, enjoy enhanced perceptions and knowledge, and be free from pollution. They would "neither pass water, nor void excrement, nor suffer from catarrh, nor will they spit, and their combs will be made of gold, and their sweat would be musk."

There would be an everlasting banquet with drinks that would be delightful but not intoxicating, served by immortal young boys fair as virgin pearls (beings who seem to be objects in the same way as the carpets and cushions and fine foods). Each man would have the sexual strength of a hundred men and never be without a wife. One hadith promises two wives per man, and they might also be awarded houris for their upright conduct on earth.

The houris, who are companions rather than servants, are an enduring theme that reflect writers' efforts to make the Garden ever more attractive. They are celebrated for the color of their faces, the attributes of their bodies, their smell and lack of pollution. Not only do they have large lustrous eyes as mentioned in the Qur'an, but their limbs are so fair that their bones can be seen. They are marvelously fragrant, and might even be composed of saffron. Of course a houri does not spit or defecate or menstruate. Houris speak in musical voices: "We live forever and never pass away, we are affluent and never austere, we are content and never discontent. Blessed are those who belong to us and to whom we belong." One hadith says the voices of the houris are the only other sound besides laughter in the Garden.

The career of the houri began as a nurse to the wounded, but as the tradition developed, she was described in increasingly erotic ways and became one of the most elaborately explored rewards of the Garden. She was untouched, virginal, although in some accounts her sexuality was exaggerated and she appeared to be more of a concubine. The houri also appeared as a virgin designated to each man (there were no such rewards for women). Often the houri greeted the soul as it entered the Garden. The ninth-century philosopher al-Muhasibi wrote of a dreamlike encounter between the believer and the houri, adorned with silks and jewels, with a face that would light the morning. As they gazed at each other, angels circled, trees inclined, and rivers flowed with wine, honey, and milk that the houri served up in pearl and silver cups.

Some traditions described the houri as an object, a reward for the believer, while in others she was the embodiment of the beneficence of the Garden, or a departed wife who united with her beloved when he entered the Garden. The distinction between a houri and a wife was fluid, however, and discussion of earthly wives and children was rare in hadith collections. Some writers brought them up, but only to discuss the continuity of family structure. If a woman was married twice on earth, who would be her husband in the Garden? (Her first.) Would it be possible to have a child in the Garden? The answer was that if a couple wanted one, a child lovely as a pearl would appear in an instant.

As the tradition matured, houris rose in status—they even had their own servant girls. Efforts to make the afterworld attractive (to men, of course) drove the gradual evolution from a familial to an individual form of paradise, where companionship was replaced by sensual pleasure. Women faced great challenges to entering the Garden: their nature was deficient, their status secondary, and Garden pleasures were designed for individual men. By the twelfth century, when the scholar al-Qadi wrote his account of the Garden, women, along with children and other family members, had disappeared—while the houris remained. This is not to say that women will not be admitted to paradise; they are certainly held to the same standards as men for the practice of Islam and merit reward. But women had no role in imagining the Garden, and the men who spun these visions did not make room for them.

———

ALONG WITH THE THEME of the afterworld as a lush Garden, there is a deeply spiritual thread in Muslim conceptions of the afterlife, that of the *ru'yat Allâh*, the beatific vision of God. The Qur'an teaches that "the greatest bliss is the Good Pleasure of Allah: that is the supreme felicity." God will bring the elect near to his Throne, and "Some faces, that day, will beam in brightness and beauty—Looking towards their Lord." While some Muslim scholars interpret this vision metaphorically, others take the promise literally and elaborate on the vision. It will take place each Friday in the Garden. The veil of light will lift and God will appear to his guests like a full moon. He will greet each one with "Peace be with you," and the angels will serve them. They will experience supreme bliss that will surpass all other joy.

TWENTY-ONE

The Goal of You All Is Allah

If Allah had so willed,
He would have made you a single people,
but (His
Plan is) to test you in what
He hath given you: so strive
as in a race in all virtues.
The goal of you all is Allah;
it is He that will show you
the truth of the matters in which ye dispute.

• THE HOLY QUR'AN

The pursuit of enticing rewards in paradise is not the only way Muslims think about the afterlife. Muslim philosophy took up the challenge, not through theoretical reflection but through disputation, as called for in the Qur'an. As early as the late seventh century, Muslim groups were debating the nature of God, judgment, and our ultimate fate, even though the Postponers (Mustija) cautioned that such disputes could not be resolved until the afterlife. The rationalist Mutazila, active in the eighth to tenth centuries, took up the matter of free will versus predestination, both of which could be argued on the basis of the Qur'an. They concluded that people possess free will and that God is not all-powerful. If he were, he alone would be responsible for both good and evil, and the Mutazila did not see how such a God could perform the all-important work of administering justice.

The eleventh-century philosopher and mystic Abu Hamid al-Ghazali challenged Muslim philosophers who argued that the universe runs itself, leaving no room for divine initiative or providence—for al-Ghazali, it was religious faith that ensured cosmic order. He also engaged in a famous controversy over Muslim teaching on resurrection and the afterlife. In *The Incoherence of Philosophers*, al-Ghazali called his opponents unbelievers for focusing on the immortality of the soul while denying the resurrection and the gathering of bodies on the Day of Judgment.

Ibn Rushd, also known as Averroes, responded with *The Incoherence of the Incoherence*, making the case that philosophy pursues the truth, though in a different language than that of religion. He argued that philosophers did indeed uphold the promise of resurrection but considered the afterlife to be of a higher order than this world. Unlike the manual writers, Ibn Rushd was reticent in describing it, quoting Muhammad: "In [Paradise] there is what no eye has seen, no ear heard, nor ever entered the mind of man." However, he acknowledged that describing the afterlife in material terms was effective in encouraging moral behavior among the faithful. Ibn Rushd was downright lenient compared to another philosopher, Ibn Sina, who was adamant that the pleasures in paradise would be those of the imagination. He despised physical delights—they were for the weak-minded, who were incapable of exercising their intellect.

Such philosophical and theological disputation, however, does not express God's guidance for Muslims in the way Islamic law does. It is the blueprint for a morally upright individual and community life, a concrete path to reward in the afterlife. By the tenth century a comprehensive code of law had been institutionalized, drawing on Qur'anic reforms and Muhammad's moral example. Powerful religious figures known as the ulama enforced this law according to its basis in reason, the Qur'an, and the consensus of the community. So important is the law to Muslims that any innovation or deviation from the law is tantamount to heresy, both a crime and a sin that will be punished in this life and beyond.

SUFISM, the mystical path in Islam that emerged in the seventh and eighth
centuries, stands in direct contrast to the system enforced by the ulama.
Through their interior path, Sufis reach beyond institutionalized religion to
its source—Allah—by purifying and spiritualizing Islam. Sufis are scrupulous in keeping what they regard as divine law, which is essential to their goal
of experiencing God directly. But they are not content simply to follow the
path ordered by God's law, awaiting judgment and reward in paradise. Sufis
desire and endeavor to encounter God directly, now.

An early Sufi mystic, Rabi'a al-Adawiyya—she of the fire and water—
taught that God's love was at the core of the universe: to immerse oneself
in this love, and to share it with others, was life's highest calling. Rabi'a's
message of devotional love and ecstatic experience of God is beautifully
expressed in the work of the great Sufi poet Rumi. In a poem reflecting
the Qur'anic text "He loves them and they love Him," he writes,

> Never does the lover seek without being sought by his beloved.
> When the lightning of love has shot into this heart,
> know that there is love in that heart.

Sufis believe that love mysticism yields heart knowledge and that mystical practice yields intellectual knowledge. They consider the things of the
world to be a veil God wears—and as they see God through this veil, it
becomes more and more transparent. To reach beyond, Sufis use symbols
as stepping-stones—they believe that each verse of the Qur'an carries at
least seven hidden meanings. Indeed, al-Ghazali regarded symbolism as
"the science of the relation between multiple levels of reality."

The transcendence of God, his independence from the material universe, is a central teaching of Islam, but Sufis also emphasize God's immanence, his indwelling in us. The God who is apart from the world can
also be encountered within, during this life. Sufis seek to overcome the

separation from God that our earthly existence imposes through what they call fana, the annihilation of the ego-centered self. Fana can be achieved in this life through renunciation of this transient world. Through meditation, one becomes aware of and absorbed by the immanent God in anticipation of ultimate union. The self that has been annihilated is restored in *baqa*, which is resting in God. Sufis consider the soul to be capable of a form of death and resurrection in this lifetime. Some Sufis see themselves as martyrs, their lower self having been killed in interior struggle. Sufi mystical practice is a sort of fast track to paradise: whereas regular Muslims have to wait for judgment, there are two exceptions: martyrs, who go straight to heaven, and mystics, who have a preview and consider their joy in meditation to be a foretaste of their ultimate reward.

Sufis also seek ecstasy through rhythmic, repetitive forms of prayer as well as devotional music, poetry, and dance. Best known perhaps is the practice of the whirling dervishes, an order founded by Rumi: they achieved ecstatic union with God through spinning in a circle around their master as planets revolving around the sun. The principal basis for the Sufi ecstatic tradition is the Night Journey, in which Muhammad traveled to heaven, where he met with notable personages and then with God himself. In so doing, he both demonstrated and verified his teachings to his followers.

The stories of Sufi ecstatic ascents serve the same purpose. One of the most famous is that of a Persian Sufi, Abu Yazid al-Bistami, a wondrous figure who walked on water and flew in the air. Al-Bistami's ecstatic sayings are revered, one being "Glory be to me, how great is my majesty." (Although Sufis debate whether such a statement was evidence of a profound experience of God or of madness.) By his own account, al-Bistami crossed multiple seas until he came to the throne of the Compassionate, who was accompanied by throne-bearers and angels. Al-Bistami declared that the wonders he was shown would wear out his tongue to describe.

He protested continuously, however, that his goal was not to witness such things, and God, recognizing his sincerity, called out, "To me, to me!" and "O, my chosen one, come near to me and look upon the plains of my splendor and the domains of my brightness. Sit upon the carpet of my holiness until you see the subtleties of my artisanship I-ness [sic]. You are my chosen one, my beloved." At this, al-Bistami felt as though he were melting like lead. God gave him a drink from the spring of graciousness with the cup of intimacy, and "He brought me closer and closer to him until I was nearer to him than the spirit is to the body."

The spirits of the prophets then saluted and praised al-Bistami and declared: *"Allah has preferred you over many of his creatures. When you return to earth, bear to my community my salutation and give them sincere advice as much as you can and call them to Allah."* Al-Bistami eventually arrived at a state wherein he experienced what God felt before creation: "Only the real remained without being or relation or place or position or quality."

Another Sufi otherworld traveler, the twelfth-century Persian mystic Ruzbihan Baqli, recorded a diary of his revelations called *The Unveiling of Secrets*. He beheld the ocean of sanctity and the castle of sanctity—unlimited in height, with innumerable windows, and God manifesting himself in each one. He found Munkar and Nakir, angels of indescribable beauty who interrogate the dead, playing the lute on his tombstone and uttering reassuring words: "We are lovers for you; we shall enter your tomb in this form." He witnessed the spectacles of the Prophet drunk, afloat in a deep ocean of wine, and of al-Bistami and other Sufi masters clad in patched cloaks, dancing in ecstasy around the prophets from Adam to Muhammad. Ruzbihan saw all existence like an atom in the fingers of God and was given the ultimate call from God: "Seek me in the station of love, for the world and everything in it are no match for the assaults of my glory."

FOR ISLAM, the eleventh and twelfth centuries were turbulent times. The universal caliphate that had reigned through various dynasties since Muhammad's time splintered into decentralized, competing states. Sufism spread widely, and the control of ulama loosened. It was during this time that al-Ghazali revived Islam through his reconciliation of religious and philosophical thought. But in the middle of a brilliant academic career, he experienced a spiritual crisis, became unable to speak, and fell apart both physically and psychologically. In his words, "Worldly desires were trying to keep me chained where I was, while the herald of faith was summoning, 'To the road! To the road! Little of life is left, and before you is a long journey. Your intellectual and practical involvements are hypocrisy and delusion.'"

As a result of this crisis, al-Ghazali turned to Sufism: "I saw clearly that the mystics were men of personal experience not of words, and that I had gone as far as possible by way of study and intellectual application, so that only personal experience and walking in the mystic way were left." He subsequently wrote *The Revivification of Religious Sciences*, a synthesis of law, theology, and mysticism. So persuasive were al-Ghazali's ideas that the ulama came to accept Sufi practice as orthodox. The mystical pursuit of direct experience of God in the here and now had proved more inspirational than the pursuit of heavenly reward through rigorous observation of the law.

TWENTY-TWO

For God to Decide

We are nearer to him than the jugular vein.

• THE HOLY QUR'AN

By the mid-twentieth century, Muslim religious fervor had waned, and Islam was facing great challenges in accommodating modernity and maintaining its truth in a pluralistic age. The traditional authority of the ulama, the enforcers of Islam law, had eroded, and Muslim leaders such as Indonesian president Abdurrahman Wahid were calling for a new path forward. He proposed the separation of religion and state, equal respect for Muslims and non-Muslims, and freedom for Muslims to continually reinterpret the Qur'an in light of their changing situations.

On the ground, however, economic hardship and public unrest gave rise to Islamic movements such as the Egyptian Muslim Brotherhood that in many countries became part of mainstream Muslim life. But in groups such as al-Qaeda and ISIS, this ultraconservative, exclusivist theology has become militant religious extremism whereby God's will is carried out through a violent and terrorist form of jihad. The rewards in paradise that await those who wage jihad play an essential role in this ideology.

IT IS IMPORTANT TO UNDERSTAND the significance of jihad and its two distinct forms in Muslim tradition. The "greater" jihad is the nonviolent struggle with greed, ego, and evil in order to lead a morally upright personal life and to do God's will. The "lesser" jihad is the struggle of war against the enemies of Islam, going back to Muhammad's days as a warlord in holy combat with the pagan inhabitants of Mecca. Some of his revelations describe the defensive nature of warfare: "Fight in the cause of Allah those who fight you, but do not transgress limits; for Allah loveth not transgressors." But this admonition is immediately followed by a "sword verse": "And slay them wherever ye catch them, and turn them out from where they have turned you out; for tumult and oppression are worse than slaughter."

To this day, the interpretation of these passages and their implications for Islam are the subject of fierce debate. The Qur'an states that peace is the norm: "But if the enemy incline towards peace, do thou also incline towards peace, and trust in Allah." However, many have used the sword verses to legitimize aggression. Those engaged in the current resurgence of unconditional war against unbelievers see them as a religious imperative for all true Muslims, the only way to bring about a new Islamic order.

The personal implications of the lesser jihad have profoundly shaped the Muslim view of life, death, and subsequent reward. Allah rules over life and death and decides when and how a person dies. So a person might as well risk his life for Allah, particularly when faced with persecution: "Let those fight in the cause of Allah who sell the life of this world for the hereafter. To him who fighteth in the cause of Allah—whether he is slain or gets victory—soon shall we give him a reward of great value."

The Islamic view of martyrdom goes back to the Battle of Badr in March 624, when Muhammad's greatly outnumbered followers faced Meccan forces. After extensive prayer, Muhammad proclaimed that the soul of anyone killed would be transported straight to paradise. With the assistance of the angel Jibril and his whole angelic host, Muhammad's forces won. After the community emigrated back to Mecca, warfare became a regular part of life. Thus early writings declare that jihad would be rewarded by either martyrdom or passage home with material rewards. Those warriors who were holy, and who died "in the way of God," are alive with him in the privileged place lost by Adam and Eve. A generous teaching promises ordinary Muslims the chance to achieve such a state as well: "One who prays for martyrdom sincerely: God will place him among the ranks of the martyrs, even if he dies in his bed."

Jihadist movements, with their invitation to martyrdom, provide a powerful incentive: the promise of seventy-two virgins for each man. There may be no more enticing (to men) description of paradise than that of Qur'anic scholar al-Suyuti: "Each time we sleep with a *houri* we find her virgin. Besides, the penis of the Elected never softens. The erection is eternal; the sensation that you feel each time you make love is utterly delicious and out of this world and were you to experience it in this world you would faint. Each chosen one [Muslim] will marry seventy [*sic*] *houris*, besides the women he married on earth, and all will have appetising vaginas."

SUCH VISIONS OF PARADISE have inspired a generation of suicide bombers. In a 2012 report for ABC News, journalist Barbara Walters visits an Israeli maximum-security prison in which she interviews a young Palestinian named Jihad Jarrar who was recruited by an uncle into a religious extremist group, Islamic Jihad. At seventeen, he was sent off to carry out a suicide bombing in an Israeli town. But the bomb did not go off, and we see him alive, in prison— and truth to tell, still rather naive. When Walters asks him where'd he be if the bomb had gone off, he replies that he would be in paradise: there would be "everything you want, everything good is in the garden, is in paradise. There are rivers: rivers of milk, rivers of honey wine, rivers of wine. There is everything." When Walters asks him if there are virgins in paradise, he says, "There are a lot, but for a *shahid*, for a martyr, there are seventy-two." Walters then asks whether she will go to hell, as she is not a Muslim. Jarrar replies that it's not what he wants, but what God wants, and that she should follow Muhammad. If she does not, he says, "then of course you are going to hell."

Walters later asks scholar Feisal Abdul Rauf about Jarrar's beliefs. He explains that the number seventy-two is used in Arabic to mean "countless," and the killing of innocents and of oneself is prohibited in Islam. And Muslims must never say somebody will go to hell or to heaven—that is for God to decide. Clearly, the version of Islam that called for young Jarrar to blow himself up, exploiting his youthful sexual longings in a cartoon of paradise, is a grotesque perversion of religious faith and authority.

Speculation on the nature of the seventy-two houris persists, including a recent theory involving an error in translation. Scholar Christoph Luxenberg argues that certain words in the Qur'an are Syriac rather than Arabic. The word *hur* refers to white raisins, and what the blessed will receive will be chilled raisins or drinks, in contrast to the damned, who will receive boiling drinks. Debate on this and other issues around paradisal sex partners rages on the internet, and you enter at your peril. There seem to be as many interpretations of the Qur'an and hadiths as there are bloggers. It is an extreme manifestation of how we humans express our hopes for the afterlife in ways that directly reflect our own longings, pouring our own meanings into ancient texts and traditions, and then proclaiming them loudly for all to follow.

THE HUBBUB ABOUT SEVENTY-TWO VIRGINS comes as no surprise; it reflects a paradise that remains oriented toward male gratification. Women have never had much of a presence in Muslim paradise or in Muslim public life on earth. The concern for women expressed in the Qur'an was not developed in the patriarchal societies in which Islam took root. Over the centuries, women's role in religious practice, in education and public worship, has been severely restricted to protect them from decadent society and to prevent the social discord their very presence might cause.

In contrast, contemporary scholar Hamza Yusuf has an idealized notion of women's nature: indeed, women are so chaste and pure that men should emulate them. Their physical attraction is a power they hold over men, causing vile men to dominate them but virtuous men to protect them. In any case, men must avoid getting caught up in carnality. Women are to be elevated, and when women's virtues of love and compassion predominate in men, men will overcome their natural vices and realize their full humanity. Hamza Yusuf's view of women serves as an antidote to the base version of femininity embodied in the seventy-two virgins, but a flesh and blood woman would not see her reflection in either. Nor would she know what to look forward to in the afterlife.

Farhat Hashmi, a Muslim woman, scholar, and preacher who straddles traditional and progressive Islam, sponsors a website that takes up the question of what women can look forward to in paradise. Women are reminded that our knowledge of things to come is limited, that God is just and merciful, and that he created men and women differently. In paradise, the righteous woman will be married to her husband and she will be happy with that arrangement. Those who had no husband on earth will be married to a man in paradise, and they will all live with their families in their own realms. Above all, there will be no jealousy, even if the men have their houris. The believing woman will be higher in status and more beautiful than the houris. After all, the houri is just a creation of paradise, and the righteous woman will have earned her reward and honor from Allah. Muslim women are finding their voice, and perhaps someday they will project onto the cosmic screen their own version of the Garden.

I WENT LOOKING for Muslim views of heaven with scant knowledge of Islam, in a quixotic effort to grasp its extraordinarily varied range of belief and practice down the centuries. As a Westerner, I did not have the readily accessible resources I'd relied on while studying Judaism and Christianity. Two Muslim women became my guides, one as a bridge between Christianity and Islam, one as, well, a saint.

Colleen Keyes, a dean at Zaytuna College in Berkeley, California, readily admitted that her beliefs were not strictly orthodox. She was raised in an American Roman Catholic family and converted to Islam as an adult. She laughingly called herself a "Chrislim," stressing the common ground between Islam and Christianity, in particular the importance of Jesus. But as a Muslim, she does not believe that Jesus was a savior or that he actually died on the cross. (There are conflicting opinions among Muslims about whether he died at all.) But Jesus did ascend bodily to heaven and will return in the end times to usher in the millennium.

Colleen described the Muslim view of the interim period between life and death in terms that were close to Christian Purgatory—testing and mental torture. There will also be terror that you may not be among the elect come Judgment Day. The spirit undergoes this ordeal while suspended above the decaying body. The spirit is aware and can be reached—when Colleen goes to visit her parents' graves, she tells them everything that's going on, speaking out loud so they can hear her.

Colleen believes that when the body rises again, it will be perfected, in a beautiful place imbued with the beauty and love of God. As she put it, "The overarching wonderfulness of what I imagine God to be is love and mercy and all the things that we think of as good. My imagination of this perfection is my human anthropomorphic idea of what is the good. So whatever it is, it's okay with me." As for hell as a temporary or final destination, she is cautious, recognizing again the human limitations in describing such things. I came away from our conversation with a sense that I had far more in common with this Muslim than with anyone who might dismiss religious calling and curiosity. Our beliefs may vary, but all we require to understand each other is humility, for that which we long for is far beyond our comprehension.

SUFI HABIBE HUSAIN turned out to be a different kind of guide. We sat together with her husband, Ishrat, in a large warehouse in Northern California full of people sorting food and clothing, about as far from a mystical setting as could be. She traced for me the Sufi path of love all the way back to Muhammad's Ascension, during which he saw everything, experienced everything, and then returned to share his experience. Through his friend Abu

Bakr came the Golden Chain of Sufi; the thirty-nine other paths came from Ali, for Muhammad had declared that while he was knowledge, Ali was the gate to knowledge. All Sufis aspire to attain divine love, for in the beginning, God said: "I was a hidden treasure, and I would love to be known, therefore I created the creation." Sufis also fear God, but it is a fear of displeasing their beloved—Habibe's prayer is "Oh Lord, don't be displeased; I am afraid I can displease you." Their path is full of trials and tribulations, paying for their love with tears and yearning and the suffering of being away from the Beloved.

Habibe spoke of having been created as a spirit by God, along with all other spirits, and of his question to them: "Am I not your Lord?" They responded, "Yes, you are our Lord," and thereupon fell in love with him. Eons later, in 1944, she entered her mother's womb. During her life on earth, her yearning to return to God was awakened by serious illness. Her mother discerned it to be a spiritual illness and revealed to Habibe that as a child she had been initiated into Sufism by a Sufi sheikh and that she needed to find such a teacher and guide to help her.

Habibe sought out Sheikh Nazim al-Haqqani, to whom her father and she are linked in a spiritual chain, and was filled with pure love the moment she met him. She realized that she was attracted to the light of God he was reflecting onto her. Sheik Nazim told her that God chooses certain people for himself and puts them through trials. Her illness was actually a purification, and she would be tried continually as God drew her closer and closer to himself. Sheik Nazim told her to limit useless social interactions, which she did for some twelve years. She learned during that time that she did not dream but rather *saw* reality—beautiful things, but ugly things, too, like the ego, the me-worship, which must be subdued. She also learned that her purpose in life should be twofold: devotion to God and service to humanity. It is through surrendering one's will to the will of God that one attains a peaceful existence. Habibe is continuing to "polish her heart" through remembrance of God to reach that state.

Habibe's acceptance of God's will led to a very concrete mission to help the needy people who were increasingly coming to her for help, and she started the Rahima Foundation. Through the last twenty-five years, it has moved from her carport through a series of ever larger warehouses to its own permanent place. Habibe and her husband are passing the work on to others—her health is failing, and she needs "to get the journey started to seeing God," who is for her but a step away. She recalled a poem of Rumi's where he says not to weep and pity him when he is gone—her death will be her wedding night, for she will be meeting her beloved.

I HAD BY THEN REALIZED that her husband, Ishrat, was there as Habibe's protector, as someone who guided and supported her in both her spiritual and her charitable work, and perhaps in speaking with strangers like me. But after Habibe told her story, he joined in the conversation, and we talked at length about what lies ahead—not so very far ahead, in Habibe's case. They stressed that death can come at any time, when God wills it, so that although they wished for a serene death surrounded by loved ones, they would submit when the Angel of Death arrived. They spoke of the trials and purification that would take place in the grave, purification that should begin in this life while the spirit is still in the body, so that the heart becomes a mirror of God's face. Mainstream Muslims speak of the Garden or the Fire, but for Sufis, there is always hope. God's mercy, hundreds of oceans of it, an infinity of it, will prevail: now and then he will turn to hell, take untold numbers of humans into his blessedly merciful hands, and say "I forgive you."

Prayers, good deeds, and a life lived in gratitude continue to yield benefit not only to the living. One's reward will continue to grow, even after death. What that reward may look like cannot be apprehended through our senses but through the spirit. Habibe likened it to the way we feel love and see the effects of it but cannot explain it. As she said, we cannot speak well about these realities. I asked Habibe if such intimations were for her a glimpse of the Garden, but she said they just brought her a feeling of total surrender and peace. There may be wonderful fruit and jewels in paradise, but they will not be important, for we will be "in the love of God . . . impregnated with his light and love."

I have had the privilege and the joy of encountering many wise and holy people in my life, particularly in the course of this search for life beyond. But that morning in the warehouse I knew myself to be in the presence of someone who had already, in some way, transcended this life. Habibe is a citizen of earth, working and suffering and longing, and she is a citizen of paradise, basking in the love of God. In her presence I was uplifted by the bustle of her staff organizing their gifts for the needy; I also had a glimpse, ever so fleeting, of what she is looking forward to.

Part VI

HINDUISM AND BUDDHISM

Looking East

Seekers, listen:
Wherever you are
Is the entry point.

• KABIR

I have come to understand that being immersed in my own religious tradition has enabled me to appreciate others more fully. And I have tried to share that understanding, along with sufficient background for various religious traditions, so that my readers might appreciate the roots and evolution of their various views of life beyond. Still, it wasn't until I encountered Hinduism and Buddhism that I became acutely aware of the limits of my own assumptions about religion and the afterlife. Faiths such as Zoroastrianism, Judaism, and Islam all fit my Christian framework regarding creation; forces of good and evil; aspirations for union with God in a heavenly life beyond this one; the coming of the end times and a final reckoning. But in Hinduism and Buddhism, I encountered ways of reaching beyond this life that are essentially different from those offered by Western faiths.

I realized that I had been working with a particular understanding of religion itself, one that is entirely Western. This understanding was articulated in the early eighteenth century by Jean-Frédéric Bernard and Bernard Picart in *Religious Ceremonies and Customs of All the Peoples in the World*. In Bernard's words, "All religions resemble each other in something. It is this resemblance that encourages minds of a certain boldness to risk the establishment of a project of universal syncretism . . . with the help of charity one finds everywhere *brothers*." Bernard and Picart's aims were laudable: they were attempting to meet the challenges to the European understanding of religion brought about by exploration and colonization. However, they lived in a culture where the secular and the sacred—in their case, Christianity—had become separate, distinct domains. They assumed that every religion was similarly separate from its culture and that they could readily be compared with each other. Their ideas were broadly influential and were reflected in the Protestant American view manifest in the 1893 World's Parliament of Religions in Chicago: there could be a generic religion whose truth all specific religions could acknowledge without renouncing their respective identities.

In his book *Salvations: Truth and Difference in Religion*, S. Mark Heim challenges these assumptions about the uniform nature of religions and their common truth. He explores three ways in which religious belief and aspirations for salvation can be considered. Exclusivists hold that Christianity alone has religious truth and the path to salvation. Inclusivists acknowledge that salvation can be achieved through other faiths because God, while most fully active through Christ, offers them redemption as well. Pluralists regard different faiths as "independently valid paths to salvation." Heim proposes another possibility: God may have provided humans not only different religious belief systems but also different religious ends.

This is a marked departure from my usual way of thinking, which is that all religions are drawn toward the same pole of truth, that they are all different paths to the same destination where Catholics and Muslims and every other faithful person will be united after this life, in some way, with God. This assumption proved to be inadequate when I encountered Hinduism and Buddhism, and Heim gave me a way to acknowledge—without judging—different truths, with different ends. He sees divergence, not contradiction, in different faiths, salvations rather than salvation. Religious fulfillment comes about through a comprehensive way of living aimed at a particular end, and thus the fulfillment Christians seek and find may not be that of Hindus and Buddhists. We have profoundly different worldviews, with radically different ideas about time; the cosmos; the existence and nature of God; the soul, self, and consciousness; death; reincarnation, and what lies beyond this life. But if difference carries on through history and into eternity, what does salvation mean? And how does heaven fit in? We will have to wait to find out. God may have a plan whereby different religions have roles that are "now only dimly perceived and that will be fully disclosed in the consummation of history."

TWENTY-THREE

Life after Life after Life

Only that yogi
Whose joy is inward
Inward his peace,
And his vision inward
Shall come to Brahman
And know Nirvana,

• BHAGAVAD GITA

The origins of the Hindu tradition lie deep in prehistory. They include a vast diversity of belief and practice, and tracing sources through oral and written traditions is a complex effort. There is a body of literature in Sanskrit produced by the Brahmins, priests and scholars who comprise the highest caste in Hindu society, that has been transmitted through all classes and places. There are also vernacular works, with influences from groups that were officially silenced, such as women and Untouchables. But they share no single authoritative tradition, no central creed or ritual. Still, all Hindus consider their texts to be part of an unbroken chain, and over the last four hundred years they have considered their religion to be distinct from others.

There are common elements in the literary tradition and in popular Hinduism. Its cosmology revolves around Mount Meru in the Himalayas, the center of all the physical, metaphysical, and spiritual universes. And although there is no single creation myth, no one primeval drama that sets the stage for our ultimate return to our creator, the many versions of the origins of the universe all tell of the emergence of order out of chaos. In one passage in the Rig Veda, everything begins when God manifests himself as the creator of the universe, encompassing and animating all things. In another, gods dismember a cosmic giant, the primeval male Purusha, who is both the victim of sacrifice and the deity to whom the sacrifice is offered. In Matsya Purana the universe has dissolved, and all things are asleep. Svayambhu, the "Self-manifested Being," arises, creates the primordial waters, and infuses them with the seed of creation. The seed turns into a golden womb, Svayambhu enters it and thereafter pervades the universe.

The Hindu cosmos contains multiple worlds. There are innumerable galaxies, with innumerable tiers of finer and coarser worlds. We live in the middling world, a world of good and evil that is our spiritual training ground. Mount Meru is its axis, lying north of India, with the Himalayas as its foothills. It reaches deep into the earth and far up into the heavens. All the important gods have their own heavenly kingdom there, and those who have been devoted to them join them there to await reincarnation. There is also the moral world of inexorable karma, a just world where everybody gets what they deserve, and the ever-changing world of maya that we ourselves create out of our own ignorance. Finally, there is *lila*, a world where the divine engages in an unending cosmic dance. *Lila* is manifest in many ways, from the god Krishna's erotic sport with milkmaids to the playful goodness of the universe.

The Hindu cosmos involves countless cycles of time, wherein things generally get worse and worse. In the beginning times, there is no need for a social system or for classes or stages of life. But as time goes on, such systems arise, until it is no longer possible to maintain them. Human life fades into the wilderness, and the next cycle of civilization ensues. A description of successive ages is found in *Linga Purana*: The Four Ages of humankind extend from the Golden Age of goodness to Trey, the age of energy, to the Age of Deuce, characterized by a mixture of energy and darkness. The Dark Age follows, a desperate time when people's minds will be numbed by suffering that will balance the mind so that it is capable of understanding and dedication to dharma (cosmic order). Those left at the end will have mental peace. In a day and a night, the age will be transformed, and the Golden Age will begin anew. Fortunately, those who suffered to the end will be born again into this new Golden Age.

But as humanity declines, each age, or *yuga*, gets shorter. Four *yuga*s make up the great *yuga*, and two thousand great *yuga*s make up the basic cosmic cycle, the *kalpa*. We are living in the last age, Kali, and at the end the world will be destroyed. Nothing that exists in time and space and subject to causality will survive—even Brahman, the world-soul. But the cycle does begin again, and again. There will be infinitely more creation stories in the ages to come.

ALONG WITH HARMONIOUS VERSIONS of the cosmos, there are essential Hindu principles. *Dharma*, cosmic order, is the basis for Hindu religion, law, and justice. *Karma* is the natural law of the moral world by which the course of a person's life after life after life is determined. In terms of practice, much of Hindu religious life is characterized by *bhakti*, mystical devotion, the mutual love between devotee and deity. Bhakti is often expressed through pious practices such as ritual offering of fruit and flowers, sacrificial offerings, and pilgrimages to worship local gods and goddesses.

In ancient Hinduism, *dharma* was the cosmic law bringing order to chaos, and was codified beginning in the third century BCE. *Dharma* came to mean the right way of living in both social and individual contexts; the duties, rights, and moral behaviors that would maintain order in the world. All must act in accordance with general laws such as truthfulness and generosity, while also following their individual *dharma*, their true role in life. Along with material gain, physical pleasure, and salvation, it is one of the four goals of life on earth.

The yogas are pathways that lead beyond rational knowledge to the infinite. But instead of reaching outside and upward toward a God who resides in a heavenly realm, Hindus reach deep into our being—"the beyond within." Their religion is their guide to the fulfillment of their human potential, to the transformation of their nature, to ever-higher states of being and union with God. It is a process of "involution," sustained by the atman, God within. Which path one chooses, and where one starts, depends on what kind of person one is and on one's status and stage in life.

Hatha yoga is the way to God through cultivation and control of the body in order to bring about spiritual growth. Jnana yoga, the path of knowledge, is the shortest and steepest path toward God, for reflective people capable of being transformed through their own intuitive discernment. Bhakti yoga is the path through love for those whose feelings are more real than their thoughts; karma yoga is the way of work, for those who are active, either through knowledge or devoted service. Raja yoga is for those with a scientific bent, "the royal road to reintegration" through the discipline of meditation, turning from the external to the internal world. As the Bhagavad Gita says,

> Only that yogi
> Whose joy is inward
> Inward his peace,
> And his vision inward
> Shall come to Brahman
> And know Nirvana.

The word *karma* carries multiple meanings. It is action; or ritual action; or morally charged action, as well as the consequences for the future brought about by such action. Karma is the result of past lives and accounts for a person's role in life. Every good and every bad deed returns to a person with commensurate reward or punishment. The winds of karma blow a person to successive lifetimes in which she reaps her karma, both bad and good. She may experience life as a leech or a human or a goddess, but they all serve as the training ground for ultimate liberation.

Mercifully, and in seeming defiance of its strict logic of reward and

punishment, karma can be transferred to others. This belief parallels notions of intercession that we find in Christianity and elsewhere. In the
Markandeya Purana, a king in a heaven can release sinners from a hell; they
nevertheless are reborn as they deserve, according to the law of karma.
One might not always benefit from the transfer of karma, however. The
eighth-century poet Cuntarar laments that Shiva refuses to remove his bad
karma, leaving him to work it out by himself:

> You won't remove the fierce karma
> that afflicts us
> Together with your great demon,
> You abide in the wilderness . . .

My introduction to Hindu notions of reincarnation and the soul came
through Swami Prasannatmananda of the Vedanta school of Hindu philosophy, whom I met through a mutual friend. As we talked, I became aware
of (and somewhat embarrassed by) my assumption that Eastern religion
would involve theology and philosophy as it does in the West. Swami
Prasannatmananda, a bit amused by my confusion, said, "But Catherine,
we don't have a theology, we have a religion." He described humans as "tri-
chotomous," with a mind, a body, and an atman, and spoke of the unity of
the individual soul, atman, with Brahman, the world-soul.

Swami Prasannatmananda told me about the *Katha Upanishad* from the
fifth century BCE, which tells the story of a little boy named Nachiketa who
meets Yama, the Indian deity of death. He is granted three favors, and so
he asks for peace for his father and himself; how to make the sacred fire
sacrifice; and finally for the answer to what happens after death. Yama replies that this is a mystery even for the gods, and tries to get Nachiketa to
ask for something else. But the boy perseveres, secretly pleasing Yama, who
delivers a great teaching on the true self—the atman—that persists beyond death.

The atman is formless and all-pervasive, smaller than the smallest and
larger than the largest. It is free, birthless, deathless, perfect, and illumined.

It connects an individual human with the divine, untouched by time and circumstance. In the Vedanta view, the atman, our real nature, makes humans naturally moral, not flawed or marked by sin as in Christianity. Yet it is trapped in samsara, the cycle of death and rebirth into lives as cockroaches or eagles, in hellish realms or on the heavenly slopes of Mount Meru. The wise person (such as Nachiketa went on to be) dedicates himself to knowing the atman, and distinguishes it from the body, the locus of desire. Such knowledge brings peace, inner serenity, as it is beyond laws, beyond heavens. It allows the body to drop away, and the person to merge with Brahman, the ultimate reality.

THE RIG VEDA PRESENTS the universe as an egg, with the sun as the yolk between the two halves of heaven and earth. The universe is a sealed space, with a given number of souls and a given amount of good and evil. But this concept of the universe was challenged by the emergence of the idea of bhakti, mystical devotion to God. The universe became a place where good and bhakti could expand infinitely. First mentioned in the Bhagavad Gita (Song of God), bhakti led to a flowering of ecstatic poetry that spread across India from the sixth century on.

One of the most distinguished bhakti poets, who wrote extensively on death, rebirth, and release, was Kabir, a fifteenth-century North Indian bhakti saint. Like many of his contemporaries, he melded Sufi Islam with Hinduism, going so far as to form a religion of his own. In his collection *Seedling or Map for Hidden Treasure*, sacred to many religious sects, Kabir describes how his deep faith in God, whom he calls Hari, informs his beliefs about heaven and hell:

> Heaven and hell are for the ignorant,
> Not for those who know Hari.
> The fearful things that everyone fears,
> I don't fear.
> I'm not confused about sin and purity,

Heaven and hell.
Kabir says, *seekers, listen:*
Wherever you are
Is the entry point.

Kabir reminds us that even gods die, while the Original One does not:

Brahma, Vishnu and Shiva died,
Parvati's son Ganesha died,
So many suns and moons died,
Hanuman the bridgebuilder died,
Krishna died, the maker died.
One, the Original, didn't die.

It is into this One that Kabir longs for his soul to be reabsorbed. He sets aside thoughts of heavenly reward and hellish punishment, for he has met with Hari, he knows and understands him, and this understanding has freed him. He knows he will not die like the rest of the world, for his soul is free from birth and death. His gaze even in this life is on God, and thus he is already absorbed in the infinite.

Kabir is living the great paradox of the already and the not yet. Such absorption may be unfathomable to those of us who are not mystics, but bhakti poets such as Tukaram of Maharashtra dreamed of it:

I've built a house in boundless space,
I live in formless infinity.
I've become completely without illusions, serene,
I've reached unbroken unity.
Tuka says, Now there's no ego,
I've become suddenly continuously pure.

Unlike Tukaram, the rest of us will most likely not achieve liberation and absorption into the infinite. When our soul leaves our bodies, our prana (life breath) will follow, and our organs will die. Our soul will receive a particular consciousness and enter into the body that is related to the consciousness, followed by our past experiences, our deeds, and our knowledge. We will then take one of four paths. *Devayana*, the way of the gods, is for advanced souls who led a pure life of meditation but who have not yet achieved complete knowledge of their selves. They go to the highest heaven, *Brahmaloka*, and eventually on to liberation. *Pitriyana*, the way of the fathers, is for people who looked for rewards for their charity, austerity, and piety. Their path leads to *Chandraloka*, the lunar sphere, where they will be immensely happy, but they need eventually to return to earth to rid themselves of earthly desires.

The souls of those who have led impure lives take a path leading to hell. They are born into subhuman species to make up for their evil so as to be reborn as humans. An even lower path is for those who were utterly vile: they become mosquitoes or fleas or some other mean, noxious creature—but even they can and will work their way back up to human status. When the soul's karma results in a human body, it takes up the thread of spiritual evolution from its previous human life and continues to evolve toward self-knowledge and liberation. Whether we retain our separate identities when we are finally liberated is an open question for Hindus. Some believe that a remnant of ourselves remains so we are able fully to enjoy union with the divine. Others believe that we lose all traces of separateness, that we are fully absorbed into the One.

TWENTY-FOUR

Gone to God

Although he is Unity, God finds, it seems,
his recreation in variety.

• PREMA CHAITANYA

There are many Hindu stories of the heavens and hells a soul might experience in its long journey. One of the most famous is the trip the hero Arjuna makes to heaven, chronicled in the epic poem *Mahabharata*.

Arjuna is sent to the Himalayas to obtain weapons from Indra, king of the gods, to vanquish the family's enemies. Prepared with mantras, he travels at the speed of mind and arrives in a heavenly place full of peacocks, blossoming trees, and rivers the color of lapis lazuli. Indra appears to him as an old ascetic who advises him that since Arjuna has already attained a state of high purity, he can throw his weapons away. Arjuna will do no such thing, and Indra, impressed by his dedication to duty, grants him a boon. Bold Arjuna, recognizing the god, asks for Indra's weapons! Indra makes a counteroffer of life in the heavenly realms, but Arjuna persists, and Indra promises to give him his weapons when he meets Shiva, destroyer of worlds.

Arjuna thereupon undertakes a series of ascetic practices to prepare for the encounter. He eats fruit but fasts for longer and longer periods so that by the fourth month he is living on air. He stands on his tiptoes, arms raised, and his hair becomes like lightning. The whole world is overheated by Arjuna's austerities, smoking in all directions, and the heavenly sages plead with Shiva to stop him. Shiva reassures them and sends them away. He assumes the form of a powerful hunter and finds Arjuna being challenged by a demonic boar. They shoot their arrows simultaneously, and the boar is killed. Our heroes then get into a fierce argument about who has killed the boar. Arjuna, enraged, lets loose two volleys of arrows that have no effect at all. He then unleashes arrows blazing like the sun, rocks and boulders, trees, and his own fists, causing sparks and smoke to fly from their bodies.

The hunter is still unaffected, unmoved, and Arjuna realizes that he may be Shiva himself. He retreats, makes an earthen image of Shiva, and worships it with flowers. As he does so, he sees flowers falling on the hunter's head and flings himself at his feet. Shiva praises him, promises him weapons, and reveals himself to Arjuna in all his glory. Arjuna asks for Pashupata, the powerful irresistible weapon with which Shiva destroys the universe at the end of creation. Shiva gives it to him, warning that it be used only on heavenly fighters lest Arjuna inadvertently destroy creation. He gives Arjuna the mantras to power the weapon; the earth trembles, and trumpets and conches resound.

Arjuna is then sent off to collect Indra's weapons. In the distance, he sees Indra and his queen atop a heavenly elephant, shining like the sun. Many gods appear and bestow weapons on him: divine eyes, a celestial mace, inescapable nooses. Indra proclaims that Arjuna will do great work for the gods and carries him up in his own mighty chariot equipped with swords and maces, axes and spears, missiles and silver cannons. When they reach heaven, Arjuna beholds shining beings, kings and warriors, who illuminate the realm with the light of their merits—they are pious persons whose shining abodes are seen as stars from earth.

Arjuna arrives at last at Amaravati, Indra's capital city. Breezes produce cascades of light as they flow through sacred golden trees; there are palaces and gardens where gods play with celestial nymphs who sing and dance and provide all manner of pleasure. Arjuna wonders at the chariots driven around heaven by their driver's will, and the celestial music of conch shells and drums. His guide tells him that to reach this heaven, one must not turn his back in battle or neglect to sacrifice to the gods, bathe in holy rivers, or provide charity to Brahmins. Arjuna enters a great hall full of saints, pure Brahmins, and other heavenly beings, presided over by Indra on a great bejeweled throne. He throws himself at Indra's feet, where they gaze at each other, appearing as the sun and moon together. Indra grants Arjuna celestial sight so that he can enjoy heaven in all its splendor.

Although Arjuna is ever mindful of his earthly family, he lives in the heavenly capital for five years, learning how to use his new weapons. Toward the end, Indra arranges for him to be seduced by a ravishing nymph. Despite her beauty and best efforts, Arjuna resists her seductions. Thousands of years ago she was the mother of his dynastic family, and he bows his head to her not as lover but as son. She curses him, denying him his manhood. But Indra is impressed with Arjuna's fortitude and propriety and lifts the curse. Eventually, Arjuna returns to earth, and his tale of heavenly travel is still told here, in the twenty-first century, by a Westerner who has learned of it through the relatively recent spread—just a few hundred years—of the religion of the Hindus.

THE PRESENT-DAY HINDUS I INTERVIEWED had their own ways of understanding and practicing their religion, evidence of the great diversity of this ancient and resilient tradition. This may be God's plan, indeed God's delight, for "although he is Unity, God finds, it seems, his recreation in variety." All spoke of their desire for union with God and how that is possible in the present. They do not need nor intend to wait for some form of heaven.

Punita, whom I met in a roundtable discussion of the afterlife, believes that one's connection with the atman plays out not just at the end of this life but in every moment, every *now*. A restless, questioning person, she felt that our customary ways of identifying ourselves—parent, engineer, teacher—were not enough for her. She sought a deeper identification, a reality that would transcend religious, educational, and national boundaries. Punita found her answer in the teachings of Ramana Maharshi, a Hindu sage—some say an enlightened being—who as a teenager had a near-death experience that was so powerful that he thereafter lived in quiet seclusion into old age. He had discovered a force that he identified as his true self and taught a process of negation whereby one might acknowledge that, as Punita described it, "this body I am not; these material possessions I am not—one by one you go, but something remains: a very pure sense of being. It's who you are."

Punita believes that everyone can come to this realization, either in one's current body or in some future form. For though a body might end, life does not. It is a continuum, and what endures is not an individual spirit but life itself. To explain this idea, Punita spoke of how we lose ourselves in deep sleep: we have no relation to the world, but we return refreshed. Energy, life, flows unceasingly through us, in sleep and waking states, and it is the same with the transition from one body to another at death. This deep, pure being is stable and eternal, and Punita continually aspires to be in touch with it. She said that if she could just stay there, she could see this entire chapter of life going on, her own and that of the entire set of beings around her. She could thus be indifferent to this life and earth, regarding it as karma playing itself out. When she is centered in this realization of her core self, she is in heaven; when she deviates from it, she is in hell.

RASHMITA JANI'S FAITH is a powerful example of traditional Hindu bhakti, living a life of loving devotion to one's god. Her family is part of the five-hundred-year-old Pushtimarg (Path of Grace) sect, devotees of Krishna, the Supreme Being, one with the creator Vishnu. Her goal is to get to Krishna, and her present life is devoted to his service: "All I need to do is love the lord and serve him."

Rashmita's service of Krishna is an end in itself: it does not earn or result in the reward of union with her god. And she would never ask anything of Krishna, as he has already decided what is best for her. Lifting one hand, she said to me: "When I am in distress, I am in one hand of Krishna." Lifting the other, she said, "And when I am in happiness, I am in the other hand of Krishna. I am always in the hands of Krishna, so there's nothing to worry about presently! Nothing good, nothing bad, things just the way they should be." Activist Westerner though I am, I was deeply moved by her radical trust.

Rashmita's version of karma is different from the common understanding that one accumulates credit toward fortunate rebirths. She was born into a human body because she is a follower of Krishna, a sign that she may be further along her path than someone in a less fortunate situation. When Rashmita dies, she says, she will "leave her body like a set of clothes, and my spirit-soul will go into another body, if that is where I am to be, and I will pick up where I left off, and ultimately get to Krishna and the heavenly abode when it is time, back to the Godhead." When and how she gets there is all up to Krishna.

Rashmita trains her mind on the poor, second only to God, but her service to them is strictly devotion to Krishna, whom she keeps in mind as she cooks and serves food in the temple. I challenged her at this point— Jesus also teaches us to serve the poor, and we believe we are worshipping God through our generous actions. But Jesus also taught that it is through the poor that we find our way to God—"Whatsoever you do for the least of these, you do for me." Rashmita acknowledged that it seems cruel that it is not necessary for her to be doing good for others, because they are in their life situation for a reason. She pointed out that we are not to judge whether someone on the street might be in a better or worse situation than we are. Similarly, it is not her place to evangelize for Krishna, for it is not up to her whether a person comes to Krishna or not.

Along with service, life in Rashmita's community revolves around devotional practice. While she lives in the middle of twenty-first-century life in the Bay Area, she aspires to live in God's time. Every fifteen days she and her fellow believers take a day to focus on Krishna, remembering him in everything they do, fasting and practicing bhakti yoga, the constant chanting of the holy names of God. This puts them in a meditative state, but they do not aspire to actual meditation. In this yuga, this age in the cycle of history, people do not have the "mindset to meditate." Our minds are filled with too many things; the force of illusion—maya—is so powerful that it is impossible to stabilize the mind. Krishna is the only refuge, and we can only cry out to him like a child to its mother.

Rashmita's approach to prayer seems to deny the possibility of simply resting in God, and indeed Rashmita finds any sense of merging with God to be somewhat disrespectful. Chanting puts your faith outside yourself, and it is easier. And she does not long to merge with Krishna in some future life, just to serve him. In any case, she believes that if you are inspired to return to God, and have received his mercy, your spirit is already with Krishna. You are in your material body by force, and eventually it will be cast off, but you are actually already gone to God.

MY FRIEND JEFFREY MYERS is a Westerner who found his own way into the Hindu tradition. As a boy he had a sense that there was life beyond this one, due to a recurring dream: "I'm lying on a beach, immobile, looking sideways. It's a battle scene; there is a shattered palm tree, some mangled bodies, pieces of equipment all busted up. Totally quiet, peaceful, waves lapping on the black-sand beach. Nothing moving except the water. It is totally peaceful, and always exactly the same."

This experience made Jeff intensely curious, and he eventually came upon the teachings of Paramahansa Yogananda, which are rooted in the Vedas, ancient Hindu scriptures. Yogananda was a monotheist, regarding Brahma as the overarching God while allowing for different aspects and avatars of God such as Jesus and the Buddha. He taught that we are already in possession of the kingdom of God: we just have to improve our consciousness, life after life, until we are in a state of perfect consciousness in which we express divinity.

Yogananda stressed the unity of religions and their scriptures and read the Book of Revelation through the Vedas. In his view, what is described in terms of seals and churches and beasts is all out of the Vedas and is in reality time, space, and matter. His ideas hold great appeal to Jeff, who is a scientist. He was trained to be curious and reveres Albert Einstein as a scientist who was open to the divine. Jeff has found references in the Vedas that allude to atoms, to energy and matter, early hints of Einstein's ideas. For Jeff, the universe is an illusion condensed out of the mind of God.

For forty years, Jeff has practiced Kriya Yoga, a form of meditation that Yogananda regarded as the most effective way to achieve union with the divine. Kriya Yoga is quite efficient: thirty seconds of the practice is equal to one year of natural spiritual growth. Meditation is managing the life force (prana), for which the spinal cord acts as a kind of antenna. The practice is aimed to increase the flow of the life force from the head down seven spinal centers, each of which channels part of the life force: heart, digestive tract, cerebral functioning. Meditation activates these channels, and we become conscious of the flow and able to manage it. If we are really concentrating, we can hear distinct sounds from each: running water, a bell, a turtledove. When an adept Kriya yogi does this, he loses consciousness of his body; it goes into suspended animation; he stops breathing and his heart stops beating.

Jeff's medical friends tell him this is impossible, but he accepts Yogananda's explanation: when we draw all the life force from our external, sense organs, we are shutting down our metabolism, and if we are not metabolizing, we no longer need oxygen. We are basically running on light.

Kriya Yoga is said to incinerate lifetimes of bad karma, so we don't have to reincarnate on the present physical level, which is the lowest level of existence for a human. Our souls have been evolving from the mineral kingdom up through plants and animals, but Yogananda tells us to concentrate on where we are now. Some of us are old souls who have had more time to sort through their karma and to eliminate their desires. They will move to the next level, the astral planes, different worlds in this universe where we are magnetically attracted to people who are like-minded or with whom we have had common experiences. God gives us a glimpse of the astral plane when we go to sleep—indeed, Yogananda taught that in a sense we die when we go to sleep and are reincarnated when we wake up.

In Yogananda's universe, people generally reincarnate every five hundred years, unless they die prematurely, in which case they have a strong desire to reincarnate sooner. Jeff sees this as the reason for big baby booms after wars. People who had a good life and died a relatively natural death don't want to leave the astral planes to go back to the pain, the work, the annoyances of this existence. But if you want to reach the highest spiritual realm, you need to incarnate between the astral and the causal. The causal plane is the realm of pure idea, the highest place in the world of form and energy. Eventually you lose your sense of individuality and merge with the oneness of God. As Jeff puts it, the universe is now your body. *"You become God. We are God, we just don't realize it."*

TWENTY-FIVE

The Path to Enlightenment

Life and death are in the mind,
and nowhere else.

· SOGYAL RINPOCHE

B uddhism appeared over a relatively short time, the result of the teachings of Siddhartha Gautama, whom we know as the Buddha. In the traditional chronology, he was born in 486 BCE, was awakened to enlightenment at the age of thirty-five, and for the rest of his life taught the path to liberation, to Nirvana. At eighty the Buddha died and achieved liberation and enlightenment.

Gautama was a Hindu prince, so Buddhism shares with Hinduism a common past, as well as beliefs in samsara, karma, dharma, the path of the soul toward release through the cycle of rebirths, and the practice of meditation. By the Buddha's time on earth, Hinduism had become rigid and lifeless in authority, tradition, and ritual. The Buddha rejected the authority of the Vedas and the Brahmin priests, relying instead on intense self-discipline aimed at achieving enlightenment. Yet he did not claim that his was new teaching; rather, it was truth that had been forgotten.

The Buddha never delivered divine words like Moses, Jesus, and Muhammad, and he never wrote anything down. His words appear in sutras—discourses—preserved orally through elaborate mnemonic devices. Some four hundred years after his death, the Mahayana sutras were recorded in India. Although these are not universally held to be the authentic words of the Buddha, Mahayana Buddhism, devoted to that single text, became the dominant form of Buddhism in many other parts of the world outside India. The range of Buddhist belief and practice is wide and complex, given its spread throughout Asia and the many diverse sects that formed. Still, there is general agreement that in his first sermon, the Buddha proclaimed the Four Noble Truths, which contain the essence of his message. And all Buddhists are on the path to their ultimate destination, Nirvana: liberation from samsara, and enlightenment.

LIKE HINDUISM, Buddhism holds that the universe has no beginning—world systems come in and out of existence. Nevertheless, there are Buddhist myths about the creation of our particular world. One tells of the first beings living on "Rose Apple Island" in a great sea. This island is one of four continents on a flat world, with Mount Meru at the center. Meru is a great cube, with four faces of different precious stones, inhabited, as in Hindu belief, by gods. The Buddha discouraged speculation about the universe, refusing to say when it began or when it would end. But Hindus and Buddhists have a long tradition of depicting the cosmos in mandalas used to establish a sacred space and provide a focus for meditation. A sacred mandala in the Toji Temple in Kyoto is an early example showing the Buddha surrounded by twelve courts containing 414 deities, representing stages on the way to enlightenment. Bodhisattvas (those who desire to attain Buddhahood) are stationed at strategic points, reminding us that the Buddha promised to come to the aid of all sentient beings.

The Buddha's essential teaching concerned individuals caught in samsara, the cycle of rebirth, endlessly wandering on a path that has no beginning or end. The Buddha provided the way to put an end to that existence. Buddhists do not believe in an independent soul that survives the death of the body (in contrast to the Hindu concept of the atman, the imperishable soul). However, successive rebirths do allow for a "continuity of mind" that stretches from moment to moment, on to enlightenment. This continuity

Sacred mandala in Toji Temple, Kyoto

is provided through the ultimately subtlest level of consciousness, that of the "Clear Light."

Life after life goes on in a hierarchy of realms. At the top is the Formless Realm, where gods exist only in consciousness. They are named for that which absorbs their minds: Infinite Space, Infinite Consciousness, Nothingness, or Neither-Perception-Nor-Non-Perception. One enters the Formless Realm through deep meditation. Just below is the Realm of Form, where the gods are invisible to humans and do not require food or drink. Life in these realms goes on for millennia.

Further down is the Realm of Desire, where all seek the pleasure of the senses. There are six sub-realms, beginning with one for gods who live on Mount Meru and in the heavens above it. Their stay is lengthy: one thousand years wherein each day is composed of one hundred human years. To be reborn as a god on Mount Meru, a person must have been generous and charitable in a former life. One might think that given their exalted state, the gods would foster moral development or salvation for others, but they are unconcerned.

The next realm down is that of the demigods, spirits who might be benign or malevolent, whose powers—such as celestial musicians sustained by fragrances—exceed those of humans. However, our lower, human, "middling" realm is ideal for practicing the Buddhist path: life on earth is neither too painful nor too pleasurable. There is enough suffering that we want to escape, and not so much pleasure that we are seduced into staying. One is reborn as a human as a result of living an ethical life, in particular keeping the five traditional commandments to abstain from killing humans, stealing, sexual misconduct, lying, and intoxicants.

The realms of the gods and humans are fortunate, the results of virtuous actions. Though their inhabitants experience suffering, it is less harsh than the suffering endured in the lower realms. In the realm below humans, a person motivated by ignorance is reincarnated as an animal, condemned to find food without becoming food in turn. Those motivated by greed dwell five hundred leagues below the earth's surface. They are constantly hungry and thirsty and face continuous obstacles: knots in their throats or water turning to blood as they drink. These "hungry ghosts" can enter the human world, where monks endowed with supernatural powers can see them and are obliged to feed them.

Finally, there is hell, for those who killed their parents or an arhat (one who will reach Nirvana at death), those who wounded the Buddha, and those who caused dissension within a community of monks or nuns. There are many dreadful regions, including eight hot and eight cold. People are tortured by burning iron, or wander naked in dark, freezing lands where there is neither light nor heat. This agony goes on for millions of years, but fortunately not forever.

This cycle of samsara is vividly depicted in the dharmachakra, the wheel of transmigratory existence. In the upper realms are scenes of gods disporting themselves; lower down, hungry ghosts writhe torturously; in hell there is fire and mayhem. All are caught within the body of Yama, the

**Tibetan school depiction of dharmachakra,
the wheel of transmigratory existence,
in the American Museum of Natural History**

god of death. Escape seems impossible, but Buddhists trust they can follow
their Buddha out to Nirvana.

IN BUDDHISM, there is no God, no ultimate judge. As in Hinduism, karma is
the natural law in a moral universe, and good and bad rebirths are not rewards
or punishments but the natural result of one's actions. However, Buddhism

stresses not only the efficacy of ritual and ethical action but also one's motivations, in a chain of causes that yields karmic results. Thus vows are central to Buddhist practice, lifetime commitments to refrain from negative actions and thus to generate good karma every moment of one's life.

In Buddhism, karma functions differently in more or less spiritually developed persons: a moral slip will be diluted by a refined nature but has a greater impact on one who is undeveloped, who has a "small self." However, one can lessen the karmic result of a bad action by being genuinely remorseful. And one can both bestow and receive karmic merit. Good deeds are performed with the intention of transferring merit, and the very act of transference enhances good karma. Those stuck in unfortunate realms can accrue transferred merit until they are reborn in a more felicitous situation.

ON A BUDDHIST'S PATH there are three refuges, three sources of inspiration. The first is the Buddha himself, the second his teachings, and the third the Buddhist community of monks and nuns and devout laypersons—spiritually developed people who glimpse the final goal of enlightenment day to day.

A common source for coming to know the Buddha is the voluminous collection of Jataka tales of his previous lives—as a god, a human, an animal. But the Buddha is actually just one in the line of buddhas who appear in the world at rare, deeply significant times, when their teachings have been forgotten and escape from suffering has become impossible. So momentous was the arrival of Siddhartha (miraculously conceived while his mother dreamed of a white elephant, then springing from his mother's side) that Brahma, the Hindu god of creation, implored him to teach him how to escape the cycle of samsara.

THE SECOND REFUGE, DHARMA, is the truth the Buddha taught, not to be simply accepted but explored and confirmed in experience. The Four Noble

Truths comprise the core teachings of the Buddha for persons on the path to enlightenment.

The first truth is that our lives here on earth are composed of suffering arising from our actions during past lives. The second is that there are two causes of suffering: bad karma, formed by actions of the body, the voice, and the mind; and affliction—desire, hatred, ignorance, and holding false beliefs such as the permanence of an independent soul. Buddhists believe that a person is a collection of perishable parts, with a false transitory self that reincarnates again and again.

The third truth is the cessation of suffering, which requires wisdom, the confident knowledge that there is no self. Wisdom destroys ignorance and samsara so that one can experience Nirvana. The fourth noble truth is the eightfold path to cessation, requiring "right" understanding, resolve, speech, action, livelihood, effort, mindfulness, and concentration. It is said that on entering this path, one has a glimpse of Nirvana and the way that leads there.

The eightfold path can be achieved through training in ethics, wisdom, and meditation. Meditation awakens in us the Clear Light that continues throughout lives and deaths into life beyond samsara and is aimed at concentration and insight. Concentration does not necessarily result in wisdom or liberation, but if it concerns loving-kindness, compassion, sympathetic joy, and equanimity, it may enable one to be reborn as a god. Meditation aimed at insight allows for reflection and analysis. The insight achieved in meditation reveals the nature of a person and of all reality.

The original words for meditation carry the sense of awareness expressed in our modern English term "mindfulness." The Buddha taught four modes of mindfulness and promised that it was the straight path to Nirvana: indeed, it was possible to get there in seven days. Mindfulness of the body includes "charnel house meditations" that make one aware of the body's impure and transient nature. Further modes are mindfulness of physical and emotional feelings as they come and go, of one's mental state, and of dharma, in which one meditates on various truths set forth by the

Buddha. The practice of mindfulness allows one to be more aware of one's intentions and motives, and produces "clear comprehension" so that one's actions are in harmony with one's ideals. Such cultivation of the mind enables the practitioner to achieve luminous, unobscured awareness.

WESTERN AND EASTERN DESCRIPTIONS of heaven, as an ultimate destination or a pleasant reincarnation, rely on imagery drawn from our mental and physical human reality. But it is impossible to describe such a state as luminous awareness. It will not be the beatific vision of God or the realm of a personal god who created the universe. Our identity, our mental and physical being will have been extinguished. Nirvana will be liberation, enlightenment, boundless life achieved after the cessation of samsara.

Thus in the Buddha's *Great Discourse on Nirvana*, he gives no word on what Nirvana might actually be like. As he lay dying between trees bursting into blossom, he instructed his attendant not to block his view of the gods who were gathering to bid him farewell. He delivered teachings on pilgrimage, instructions on how his body should be dealt with, and chastised his former charioteer for siding with nuns in disputes with monks. He asked his disciples if they had any remaining questions for him, and hearing none, the Buddha uttered his last words: "All conditioned things are of a nature to decay—strive on untiringly."

The Buddha's mind then passed up through eight levels of concentration, the *jhana*s. He passed through the fifth level, the Sphere of Infinite Space, on to the Spheres of Infinite Consciousness, Nothingness, Neither-Perception-Nor-Non-Perception, and finally the Cessation of Feeling and Perception. He then passed down through all the spheres and back again up to the fourth *jhana* of Purity and Equanimity and Mindfulness, whereupon the earth quaked, and he died.

There have been no travelers who have returned to tell us about Nirvana, but an ancient Buddhist text called the Atthakavagga—the Chapter on the Goal—contains eight "stanzas on the ultimate" that describe what a person will be like there. He will fashion no preconceptions, establish no preferences, form no belief even about what is true. He will not be led by moral habits or by vows. "Having crossed over to the other shore, only being the way he is, he does not rely on beliefs about anything."

Enlightenment remains a matter for interpretation. An Indian view is that it is the culmination of a gradual process of purification through ethics, meditation, and wisdom. A Chinese view does not consider enlightenment to be the result of long practice but rather the recognition of the intrinsic nature of the mind itself, which could be achieved by entering a "state of awareness beyond all distinctions." Similarly, Tibetan Buddhism strives for the realization of the primordial, luminous mind and consequent liberation. And Mahayana Buddhism allows for universal salvation, whereby all beings will become buddhas someday.

DESPITE THE ULTIMATE GOAL of enlightenment, the Buddha taught the path to heavenly realms as well—some say for people who are not yet capable of achieving the insight into reality necessary for liberation. One is reborn in a heavenly realm as a result of living a virtuous life but eventually will be reborn again into a less propitious realm. Mahayana Buddhism offers a more hopeful alternative. There are many world systems similar to ours in this vast universe. Some are fortunate enough to have their own buddha to purify and teach, and who will help them reincarnate into his buddha-field. These are the Pure Lands, the most famous of which is Sukhavati, the Land of Bliss.

The Buddha tells the story of a monk named Dharmakara who asked a buddha to describe the qualities of a buddha-field. There were so many fields it took a million years to list them all. The monk then meditated for five eons in order to synthesize all of the wonderful qualities of the millions of buddha-fields into one single pure one. He promised to turn his dream into a place for rebirth for fortunate beings and set out on the long bodhisattva path to become buddha of the new buddha-field. Dharmakara took a series of forty-eight vows that give us a sense of what his heaven, the

Western Paradise, would be like. All the inhabitants would be golden-colored; they would not have private property or have to wash, dry, sew, or bleach their own robes; and they could hear the dharma in whatever form they wished. An added blessing (less appreciated by modern women) was that any woman who aspired to enlightenment, who felt disgust at her female form and heard Dharmakara's name, would never have to be reborn as a woman. Dharmakara succeeded in establishing his heaven, and presides over it as Amitabha, Infinite Light.

Dharmakara made other vows, of great interest and comfort to those on earth. He would appear at the moment of death to anyone who aspired to enlightenment, heard his name, and remembered him with faith. Those who wished to hear his name and be reborn in his pure land, and who dedicated their merit to do so (even if they promised this just a handful of times in their lives), would enter there. The only exceptions were those who would become denizens of hell for the traditional reasons: killing their parents or an arhat, wounding a buddha, or creating dissension in their community. The aspiration to enter Amitabha's Pure Land became widespread among both monastic and lay Buddhists in India, Tibet, and East Asia. And it was the subject of much artistic interpretation, as in the Nectar Ritual Paintings. A seventeenth-century Korean version shows a whole cast of characters in attendance—buddhas, bodhisattvas, even hungry ghosts—while monks perform rituals and people process bearing fruit and flowers to the central altar, all to ensure that the departing soul arrives safely in the Pure Land.

This Pure Land is described in *The Sukhavativyuha Sutra* in terms of the beauty that is available to human senses, and thus is similar to heavens we have explored. It is immeasurable, home to incalculable numbers of disciples, bodhisattvas, humans, and gods. Jewel lotuses fill the realm, each with a hundred thousand million petals, radiant with color. Some people sit cross-legged on lotus blossoms, some within the lotus—if one is still doubtful, he will stay inside a lotus for five hundred years, gazing at the

Amitabha, the Buddha of the Western Pure Land,
by an unknown artist

buddha-field but unable to hear the marvelous sounds of dharma flowing
through the buddha-realms.

The Pure Land is full of trees made of precious materials: "some jewel
trees have roots made of coral, trunks of agate, branches of mother-of-
pearl, boughs of purple gold, leaves of white silver, flowers of lapis-lazuli,

and fruits of crystal." Pure, harmonious breezes blow in these trees, scattering flowers in patterns and sounding five harmonious tones, and each piece of music is better than the other by ten thousand billion times. There are lecture halls, palaces, monks' quarters, ponds to bathe in that are up to a hundred thousand leagues long. Their water rises to the desired level on the bather's body, at the desired temperature, and "opens the mind, delights the body, and washes away all impurities from the heart."

One can hear any sound one wants in the Pure Land, that of the name of the Buddha; or the sound of "empty and without a self," or of "neither arising nor ceasing." Anything one might wish to eat appears instantly, served up in precious vessels, although simply the sight of it miraculously satisfies hunger. The inhabitants are all endowed with supernatural powers and great wisdom. They all have the same perfect form, bodies that are like empty space. The Buddha taught that they are all assured of certain success in the Path, for none has fallen astray, although he did not say whether this Path leads on to enlightenment.

In Japan, Pure Land Buddhism emerged as a way of waiting for the next Buddha, possibly millions of years in the future. There were significant refinements in the devotion to Amitabha. A twelfth-century monk named Honen taught that while it was important to live an ethical life, chanting the name of Amitabha was the true path to salvation. Honen did so seventy thousand times a day. His disciple Shinran believed that nothing we could do could earn our freedom from rebirth but that we could turn to Amitabha, whose power was absolute. Hearing his name in your heart was a sign of his saving power, and one needed only to say it once, ever. Even the wicked could be reborn in the Pure Land in this way. Shinran went so far as to teach that liberation came about not at death but at the moment of faith in Amitabha, and that moment is the manifestation of Amitabha's mind. He believed that the only reason the Buddha came into the world was to proclaim Amitabha's Pure Land.

TWENTY-SIX

The Clear Light

Our innermost essence, the truth we all search
for, the key to understanding life and death.

• Sogyal Rinpoche

Beginning in the thirteenth century, Tibetan Buddhists developed
three thousand lines of incarnation (the most famous being the
Dalai Lama) that preserve the wisdom memory of the masters who
came to fully realize the true nature of reality. This realization is the source
of remarkably specific ways to make our passage through death, which is
just the beginning of another chapter in life.

One comes to such realization through the mind, which has three
forms. The gross mind, ignorant and deluded, depends on the body, as does
the subtle mind that draws from the senses and provides information to the
very subtle mind. The gross mind and the subtle mind, as well as individual
identity and ego, end at the death of the material body. But the very subtle
mind—that of the Clear Light—persists: it is "our innermost essence, the
truth we all search for, the key to understanding life and death." Knowledge of this true "nature of mind" is knowledge of knowledge itself. It enables us to realize the impermanence and interdependence of all things,
and to glimpse the primordial, pristine, intelligent, radiant awareness of
the Clear Light. Very advanced practitioners of Tibetan Buddhism are able
to maintain their conscious identity as they enter the dying process, to
achieve liberation or to choose their situation on rebirth.

The living can help a person at the moment of death, which is crucial because that is when the person's fate will be determined. Every person has a vast store of seeds for future lives, good and bad, and one's mental state at the moment of death determines which will "fructify." *The Tibetan Book of Living and Dying* offers wise guidance to anyone who takes on this important ministry. Familiar surroundings—perhaps a shrine of offerings—can be provided, and all invasive medical procedures discontinued. The companion must let go of her own tensions, practice forgiveness, and not cling to the dying person. Above all, she must be compassionate, warm and empathetic, and determined to alleviate suffering in whatever way possible. Such compassion can help the dying person feel unconditional love and spiritual inspiration, even healing. The atmosphere of the deathbed is of utmost importance because every thought and emotion the departing one experiences powerfully affects her fate.

IN MANY BRANCHES OF BUDDHISM, it is believed that there is an intermediate state between death and the next phase of a person's existence. This state can range from an instant to forty-nine days, during which time the living can assist the dead in their passage through prayer and ritual. Tibetan Buddhism provides guidance through intermediate states called bardos, and ways for the departed to become liberated from them. *The Tibetan Book of the Dead* is a manual for such rites, such as Prayers for Deliverance from the Straits of the Bardo, written by the Lama Lobsang Chökyi Gyaltsen:

> Empower us to produce strong mindfulness
> When the wind constituent begins to dissolve into consciousness . . .

And

> Empower us to be reborn in a pure land
> Through the yoga of the transformation of the outer, inner, and secret
> When the varieties of the four sounds of the reversal of the elements,
> The three frightening appearances, the uncertainties, and the signs appear.

According to *The Tibetan Book of Living and Dying*, the bardos are inter-linked realities, moments when the possibility for liberation is heightened. The first is the natural bardo of this life, in which is included the bardos of sleep and dreaming, and of meditation. The next is the painful bardo of dying, followed by the luminous bardo of *dharmata*. The final bardo is that of becoming, of rebirth. Bardos are analogous to the dream state: bodies lack substance and are subject to winds of energy while retaining their senses. Location shifts and changes, and only bardo beings can see other bardo beings. In the bardos following life, the thoughts and feelings we die with return with force. Wisdom and confusion, insight and bewilderment emerge simultaneously and require us to make powerfully consequential choices. Only the most spiritually developed people can avoid the bardos and go directly to their ultimate destination.

The Buddha realized that it was ignorance of our true nature that is the root of all the suffering of samsara, and that we need to bring the mind home to its true nature through meditation. Thus the natural bardo of this life is of utmost importance, for it gives us the opportunity to travel deep into the nature of mind, enabling its truth to unfold in us by itself. This is the supreme way of preparing for the bardos after death: to become en-lightened during this lifetime.

The process of dying is a gradual dawning of successively more subtle levels of consciousness moving toward the ultimate revelation, the Clear Light. This is the greatest opportunity for liberation. If people have pre-pared themselves through meditation, stabilizing their sense of awareness, they may succeed in purifying themselves, emptying their karma for re-birth. Those who recognize the Clear Light at the moment of death can bask in it for days, while the living observe a display of lights signaling their liberation.

Most people do not recognize the Clear Light and move on to the bardo of *dharmata*, where they take on a body of light. This bardo is the un-adorned, unconditioned truth, with four stages offering liberation. In the first, space dissolves into luminosity. A master can collect himself and become stable in this experience, thus achieving liberation, but for most it just flashes by. In the next stage, light manifests as forty-two peaceful and fifty-eight wrathful deities in dazzling mandalas. If the departed fail to stabilize at this point, they dissolve into wisdom, which also manifests as light. If they still cannot stabilize, they enter the final stage of the bardo, wherein all of reality manifests itself, all at once: deities, heavens and hells, Pure Lands. Anything is possible—the departed become clairvoyant and aware of all teachings. If they recognize all this as the Clear Light, they will be liberated.

If not, they will become grasping again, succumbing to the seductions of old habits and instincts from the realms of samsara. They will proceed to the final bardo, that of becoming, which extends from the awakening of those old tendencies to rebirth. If the departed have been highly virtuous, they will get a good rebirth right away; if they have been evil, they will go immediately to a lower birth.

But most people linger in the bardo of becoming, awaiting the karmic connection with their parents-to-be. During this period, they may visit loved ones and feel rebuffed by their inability to respond. When the departed person sees them crying, they will realize they are dead and be overwhelmed by intense suffering, like a "fish writhing on hot sand." They will relive the experiences of their past life, and all the suffering for which they were responsible. Every seven days they will go through their death again, in a way that is seven times more intense. All the negative karma of past lives will come flooding back, and some get stuck in the bardo and become spirits. But there is still a chance of liberation, if the departed acknowledge that negative emotions have no ultimate reality and come to rest in the nature of mind. They can also envision their potential parents as the Buddha or a master, or think of the Pure Lands. Otherwise the pull of a material body becomes overwhelmingly powerful, the winds of karma sweep them along, and they enter their mother's womb as the Clear Light manifests itself once again.

FOR SOULS WHO DO NOT RECOGNIZE the Clear Light as they pass through death, Tibetan Buddhism provides a way to invoke the power of Amitabha, the embodiment of luminosity. Through the practice of *phowa*, a powerful master, at the moment a person's breathing ceases, transfers her consciousness into a buddha realm, imprinting her mind stream with the master's presence. The dying person can also make a concerted wish to be reborn either in a pure realm or as a human being, in order to help others. Throughout these processes, the nature of mind is present in the dying person, who can be assisted by careful interventions by the living, such as dedicating their merit to her so that she attains a good rebirth.

Besides the practice of *phowa* in Tibetan Buddhism, there is another way of engaging with life after life by making otherworldly journeys. Rare people known as *delogs* cross over into the realms beyond death and return to tell what they find. Delog Dawa Drolma's account of her journey, *Delog: Journey to Realms Beyond Death*, was smuggled out of Tibet by her son, Chagdud Tulku, during the Chinese Cultural Revolution. Her deep meditation breached the boundaries of ordinary perception and took her to pure realms that richly manifested the nature of mind.

In this state, Dawa Drolma became aware of impure realms of being, hells where a blizzard of souls swirled around her like snow, crying out, "a year's rainfall of tears" falling from their eyes. She met a girl who had killed a snake and was now wrapped in a black snake thick as a pine tree; and a person named Abo who had a head like a big clay pot. His mouth was as small as the eye of a needle; his esophagus the width of a horsehair, and his stomach as large as a city. He had been uncharitable, stingy in his care for others, and now he was starving in a hideous way.

Dawa Drolma also visited Yulokod, the Pure Realm of the goddess Tara, where radiant mansions of rainbow light floated in the sky, trees strung with bells granted wishes, lotuses abounded, and there was no birth, illness, aging, or death. On entering the central palace, she writes, "I awoke from the deep sleep of ordinary consciousness and was free of the veils of ignorance. The inner vision of my pristine awareness expanded, and I experienced a surge of love and compassion." She encountered Ayurdevi, the goddess of longevity, and a multitude of forms of Tara herself: Tara of the Thunderous Dragon's Roar, Tara of Spontaneous Accomplishment, Tara of Inconceivability.

At this point, Dawa Drolma was overcome with an "inexpressible, unimaginable sense of infinite cosmic order, a vast and totally unimpeded panorama of purity with nothing to grasp at as ultimately real." She was granted an audience with Tara, who told Dawa Drolma that when she realized that nobody aspired to Buddhahood in a woman's body, she appeared as an ocean of women, to bring them to enlightenment.

THE ELABORATE BUDDHIST JOURNEY of the mind into the mind is played out for contemporary Westerners in a novel by George Saunders, *Lincoln in the Bardo*. It is not an exact reconstruction of what we find in the *Tibetan Book of Living and Dying*, but a vivid imagining of what such a state might be like. And why not? We go there in our minds and our imaginations, be we alive or dead.

Lincoln in the Bardo is set in a cemetery in Washington, where newly departed Willie Lincoln finds himself amid a host of stranded souls. One, the Reverend Thomas, has been turned away from heaven and remains mired in his confusion about why he was damned. Other souls endlessly repeat their stories of brutal rape or publishing woes or unloving wives. A newcomer, young Willie Lincoln, who like the others does not seem to comprehend he is dead, is visited by his father, who tenderly cradles his son's body as he grieves.

Willie is watched over by some decent souls, as young ones were "not meant to tarry" there. But he becomes ensnared in a monster constructed of tiny writhing unrepentant sinners that aims to trap him in the cemetery forever. His guardians rescue him, and he enters his father's body only to emerge again, announcing to the crowd that they are not sick but dead. Willie takes off—elated that candy, swinging on chandeliers, and flying out windows are all allowed now. Others depart as well, and though we do not know where they are headed, we do know their release was made possible when they became compassionate, reaching beyond their individual misery. Even Lincoln, still in the land of the living, is freed through a new understanding of the utterly transient nature of things—his son had been but a passing burst of energy. As for Willie, he realizes that his earthly life was never his to begin with, and returns whence he came, to beauty.

TWENTY-SEVEN

If We Could Only Awaken

Our Buddha nature, immaterial and perfectly
enlightened from the beginning, will remain . . .
it just is.

· PAULA SAUNDERS

The Buddhism that Westerners are familiar with is a relatively recent development. By 1498, when Portuguese explorer Vasco da
Gama arrived in India, Hinduism had long since reasserted itself,
claiming the Buddha as an avatar of the great god Vishnu. Modern Buddhism
emerged with the colonization of India, during which the Buddha came to
be respected by Westerners for his rational philosophy and his ethics, and
Buddhism regarded as a form of religion that was well suited to modernity.
This view of Buddhism spread in the West during the twentieth century.
Laymen and -women became Buddhist leaders, and meditation became the
central practice. This modern Buddhism is variously regarded as a philosophy, a way of life, or even a science of the mind. It has not replaced or dis-
placed other forms of Buddhism, which remains a remarkably diverse and
far-flung tradition. But it has had, along with Hinduism, a profound influence on present-day seekers who articulate their hopes and possibilities in
very different terms than those provided by Western religious traditions.

I learned about this modern form of Buddhism from a friend, writer
Paula Saunders, who told me the story of how Jesus brought her to the
Buddha. She was a faithful and searching Christian who longed for ways to

put the language of religion into practice. A Catholic nun gave her a book by Buddhist monk Thich Nhat Hanh, and she started a meditation group at her Episcopal church. But nobody knew how to proceed, and Paula finally found her way to Buddhist teachers. As she explained it, the relationship with a teacher is the conduit for a force passed down through the teacher's lineage, in theory beginning with the Buddha and transmitted down the generations. A teacher manifests a teaching in whatever way is suited to a group or a person, functioning not as an individual but as a source—that is why Buddhists have shrines with pictures of their teachers and devotional objects, not for worshipping but for reverencing their teachers.

This role of the teacher serving as a channel down through generations of students is very different from that of Christian saints. But Christians acknowledge that Jesus is our teacher; it is he who manifests the grace and wisdom we are able to receive. In Buddhism, Jesus is also recognized as a great teacher, a major bodhisattva whose words about the Kingdom taking place *now* are cherished by Buddhists. Paula uses the word *Christ*: Christ is the link, Christ is the source, Christ is the avenue, Christ is the way. Her practice enables her to recognize and partake of the living lineage of original Christianity. But as a Buddhist, she has faith in many different manifestations of the divine, including even water and sky, none of which diminish or exclude her faith in Christ.

I HAD ASSUMED THAT the practice of meditation necessitated quieting one's own mind, but Paula described how, as a relative amateur, her mind goes where it will. In her Tibetan Buddhist tradition, there is no attempt at stopping it from doing so. Rather, you are to become aware of what your mind is doing, so if you get caught in a line of thinking—like what do I need to do tomorrow?—you just acknowledge the thought, quiet it, and go back to the practice. Even adept practitioners find themselves making grocery lists, but they are less reactive to such thoughts. As Paula said, "Human minds are made to think, so it's not going to be quiet—but it could be quieter."

Thinking of the medieval Christian mystics, I wondered if her meditation had the potential for transporting her somewhere beyond herself. She replied that actually she would become more of her real self, and that there would be a quality of presence that would open things up for her. The great Buddhist masters are said to be omniscient, seeing the tendencies and possibilities of other people playing out in ways that are not evident to those limited by their sense of self. And they are capable of great compassion for people who are difficult, not so much through feeling sorry for them but in loving them for the unique beings they are.

Paula believes everyone will eventually become enlightened in this way, because our original, innate nature is the Buddha nature. Temporary defilements of this nature like reactivity, emotions, and desires are all results of our karma; we have created them ourselves. But anything created or constructed is impermanent; it will eventually fall apart. "And our Buddha nature, immaterial and perfectly enlightened from the beginning, will remain . . . it just is."

CHRISTIANS HOPE TO REACH HEAVEN and customarily think of it as the final stage of a linear trajectory. But the sense Paula described of heightened, expanded awareness, of being with others in a river of consciousness, reminded me of the Christian belief in a communion of saints that crosses all boundaries of time and space. If during intense prayer a Christian felt enveloped in the communion of saints, it seems to me that one would have breached those natural boundaries and be, in some sense, in heaven. For Paula, it is unnecessary to separate "the already" and the "not yet," because our sense of being on a linear trajectory is due only to our limited understanding. If we were to grow spiritually, we might understand reality in a nonlinear way: "And this is why we might say we are in heaven right now, if we could only awaken to it."

And yet ordinary people do not break through to enlightenment; there is life, death, the bardos, being blown by the winds of karma toward rebirth, enacting our karma once again in another life. Still, Paula cautioned against separating the moment of your death from every other moment of your life. If you are open in each moment, aware of opportunities to bring your awareness, not your self, to the moment, you can bring that practice into your experience of death—"Why not, in the moment of your passing, be aware of yet another opportunity coming along, flowing like a river?" And she assured me that becoming enlightened is not extraordinary for human beings; everyone will get there eventually. Her equanimity arises from her conviction that our intelligence leads us "to goodness, to opening, to awareness, to happiness." And it's not a matter of hope: it's just the way it is, and so every day you simply do your best.

MY SRI LANKAN FRIEND NETHRA had a traditional upbringing among conservative Theravada Buddhists. She described for me the hopes they have of their lives to come. They aspire in the long run to attain enlightenment, or be reborn as a higher being—or as a human, for indeed it is only from the human state that enlightenment comes about. They are mindful of the possibility that one could come back as a lower being. Indeed, a child might be admonished not to kill a fly because it might have been her mother in another life. Pious people are usually vegetarian in order to follow the precept of not taking life, as there is the potential of relationship with every being in the world.

Thus you are responsible not just for yourself but for the people you are very close to. If you marry someone, you have met them in a past life, and you have been born to your parents many times before. One does not move through the cycle alone; collectives of people meet again and again. The Jataka stories teach this through accounts of the Buddha's five hundred lives, in which he meets and falls in love and marries his wife over and over again. So karma, which can be used to explain all kinds of disasters, could also explain the odd feeling we have now and then that we have met someone before. I have jokingly said to such people that perhaps I knew them in a past life; Nethra really means it. And when she does have such an intuition, she gives a nod to it, acknowledging the connection, whatever it may be.

NETHRA KNOWS THE PASSAGE of death well, as it is customary in Sri Lanka to include children in caring for a dying person and mourning their loss. As in other forms of Buddhism, it is believed that the soul is in a transient state during and after death. It is important to be careful what you say as hearing is the last sense to shut down—indeed, it is best to chant around the death-bed. People who cannot face their impending loss, who cannot let the person pass on, should not be present. Nethra told of how her physician aunt tried to give her grandfather a cardiac massage on his deathbed, and how her mother made her stop so that he could be at peace. They held his hand and let him go.

When Nethra's grandmother died, her embalmed body lay in their house for days so that people could attend her body night and day. Monks visited to chant and receive alms so that the mourners could transfer their good karma to her grandmother. In her tradition, this ritual is repeated at three days, then seven months, and yearly thereafter, as the departed soul might still need assistance in gaining a fortunate rebirth.

In the old days—and sometimes even now—there was a funeral pyre, a shocking ritual to witness, given the inescapable smell of flesh and the way a corpse, engulfed in flames, would suddenly sit up. But to bear such witness is still deemed very important, even transformative: the living are forced to acknowledge that the person is truly gone, their earthly body destroyed. These days the cremation ceremony usually takes place in a cre-matorium, and the next day the family collects the ashes. Nethra spoke of a sacred moment when she was able to handle her grandmother's ashes, to sift through them to find the bits of teeth and bone that remained. And when it came time, her family placed the pot of ashes on a pole in the river, struck it so the ashes would scatter, and cast flowers after them into the river.

THE GREAT NINETEENTH-CENTURY Hindu saint Ramakrishna taught that "God has made different religions to suit different aspirations, times, and countries. All doctrines are only so many paths, but a path is by no means God Himself. Indeed, one can reach God if one follows any of the paths with whole-hearted devotion. One may eat a cake with icing either straight or sidewise. It will taste sweet either way." There are significant differences in the paths we see before us—whether we are to follow them through one life or many, and whether we will in the end join a personal God or be absorbed into pure Being. But we have much in common—the sense of a moral universe, the essential value of compassion, the yearning for life beyond and the freedom to reach for it in the present moment. There is a divine reality at the very heart of things, and all the paths we travel lead there—as Ram Dass writes, we're all just "walking each other home."

Part VII

WE SHALL
NOT CEASE
FROM
EXPLORATION

TWENTY-EIGHT

Voices from Beyond

We want a religion that you can prove.

• ARTHUR CONAN DOYLE

Spiritualism is a religious movement based in the belief that souls survive the death of the physical body and that those of us still on earth
can communicate with them. It emerged around the same time as
the Mormon faith, from the same Burned-over District of upstate New
York, and reflects the nineteenth-century sense of the afterlife as being
very close to this one. But spiritualists did not take its existence on faith;
they did not have to *believe* anymore. They *knew* there was an afterlife because they had come into direct contact with it.

Science was becoming the prevailing mode for observing and understanding material and, for some, spiritual phenomena. The spiritualists
were confident that their beliefs and practice could stand up to scientific
inquiry; indeed, American spiritualists petitioned Congress in 1854 to
fund scientific study of spiritualist phenomena. In England, the Society for
Psychical Research was founded in 1882 to study paranormal phenomena
in a scientific way. As Sir Arthur Conan Doyle, author of *The History of
Spiritualism*, declared: "We want a religion that you can prove."

WILLIAM JAMES, regarded as the father of American psychology, was a prominent member of the Society for Psychical Research. In his influential book

Varieties of Religious Experience: A Study in Human Nature, he employed a "science of religion" that applies scientific observation to personal religious experience. Evidence is to be found not in theology or any social dimension of religion but in "the feelings, acts, and experiences of individual men in their solitude, so far as they apprehend themselves to stand in relation to whatever they may consider the divine." Practice is the only sure evidence: "by their fruits ye shall know them." James is emphatic that we should not dismiss such experience as pathological, pointing out that in other branches of science researchers do not base their opinions on whether or not their subject is neurotic.

James proposes two different families of God. The "once-born" are optimists who regard God as the "spirit of a harmonious world"; they approach God easily and do not seem to believe in evil. James is not easy on the once-born: "His contentment with the finite incases him like a lobster-shell and shields him from all morbid repining at his distance from the infinite." The twice-born are decidedly more complicated and pessimistic, fraught with conflict between the spirit and flesh and plagued by impulses that thwart their best-laid plans. James appreciates their struggle and considers religions wherein pessimistic elements are best developed—notably Buddhism and Christianity—to be the most complete. "They are essentially religions of deliverance: the man must die to an unreal life before he can be born into the real life."

James explores the inspiration of religious mystics, the nature of religious conversion, and the qualities of saintly people. He concludes that religion is close to a "transmarginal" region of the brain, one that is outside but accessible to consciousness. For deeply religious people, the door into this region seems unusually wide open. But how far does transmarginal consciousness carry us if we seek to pass through into the beyond? James cannot give a scientific answer, as this is where "over-beliefs" take hold, beliefs that require more evidence than we have. James concludes that the expression of human experience, which he has viewed objectively, "invincibly urges me beyond the narrow scientific bounds," and freely acknowledges his own over-belief. The transmarginal, mystical region of the brain is the source of our ideal impulses, and we belong to it more intimately than to the visible world. If we commune with this region, we will undergo conversion of our personalities and of our lives, and anything that produces effects within our reality must be acknowledged as real. For James, God produces real effects and thus is real.

Spiritualists claim to converse with the dead, who have sent back messages describing a loving God who does not levy a final judgment but gives us an eternity of opportunities to grow spiritually in the "otherworld," much as Swedenborg's afterlife does. In Summerland, as spiritualists often call it, the individual continues the spiritual trajectory begun in this life. She is grouped on arrival with others at a similar stage of spiritual development and reevaluates her life. From then on, she is responsible for her own quest to become more knowledgeable, creative, and loving. The otherworld is full of opportunities to do so, being a busy, well-appointed place: there are spiritual hospitals and all manner of amusements. The pets we had in life greet their humans when they arrive, or join them when they themselves die, and thereafter accompany their owners as ghosts. The departed are helped along the way by spirits, and in turn guide others, including the living. Spiritualists believe that we on earth receive inspiration from the dead: fine words for orators and new discoveries for scientists.

Spiritualists believe there are different portals to the world beyond. Mediums are conduits for contact with the dead, proving that life continues after the death of the body. Ectoplasm is the physical manifestation of spiritual energy that "seems to diffuse through the tissues of the medium like a gas, and emerges through the orifices because it passes more freely through the mucus membrane than through the skin." Emerging technologies such as telegraphy and recording devices were useful to early spiritualist mediums as well—one George Valiantine claimed to pick up Confucius speaking in an extinct Chinese dialect.

Several eminent inventors from that time—including Alexander

Graham Bell, Thomas Edison, and Nikola Tesla—believed that the spirit traveled after death in a way similar to a wireless impulse. Edison even attempted to develop a device for "personalities which have left this earth to communicate with us." In his view, living beings are made up of infinitesimal life units that regroup after death as someone or something else. Edison's invention was similar to a megaphone, designed to accommodate the weak hearing of the dead. Alas, he died before completing it.

Mental telepathy, wherein one mind acts on another, was a link to the other world as well. It was officially endorsed by the Society for Psychical Research, which believed that it might account for people experiencing the sight or feeling or sound of loved ones. But one of its researchers, Richard Hodgson, who died in 1905, thereafter reported to the living that he was besieged by messages from our side and could not answer them all. His own message was that he had been biased toward the material life while neglecting the spiritual and lamented that in the afterlife, he was like a newborn babe.

In accounts of spiritualism and paranormal experience one does come upon such messages from beyond, most notably those of "post-mortem Doyle." He wrote in The History of Spiritualism that such messages require sincere intention on the part of the sender as well as the receiver. Skeptics would be unlikely recipients, and Doyle had harsh words for them, excoriating scientists who were astute inside their own fields but foolish and illogical outside, as well as clerics who were bound to an obsolete system served up like "last week's dinner." Doyle was able to communicate his own messages to us through the medium Grace Cooke, and they are edifying. There is no final judgment from a god apart from us: it happens not at the end of the world but at the end of the spirit's world of matter. God is not vindictive or cruel, rather God is infinitely loving, a divine and compassionate intelligence. And "every religion is linked to one or another of the different planes of life we are illuminating. . . . The ultimate goal of all is to attain that condition of consciousness where the personality dwindles and is absorbed, and the individuality becomes so at one with the Universal that, in losing itself, it becomes the very pulse of God."

A STORY OF SPIRITUALIST CONTACT with the dead is woven into the history of Stanford University. Leland and Jane Lathrop Stanford had been interested in spiritualism from the early days of their marriage, although they remained faithful Christians. After their only child, Leland Jr., died from typhoid at sixteen, there was even talk (quickly discredited) of their having founded Stanford University during a séance. In fact, the Stanfords had attended séances with their friends former President and Mrs. Ulysses S. Grant, and they were driven in their grief to seek contact with their son. One of Leland's brothers, Thomas Welton Stanford, urged them on—he himself had lost his beloved young wife and had become obsessed with reaching out to her through séances that became a regular feature in the society of Melbourne, Australia, where he lived. He was patron to a medium named Fred Evans, who channeled messages from the dead that came through in complete sentences written in chalk on slates.

The Stanfords came under the influence of a prominent Methodist preacher, the Reverend Dr. John P. Newman, who conducted séances in their mansion on San Francisco's Nob Hill. These gatherings featured a blend of traditional Christian piety, hypnotic trances, and various odd phenomena such as eerie music and the mysterious appearance of ancient artifacts and things that had belonged to the departed person being contacted. Leland Stanford grew skeptical and declined to participate until there were results, but Jane Stanford clung to her hopes. As her secretary, Bertha Berner, wrote, "She prayed so earnestly for the light, which meant to behold Leland, that it was pitiful. She often attended demonstrations . . . but they were never satisfying to her."

However, Fred Evans had managed to convey messages from Leland Jr. in which the boy consoled his family (and reminded Thomas to tip the medium). Thomas later donated the slates to the university, where they can be found today in its Special Collections. One reads: "My dear uncle I am pleased to meet you here this morning."

Jane continued to harbor hopes of finding Leland Jr. and traveled to Melbourne. She said at the time, "Unfortunately, so far, we have met only with charlatans, but perhaps we may yet see an honest demonstration." She found Thomas in a shocking state, reclusive and obsessed with psychic research. He arranged for one Charles Bailey to conduct a séance. It was simple and sadly uneventful, as Bertha Berner later wrote: "after a long silence—broken only by an occasional request that we have patience—the man Bailey declared that the conditions were unfavorable and that there would be no manifestations." Jane returned home, and to a faith in the hereafter that she proclaimed was based solely on the Bible.

A brief coda to this story: When Bailey found out that Thomas intended to bring a Stanford professor to Melbourne to test his abilities, he fled abroad, only to resurface as a favorite of none other than Arthur Conan Doyle.

TWENTY-NINE

The Beyond Within

Science without religion is lame, religion
without science is blind.

• ALBERT EINSTEIN

What do we talk about when we talk about consciousness? To understand the range of phenomena that lie beyond normal human experience and scientific understanding—from reincarnation to mysticism to out-of-body travel to near-death experience—we need to consider the different ways we define consciousness.

Scientific materialists, who believe that physical reality is all that actually exists, explain consciousness solely in terms of how our neural constitution interacts with the concrete world. But for those involved in the broad range of religious and New Age movements advancing human spirituality, this view is thoroughly inadequate. Not everything can be explained in terms of chemistry or biology or electric activity in the brain. In the words of neurophysiologist Sir John Eccles, "We have to recognize that we are spiritual beings with souls existing in a spiritual world as well as material beings with bodies and brains existing in a material world."

Indeed, no single organ in the brain actually corresponds to consciousness. It is the result of our unconsciously synthesizing and harmonizing our perceptions, cognitions, memories, and other functions. Consciousness leads to self-consciousness, which in turn is shaped by one's cultural understanding. The ancient Greeks considered the self to be transcendent, expressed in the immortality of the soul. For Hindus, self-consciousness reaches beyond the individual to the infinite identity with the atman, and for Buddhists, consciousness refers to pure unchanging awareness, the subtlest consciousness that continues throughout the cycle of rebirths.

Our understanding of consciousness has also been influenced by the scientific notion of a quantum universe based on webs of relations. Subatomic particles with no physical link can somehow be connected or entangled, exerting influence on each other even when they are separated—what Einstein called "spooky action at a distance." Moreover, their properties can only be understood in terms of interaction with an observer. According to psychologist Dean Radin of the Institute for Noetic Sciences, "Quantum theory and a vast body of supporting experiments tell us that something unaccounted for is connecting otherwise isolated objects"—and we experience this quantum interconnectedness through parapsychological phenomena.

Neuropsychiatrist Jeffrey Schwartz and psychologist Mario Beauregard have developed a theory of quantum mind in an effort to explain the relationship between the mind and the brain. Rather than seeing the mind as what the brain does, they propose that we think of the mind as the controller of the brain. Their theory is based on "neuroplasticity," whereby brain cells change in response to will or intention—"When the mind gives a signal, possibilities coalesce and become a thought in the brain."

We need to take this evolving understanding of consciousness into account as we explore the nature of the reality we live in—and whether there is a reality in which we will live after the death of our physical bodies (even if they are eventually resurrected in some mysterious way). We live in a participatory universe: there is a vast interconnectedness of things; the observer cannot be separated from the observed, and the mind is an intentional force that controls the brain. The Hindu atman and the Buddhist sense of shared awareness both rhyme with this new perspective, but we have come a long way from Western notions of a God way up in the sky who is in charge of everything. Barbara Bradley Hagerty suggests in *Finger-prints of God* that the quantum reading of reality is "where mysticism meets science" and that the medium through which our thoughts are transmitted to others may in fact be God.

IN *THE MAP OF HEAVEN*, neurosurgeon Eben Alexander laments that we have lost a deep, hidden side of our lives, a side that we keep secret even from ourselves because our culture has no place for it. His concern puts me in mind of the sense Mary Ann Evans (George Eliot) had of a vast and overwhelming hidden reality: "If we had a keen vision and feeling of all ordinary human life, it would be like hearing the grass grow and the squirrel's heart beat, and we should die of that roar which lies on the other side of silence." If we were to awaken such consciousness, we would not be overcome by it, but we might find we have drawn unnecessary boundaries around who we really are and who we can become. We might discover a self that is unfolding through life and on after death into a much larger life, and we might begin to prepare ourselves. These aspirations have been at the heart of religion, and they increasingly drive the exploration of parapsychological experience.

In every culture, people experience visions, ecstasies, ghostly visitations, and various states of altered consciousness that are usually explained through mythology or religion. They are not considered impossible, or evidence of insanity—they spring from worldviews that we may not be able (or willing) to understand. In cultures imbued with apocalyptic foreboding, accounts of otherworldly journeys such as those of Enoch or Viraz verified for believers that God's moral order was intact and that their good God would ultimately prevail over their enemies and oppressors, and evil itself. Such journeys attest to a just and glorious conclusion to the strife on earth. A modern person would be skeptical of such accounts and the conventional way in which they were delivered. But their original audience would have seen that conventionality as a sign of authenticity.

Skeptical as we might consider ourselves to be, there is a growing literature describing otherworldly journeys, deathbed visions, and return-from-death stories. It seems there is a resurgence of otherworld accounts when they are needed most, when a society sees itself as besieged by change, when our views of the universe and our place in it are unsettled and uncertain. We have no common religion or mythology with which to face these challenges, and traditional notions about death and the afterlife have lost much of their persuasive power.

But there is a great deal of creative thinking by those exploring the nature of consciousness and where it can take us. Such efforts seek, like spiritualism, to define and verify consciousness through science—in particular "noetic" science, which involves multidisciplinary efforts to study different ways of knowing to understand the spectrum of human experience, including the parapsychological. After all, the scientific method in our culture is the customary measure of validity. Whether it is the only or best way of understanding experiences that have in the past been interpreted through religion is an unsettled question.

CONSCIOUSNESS IS NOT located in or powered by one organ. Rather, it emerges from the harmonious operation of a series of processes such as memory and cognition. Neurological activity that indicates altered consciousness, such as mystical experience, is the topic of scientific research documented by Barbara Bradley Hagerty. There is nothing so clear as a brain scan for spiritual experience, but research on stress, genetics, and meditation is yielding valuable information.

As described by neurologist Patrick McNamara, a person experiencing long-term stress can reach a point where she can no longer tolerate it. This turn may cause the body to "up-regulate," so that her symptoms of anxiety and fear dissipate, cortisol levels decrease, and endorphins kick in. She may even enjoy a surge in dopamine, the neurotransmitter said to play a role in falling in love. Science can track and describe these processes, but it cannot establish definitively that they are solely physical phenomena. When these processes play out in conversion experiences or other transforming moments, some regard them as a "touch of God."

Genetic studies reveal different capacities for spiritual experience in individuals—and even in families. There may even be a "God spot" in our brains: four out of five people feel rapturous when specific regions of their temporal lobes are stimulated. Perhaps this is the physical grounding for the yearning that Longinus wrote of—human speculation reaching beyond the bounds of the material world, launching "forth at pleasure into endless space." Of course the environment and our experience play a role, but so do genes: we are wired for spirituality much as we are wired for personality or intelligence. William James was on to this when he proposed the idea that certain people are predisposed to religion and spirituality. In his terms, they are uniquely open to the "transmarginal" area of the brain that is outside of but accessible to consciousness, and which may convey us beyond ourselves.

Mary Roach, author of the book *Spook: Science Tackles the Afterlife*, writes about submitting to a test administered by neuroscientist Michael Persinger to see if she was capable of feeling the presence of spirits. Persinger's theory was that particular patterns of electromagnetic field activity can make the brain more susceptible to hallucinations. Roach was wired up and shut inside a soundproof chamber. Not much happened except for the sound of a distant police car. That turned out to be irrelevant, and she was diagnosed as "left-hemispherically dominant," in other words a "least responder." According to Persinger's theory, Roach has never seen ghosts because she was born with a neural structure that does not enable her to do so.

Science has established that brain activity correlates to one's spiritual experience, but exactly how is a matter of debate. While some researchers focus on the "God spot," others have found that many areas of the brain are involved in spiritual experience. And there is always the matter of interpretation. Work on the physiology of seizures—electrical storms that rewire the brain—indicates that they can produce enhanced emotions and hallucinations such as music and flashes of light, so that the person feels herself to be in an alternative reality. But is the person having a hallucination as the result of a purely physical event? Or is her brain wired, like a radio, to receive transmissions from beyond?

Most intriguing to me, as someone who prays, are the studies tracking the effects on the brain of different modes of prayer. Neuroscientist Andrew Newberg has found that the focused prayer of Tibetan Buddhist monks and of Catholic Franciscan nuns results in the same brain behavior: their frontal lobes light up, as a result of their willed concentration, while their parietal lobes (on the top of the head) go dark. These monks and nuns—indeed, contemplatives in every religion—follow disciplines such as focusing on a mantra or image to filter out distractions. The tests reveal that their brains behave the same way whether they are basking in a state of enlightenment or in the presence of Jesus. The transcendent state of mystical experience is physiologically the same.

In contrast, evangelical forms of prayer—such as speaking in tongues—result in the opposite brain pattern: the frontal lobes shut down, and the parietal lobes light up, indicating that people have surrendered their control. Newburg surmises that the monks and nuns go beyond their natural boundaries to merge with God, while the charismatics remain separate from God, engaged in an intense relationship.

THERE IS A LONG HISTORY of people using psychedelic substances to experience altered consciousness. Evidence for the use of mushrooms goes back as far as the Eleusinian Mysteries, and later to Mesoamerican cults (to such an extent that the Spanish suppressed their use). Present-day researchers are using psilocybin to study the neurobiology of mystical experience. In 1962, psychiatrist Walter Pahnke conducted the "Good Friday Experiment" in the chapel of Boston University. Students who had been given the substance lay down or wandered around, quietly saying things like "God is everywhere" and "Oh, the glory!"

Such experimentation continues. In his book *How to Change Your Mind: What the New Science of Psychedelics Teaches Us about Consciousness, Dying, Addiction, Depression, and Transcendence* writer Michael Pollan explores the effects of psilocybin and other psychedelic drugs and notes that observable chemical changes in the brain account for heightened perceptions and imagination—he himself experienced a new way of seeing the wonder of nature. But many have experiences that go far beyond nature. Author Aldous Huxley described experiencing on mescaline a "spiritual realm of ineffable beauty," of grace and transfiguration. And Pollan found that the effects can be so powerful as to inspire a terminally ill cancer patient who identifies as atheist to speak of being bathed in God's love, a great and gratuitous grace. Perhaps, as Pollan suggests, "'God' might be the only word in the language big enough" to convey such a gift.

Psychedelic drugs often produce a powerful sense of awe, a blurring of the boundaries of the self, and a sense of merging with a transcendent reality far beyond the material world. This transcendent reality is generally kept from our awareness by our everyday consciousness, although it is well traveled by the mystics. Psychedelics can provide a path there—indeed, the word *psychedelic* means "mind-manifesting" and was coined by psychiatrist Humphry Osmond, who wrote:

> To fathom Hell or go angelic
> Just take a pinch of psychedelic.

THIRTY

Beyond Time-Space

There are more things in heaven and earth,
Horatio, than are dreamt of in your philosophy.

• WILLIAM SHAKESPEARE

S cientific research into human spirituality is still in its infancy and has yet to capture the popular imagination in the way reports of out-of-body travel and near-death experiences have done. Both require a leap of faith regarding the possibilities of human consciousness, and both attest to the continuation of life beyond this earthly existence, as did post-mortem Doyle. But he had to wait until after his death to enter such realms, while contemporary otherworld travelers have not found that necessary.

Robert Monroe was a radio broadcast executive who discovered that "specific sound patterns have identifiable, beneficial effects on human capabilities." He developed an audio technology called Hemi-Sync that helps synchronize electrical brain waves between the left and right brain, so as to foster particular states of consciousness in the listener. Monroe believed that during sleep, we leave our bodies and travel to other realms of existence. He engaged in extensive out-of-body travel that he meticulously documented—not unlike Swedenborg—though he did not seek or find the kind of heaven religious believers desire. In *Ultimate Journey*, Monroe described making runs outside the solar system and visiting loved ones, checking in with his daughter at college. He was guided by higher spiritual beings such as the INSPEC (Intelligent Species) that he would meet just past the H Band Noise, which is "the peak of uncontrolled thought that emanates from all living forms of Earth." At one point, the INSPEC produced a flying saucer bearing W. C. Fields to demonstrate the human capacity for humor, which apparently is unique in the universe.

In the next stage in his spiritual quest, Monroe developed his theory of the Earth Life System, a "food chain predator system." In this unique creation story, a mind-consciousness foreign to the System emerged, in the form of a new species, *Homo sapiens*. Concern and empathy for other humans and for other species, along with curiosity, forged a thin layer of Human Minds who are capable of thinking beyond survival. Their (our?) analytical, scientific left-brain activity enables them to visit and return "There"—beyond time-space.

One of Monroe's most intriguing set of encounters "There" involves a wounded young man in a primitive battle scene. In the first, Monroe is shown the young man to help explain his own physical pain; in the second he intervenes, helping the young man to understand that he is dead. Monroe comes to realize that he is the one who had shown himself the young man, and that indeed the young man is himself. A future Monroe had shown the present Monroe the past Monroe.

He later visits a gathering of loving beings who turn out to be Monroe himself in all previous and present lifetimes. This is the "I-There" of Monroe, a cast of characters including a medieval architect, a rebellious priest, a "vibrationist" being that he himself does not quite understand, and of course the young warrior. The "I-There" represents the sum of love-energy distilled from over a thousand lifetimes, guiding his growth. Finally, Monroe recognizes an "Ultimate Option"—a Creator who is beyond human comprehension, who has designed, and continually retools, the process of life, who does not demand worship, does not intervene in our lives, and who does not punish. Monroe understands his vocation: not ego gratification or fame or fortune, or even the sum of all his "I-There." His calling is part of the collection of all the disparate parts of creation into One, the fullness of experience and love. This unity is the entry point beyond, leading us to the unknown.

Although Monroe does not explicitly refer to Buddhist belief, his vision of our ultimate destination is very similar to Nirvana.

ROBERT MONROE FOUNDED THE MONROE INSTITUTE, dedicated to exploring the potential of consciousness by experts such as William Buhlman, an experienced out-of-body traveler. At the heart of Buhlman's belief system is his conviction that humans are a nonphysical species in temporary biological vehicles, capable of molding our identities and our energy surroundings with our thoughts so that we ultimately achieve our "higher selves," moving through the transition at death and on up into nonphysical planes of existence.

Buhlman believes that people are prevented from realizing and using their spiritual abilities because "the density of the molecular surroundings of our material world slows the creative manifestation of thought." His view of the universe is close to that of Yogananda: after death, people carry their expectations of a pleasant place free from suffering, where they will be together with their loved ones, into a "thought-consciousness environment" on the next plane of existence, the astral. There are many different nonphysical realms on the astral plane, and most people land in one that reflects their earthly conception of reality. These notions often are religious, based on the testimony of spiritual explorers who transcended the limits of their physical bodies. Unfortunately, people who reach these group-thought-constructed heavens are stuck there in the astral plane until, inevitably, they reincarnate. Buhlman's ideas are also informed by *The Tibetan Book of the Dead*, in particular the ultimate goal, the Clear Light—"a transparent vacuum without a circumference or center"—and the bardo states. Indeed, out-of-body explorers have confirmed that the bardo (or astral) body is a nonphysical duplicate of one's physical body, comprised of dense energy.

HAVING READ SO MANY STORIES of otherworld travelers, I was eager to give Buhlman's training a shot: I might achieve transcendence in ways I'd never dreamed of. The Monroe Institute, in the rolling foothills of the Blue Ridge Mountains, is secluded, restful, and beautiful—just the kind of place people describe as heaven on earth—with plenty of delicious food provided as fuel for our intense brainwork. The dozen or so people in attendance—men and women, an airline pilot, a professor, a doctor, various government workers—were sensitive and intelligent, friendly but reserved, although they did loosen up as they shared their efforts to travel outside their bodies.

Buhlman and his wife gave lectures interspersed with sessions when we repaired to our own personal booths containing beds and built-in sound systems delivering Hemi-Sync audio-guidance designed to liberate our minds. This involved guided meditations, vibrations, and ethereal sounds—low, drawn-out sonorous tones, waves of sound, ethereal harmonies one might describe as angelic. The sleep-pod experience put us in the "hypnogogic" state between waking awareness and sleep, when vivid mental imagery occurs. It is testimony to the technology that I cannot describe the sound in detail—it really did set me afloat, carrying me away from analytical awareness. My first taste of this state was literally a trip—I flew through land and seascapes, pausing in an Edward Hopper–like café where I saw people I had not seen in years, arriving at last under the Golden Gate Bridge in a procession of ghostly hooded monks who seemed bound for a gallows.

Buhlman presented steps for spiritual awakening and liberation: most were fairly conventional, like creating a personal spiritual goal and ridding ourselves of false beliefs and unhelpful attachments. Others required new ways of thinking about reality: releasing energy anchors and false notions of the self that bind us to physical reality. Some were downright baffling, such as navigating nonphysical thought-responsive realities so that we can achieve "escape velocity" to become liberated. The goal was to have out-of-body experiences in preparation for the afterlife. This would involve travel in an "energy body" that would adapt to higher and higher vibrational frequencies in the universe, thus enabling us to "navigate unseen worlds of the spirit."

One session was dedicated to ridding ourselves of attachments and judgments. The music put me into a state of conscious resting during which a coastline emerged, and a star drew me up into a galaxy. Another session was aimed at shedding responsibilities that breed resentment. The music worked magic this time—I imagined an isthmus extending into an ocean that dissolved into quiet graciousness, a state I have gone to since I was a child. It can be triggered by curtains blowing in the afternoon breeze, by fingers of fog, by the shadows of clouds on the land, by beauty of any kind. I feel the presence of God there, and I always wish I could stay. I had to wake up, but I was refreshed and fortified and hopeful. A later session for healing took me back to a scene from my childhood, waking up from back surgery in a room full of wailing children and glaring lights. My dad was there but couldn't get the nurses to turn the lights down. So he opened his big black umbrella over my bed, a great bird with wings spread to shield me, and I slipped away into sleep.

BACK IN THE LECTURE, we considered where the self, the soul, might be headed. Buhlman described the afterlife as a place with no physical matter, no gravity or air or bodies or senses or molecular decay; a place where linear time has disappeared and reality is molded by collective thought. We must power through bardos or astral planes to the clear light, to our higher selves. Buhlman emphasized that we cannot take traditional religious pathways— they are the product of a herd mentality on the part of people who will end up as a herd in the afterlife. They are fearful people for whom their Bible or their Qur'an is all they know. They cannot rely on their scriptures to save them, nor on the money they give to their churches so they'll get to heaven. He has found people who have gone to an astral reality with others attuned to their personal vibrations, and together they have created a "consensual reality," such as Christians who think they are in heaven although they are still waiting for Jesus.

Buhlman clearly has no use for religion, convinced that it does not prepare us for the afterlife and gets us stuck on the way. He has chosen to cloister himself from people who do not foster his higher self. He describes himself as going through life like an alien, focusing on his own journey, because he is here to save himself. He believes that altruistic impulses spring from our own self-interest and advised us to concentrate on loving ourselves and those near to us. This notion of love runs in the opposite direction from that which I and countless others follow: we understand that we grow through reaching out to others, and that we find ourselves through loving others.

WE TURNED FROM SELF-INTEREST to the process of dying, to creating for those making the passage a sacred, private space and time. Despite his dim view of religion, Buhlman advised us to respect the religious preferences of the departing person. We can ask God's blessing but also have crystals nearby. Buhlman presented the Tibetan Buddhist idea of *phowa*, the transference of consciousness we can provide for the dying, and had us take turns doing a practice *phowa* on a partner to liberate them from their karma. It seemed a disrespectful exercise—a bunch of well-heeled Americans in an expensive secular retreat who had just learned the word *phowa* having the nerve to attempt such a sacred and powerful practice. We then went into our sleep-pods to visualize our own passing, and later people described going through the bardos and trying to stay on the trajectory to the higher self. I came sweetly into a sense of Jesus's presence; and if that meant I was simply participating in a bardo, stuck in a consensual reality, then so be it.

As for what happens after our passing, Buhlman explained that the soul is in constant evolution, moving through the astral planes to the conscious mind, and on to the subconscious mind. Then, having developed our minds to do so, we enter even higher mental dimensions, mastering our multidimensional capabilities. He described an out-of-body experience (OBE) that culminated in a sea of white light filled with love, radiance, knowledge, and consciousness. Our last guided visualization was designed to take us on an upward journey, toward our higher selves, but I remained in my Jesus bardo, glimpsing him along the way, arriving with him at the end at a great feast for all good souls.

My TRIPS HAD BEEN LOVELY, but they had not taken me anywhere I hadn't been before. Was I having OBEs? Do my religious upbringing or my genes predispose me to be stuck forever in the Jesus bardo? Am I just used to living in my head with an overly active imagination? We are in uncharted waters here, and whatever theoretical framework Monroe or Buhlman or anyone constructs is largely guesswork based on subjective experiences that not everybody can share. Their ideas seem fanciful to an outside observer, but so does much of religious belief. Ironically, Monroe's and Buhlman's constructs echo its essential values: the quest for transcendence, the primacy of love, the goal of union in some ultimate reality. They are apostles for a secular faith.

The last night was a grand finale of sorts. We assembled at a great fire pit, held hands, and then threw little items symbolizing our burdens into the bonfire. It reminded me of Girl Scout camp. When the group went back inside for a photo, I went to pack for home.

THIRTY-ONE

The Vastly Alerted Mind

The individual nearing death may . . . capture a
glimpse of life in harmony with the universe.

• RUSSELL NOYES AND ROY KLETTI

The practice of the living accompanying the dying is both ancient
and modern. In *phowa*, a master transfers a dying person's consciousness into a buddha realm. In the hospice ministry described
by the Buhlmans, a companion helps a person draw up and follow through
with a spiritual plan, provides a sacred space, music, and other companions
who will focus on the person's spiritual intentions. Their model also includes cremation, which is necessary so that the person can break free
from her dense physical self and all its attachments.

In *Ultimate Journey*, Robert Monroe tells a very personal story of accompanying his wife Nancy through, as he puts it, "the transition from physical
life to another energy system." As she lay dying, he promised her that they
would travel together in their minds to a way station designed to ease the
passage out of her body. Later that evening he was called back to the hos-
pital, but he could no longer sense her presence. A team from the Monroe
Institute, dedicated to serving those no longer in physical form, had taken
her spirit to the very place Monroe had promised to go, and sure enough,
she stopped breathing soon after. A few days later, Monroe was able to visit
Nancy in her new existence, and they felt an emotional explosion of love
beyond the limits of time and matter. But it took a great toll on him, and

he wondered if he'd be able to learn to live in two worlds at once. A few years later, he himself made his own transition from this life.

These are examples of a living person's participation in another's passing. In reports of near-death experiences—NDEs—we have the witness of people who become travelers beyond, returning, like visionaries such as Muhammad and Mechthild, to tell us what they have found. Their testimony is considered by many to be sound evidence that can be verified scientifically and that confirms religious or spiritual aspirations for continuing life. On the other hand, these people don't die, so we cannot assess how *near* to death they actually were, nor can we follow them into the experience as an objective observer. But NDEs should be regarded as genuine experiences even if we cannot define them medically or scientifically. As psychiatrist Russell Noyes and psychologist Roy Kletti put it: "The vastly alerted mind may be set to work upon final tasks . . . the individual nearing death may accept the reality before him, and from a transcendent perspective, capture a glimpse of his life in harmony with the universe."

THERE IS NO PARTICULAR SORT of person who tends to have an NDE, no evidence that a person is predisposed by education, age, race, sex, religion, or any other factor. Atheists, agnostics, fundamentalists, those bent on suicide have all undergone NDEs. So what produces an NDE? Impending death itself? Not for everybody—cardiologist Pim van Lommel points out that only 18 percent of patients who have been resuscitated have gone through one. He thus rules out purely medical explanations such as oxygen deprivation because most people who have been clinically dead should have had such an experience. Similarly, Eben Alexander (who documented his own NDE in *Proof of Heaven*) argues against various theories: NDEs being caused by "isolated preservation of the cortical regions of the brain," or "distorted recall of memories from deep in the limbic system," or an attempt by the primitive brainstem to ease pain and suffering. Sidestepping the argument about possible medical causes, psychiatrist Bruce Greyson suggests that as a result of cessation of brain activity in the dying person, her consciousness may become particularly attuned in a way that it normally cannot because of the distractions of life.

NDEs have been well documented, starting with Raymond Moody in his 1975 book *Life after Life*. NDEs are unique to the individual, and their characteristics vary; nobody has all of them and none show up in every account. Moody reported that patients described feelings of ineffability, of peace and quiet, and the sensation of being out of one's body, as well as sensory impressions such as hearing medical attendants pronouncing them dead and feeling as though they were being pulled through a dark tunnel. They meet others, including a being of light, and their whole lives are presented for review. Some reach a border like a door or a river, and many do not want to return to earthly life. When they do, they are changed.

Moody's ideas have inspired a great deal of research. Bruce Greyson emphasizes the sense of being out-of-body, visions of relatives and religious figures on the other side, and transcendence of boundaries of space and time and ego. Psychologist Kenneth Ring has proposed a five-stage continuum, with earlier stages being reported more frequently: feelings of peace, separation from the body, entering the darkness, seeing and then entering the light. Ring found that particularly intense NDEs tended to go farther in the continuum toward the light.

AT THE CORE of many near-death experiences is the passage from dark to light, as though one is separating from the body, approaching transcendence. And then there is the light itself: ravishingly beautiful; brilliant but restful; radiating wisdom and compassion, expanding awareness. Hieronymus Bosch must have had such a vision. In *Ascent into the Empyrean*, which hangs in the Palazzo Grimani in Venice, souls accompanied by angels make their way upward into a tunnel streaming with light, a small figure outlined against its heavenly source. Testimonies to such light occur across cultural and historical boundaries and are central to religious traditions: Zoroaster spoke of encountering God in heaven in the form of pure light; Buddhists look to the Clear

Ascent into the Empyrean by
Hieronymus Bosch in the
Palazzo Grimani, Venice

Light. Pope Gregory the Great wrote in his *Dialogues*: "Anyone who has seen a little of the light of the creator . . . is opened up by that light. . . . The soul that sees this is even raised above itself. Rapt above itself in the light of God."

The dissolution into some form of essential wholeness also occurs across religious traditions, from the Hindus merging with Brahman, Buddhists becoming enlightened, Sufi and Christian mystics succumbing in ecstasy to a foretaste of ultimate union with God. As Meister Eckhart wrote, "Into this One we are to sink from nothing to nothing."

Another central feature is that of life review, presented by the being of light. The being does not accuse or threaten the nearly dead person but inspires her to think about her life and how she might pursue ultimate self-realization. She may experience regret or guilt but within the context of being loved unconditionally, and the purpose of the review is to set her on the path to ultimate self-realization. This vision of judgment is far from the traditional verdict delivered by God and closer to Swedenborg's belief that we judge ourselves before embarking on a spiritual ascent.

Not surprisingly, people's interpretations of their NDEs often correspond to their cultural and religious beliefs. And they use sky and garden images to describe what they see beyond, rendering something essentially indescribable in familiar terms. Those who believe in guardian angels will see the benevolent being in the form of an angel or a loved one, while Hindus identify the being as an emissary from the god of death. Interestingly, people from indigenous cultures do not go through a life review—perhaps because their sense of interconnectedness and unity is woven through their earthly life, and individual accountability is less important than in Western culture.

Having undergone an NDE seems to change people: at the very least, they feel they have a second chance at life. Some switch careers or end difficult relationships. Some undergo a kind of conversion, becoming more compassionate and loving. Mario Beauregard believes an NDE can hasten a person along his spiritual path to transformation. He found that near contact with death triggered brain activity associated with encountering a spiritual reality and experiencing positive emotions and love: the same neural activity he observed in those engaged in meditative union with God.

While the majority of near-death experiences are positive, some are deeply disturbing. Bruce Greyson and Nancy Evans Bush have identified three types of negative NDEs. The experiences usually described as pleasant—such as moving through a tunnel toward a light—cause distress in some people. Others find themselves looking into a void or being stuck in a hellish place. And some undergo a life review that is not the usual loving education but rather a harsh judgment.

———

I SPOKE WITH THREE PEOPLE about their near-death experiences, and they were as diverse as the research indicates, ranging from breaks into euphoric and timeless states to a full-blown encounter with beings beyond. My friend the poet Rick Ryan has been close to death due to poor health, and, as he says, he is used to inhabiting an altered form of reality. His first NDE took place when he was middle-aged and was suffering from a brain tumor. One evening he had stepped outside a restaurant to smoke a cigarette and subsequently found himself in a world that he describes in present tense as peaceful and loving. "It doesn't have any shape or form, just a general feeling: wonderful, euphoric, one of the best things I've ever felt." He did not encounter a being—it was just a state, "a feeling of bliss. I'd really never experienced that—sort of the pleasure of an orgasm, only beyond that, and much more peaceful." He woke back into the world to find people bending over him—he had passed out and fallen into a tree. He understands now that his brain tumor had affected his grasp on reality, and his subsequent surgery restored him to "a kind of sanity." But he still has fond memories from his time lying on the ground under a tree.

The second time Rick felt near death was anything but euphoric. He was in downtown Milwaukee when a man came up to him on the street, emanating a great wave of hatred. "He looked at me and our eyes locked, and he came over and he started pounding on my face. I had this circle of people around me watching me, we were standing under a street light." Nobody came to his defense even though he cried out, and he just kept getting hit and getting up, getting hit and getting up. He was not in another place but in another time: "I had hours to think about this. Time just stopped, or maybe it was clicking along very, very slowly. I had time to really think." Since then, he has understood time to be very pliable.

A MEMBER OF MY EXTENDED FAMILY, Bruce, recounted the NDE that he had when he was only five years old but that has continued to affect his life for almost sixty years. He remembers being at home with his elderly babysitter, looking for caterpillars in his front yard, when he saw his sitter's husband in a vacant lot across the street, cutting the grass with a brand-new riding lawn mower. Bruce wanted a ride, so he bolted across the street; he was hit by a car. He found himself watching his body from above, in a space that led to a warm, intense light that was nevertheless not blinding, not frightening. He remembers feeling completely calm and comfortable, fascinated and drawn to the light. But he never did reach it. When he heard the voice of his minister saying *Everything is okay, Bruce*, he left the light and returned to the real world. He had been gone for almost four days.

This all came back vividly the day after he and several other relatives accompanied our family matriarch, Gee, through her passing. Bruce had told her not long before her death of his experience and how comforting it had been, and he was contemplating what she might have been going through as she died. A "strong feeling of Gee" came over him, a younger, very vibrant version of her that was not a physical presence but that of a healthy soul. Bruce thereupon found himself once again in the space leading to the light, but he felt much older than five, and he knew much more. He was there in a more evolved version of himself, and Gee was there in a younger version of herself: there seemed to be an agelessness to their state. It was a new dimension of his experience. It took—takes—place in a time-out-of-time, one that is still alive in some way. For Bruce, the NDE is like a precious package, a kind of security blanket he's been carrying around his whole life. He is finding that the more he pays attention to it, the more inviting it is—and he doesn't have to wait until he dies to go there.

RICK HAD GLIMPSES OF LIFE BEYOND; Bruce has gone there and still speaks of it in tones of wonderment. Dr. Robert could not have been more precise, almost matter-of-fact in telling his story. A scientist, an accomplished medical doctor, he is also a devout Catholic. Some years ago, while singing with his family in church on Christmas Eve, he felt himself going into anaphylactic shock in reaction to some cold medication he had taken. He told his wife (who fortunately is also a doctor) to call 911 or get him home fast. She drove home like a madwoman, running lights, horn blaring. Dr. Robert woke up in the driveway with his family all over him, shooting him up with Benadryl, steroids, adrenaline—the third shot of which brought him back, but with no memory of their trip home.

I listened in awe to his story of what had happened in the few minutes he was gone. He was drawn into a place that was beautiful, musical, with a bright light in front of him, and a figure with a deep voice he thinks must have been God. He can't remember his face, but he remembers feeling that the figure was a parent and that his own troubles—and accomplishments—on earth were of no importance. He felt love and happiness for which there were no words. He felt that he had come home, and they talked about many things. This all went on in a kind of timelessness, even though it took only a few minutes of our time.

At one point, his mother appeared, waved at him, and gave him the beautiful smile he remembered from his childhood. This was immensely comforting to him: his family had been Buddhist, while he himself had converted as a medical student. He had been concerned for years that perhaps one had to be a Christian to be accepted by God. His glimpse of his mother was a profound reassurance that as long as one has a led a good life, God will welcome you home.

After his mother waved at him, Dr. Robert felt himself being sucked back into his car, to his frantic family, his heart pounding from the adrenaline. He could not remember his conversation with God when he woke up, but in the ensuing years he has been in situations that he realizes they talked about. He has carried with him a profound sense of the true love of God, a feeling he longs for every day. I asked him if he thought he might have been sent back with a mission, but he is modest, saying only that he must have had responsibilities to care for other people. And his experience has made him even more willing to do so—it is the natural thing to do, as everyone will eventually join God.

I had to ask this physician/scientist about what many of his colleagues would say—that his brain had been flooded with endorphins, that there were physiological explanations for what happened to him. He smiled, so sweetly! "I know the feeling of endorphins; I have been injected with heroin—it's not that kind of feeling, not the feeling of elation or euphoria— we use that term for opioid, for morphine effects. This happiness is attached to the love, the feeling of love from God." And then Dr. Robert made a confession: "I tell you, sometimes I've thought of taking the medicine again, but with my wife beside me, ready to give me the adrenaline shots again to bring me back. Being a scientist, I like to experiment."

THIRTY-TWO

The Universe Awakening

The Christian of the future will either be a
mystic . . . or he will cease to be anything at all.

• KARL RAHNER

Throughout history we have undergone shifts in how we think about the nature of reality. Our conception of the universe changed profoundly when Nicolaus Copernicus positioned the sun in the middle of one solar system—our world was no longer the center of the universe in which Dante traveled. Darwin's *On the Origin of Species* challenged our beliefs about ourselves. He proposed that evolution is driven by the process of natural selection, a process that is random and impersonal, the result of blind chance rather than the design of an engaged and loving God. It was no longer possible to think of a Great Chain of Being extending from God down through angels to humans and on to animals, plants, and inanimate objects.

In the present day, we may be undergoing another fundamental shift in our understanding of who we are, the universe we live in, and what life after death may hold for us. The boundaries between matter and mind are dissolving, and we cannot be defined solely by our physical experience. We are coming to understand that our selves may transcend our bodies and our brains and that death is a passage in continual transformation. New ways of charting our path toward the afterlife are emerging not only in the study of parapsychological phenomena such as OBEs and NDEs but also in transhumanism and in ongoing efforts to integrate science and faith.

Scientist and theologian Ilia Delio argues that we are no longer the biological species we were when present-day adults were growing up. The human brain is changing, conditioned by technological devices. Young humans are growing up as "cybernetic mechanisms," blended systems of human and technological functions—*Homo sapiens* is becoming *techno sapiens*. We are on the cusp of transhumanism, which holds that we are essentially minds housed in bodies, and it may soon be "possible to repackage the mind in a new medium."

We have long assumed that reality is constructed of matter and energy, but we now need to consider a version of reality constructed on information: artificial intelligence. New generations of AI machines will mimic human processes for the construction of memory and imagination. In 2016, the world champion of Go, the ancient and complex board game that originated in China some twenty-five hundred years ago, was beaten by the AI AlphaGo system, acting independently during the game. Ke Jie, the human champion, had played AlphaGo previously and found it quite humanlike then. "But this year, it became like a god of Go."

Such a digitized entity will be unconstrained by the physical and temporal limitations of the flesh. AI transhumanists aim for new virtual bodies and a creation where our earthly garden will wither away and be replaced by a paradise never to be lost. They believe the age of the human as we know it is drawing to a close. Needless to say, there is a host of concerns. Who is going to be running this show, providing the energy to sustain it? Will physical human bodies become obsolete? Will digitized entities have the capacity for making moral decisions, and who would decide which values those decisions would be based on? Is there no difference between intelligence and wisdom? What of the spirit, the soul?

Further, there is the danger of "cybergnosticism," yet another iteration of the old dualism between matter and spirit. It sees the physical world as impure and inefficient and regards existence in the form of pure information as superior and thus a worthy goal. Indeed, there is talk of a postbiological future. In the words of professor of electrical engineering Bart

Kosko, "Biology is not destiny. It was never more than tendency. It was just nature's first quick and dirty way to compute with meat. Chips are destiny."

We humans are entering uncharted territory, tentatively imagining our way forward. An episode of the *Black Mirror* television series, "San Junipero," tells the story of otherworldly travel by two young women. Naive Yorkie (played by Mackenzie Davis) and party girl Kelly (Gugu Mbatha-Raw) are both tourists in a beach town devoted to fun and debauchery where it always seems to be Saturday night, and each bar is set in a different year. They fall in love and go through familiar vicissitudes, agonizing about their relationship and their sojourn in San Junipero.

The setting shifts to the familiar world when Kelly, who is actually an old woman, visits Yorkie in the facility where she has been in a coma for forty years. It turns out San Junipero is a vast system in which brains can be plugged into an AI machine that provides them with an alternative reality. Yorkie has made it known that she wants to be euthanized so she can go there for good, and Kelly observes that "being uploaded to a cloud sounds like heaven." They are hooked up to the system and meet on the beach in San Junipero, where Yorkie asks Kelly to stay forever with her. Kelly is resistant, as her beloved husband had decided to die permanently to be with their deceased daughter, but eventually she joins Yorkie and they drive off into the sunset. Forever? Perhaps—perhaps not. Aside from the technological problems of the San Junipero system being hijacked or losing electricity, there are very human dilemmas here. San Junipero inhabitants can take themselves off the system at any time. Romantic love doesn't last forever, and there is no reason to believe that discord and heartbreak will not ensue—in a year, or a thousand. The dream of heaven might become a nightmare.

IN OUR DAY, MANY PEOPLE look to science for answers sought previously through religion. For them, advances in science have demolished the belief in a God who created and sustains the universe, engages as a person with his creatures, and provides an eternal heavenly home for them. And the scientific method is the most effective—indeed the only—way to go about inquiry in all disciplines, even theology: Bertrand Russell famously declared that if he were to meet God he would say, "You gave us insufficient evidence!" But we have questions and yearnings and experiences that science does not address and can never explain. Why did we conceive of a God, and why do we continue to search for meaning? How is it that mystics believe they have encountered God? Why do humans long for heaven, for enlightenment?

Anyway, why limit ourselves to one way of knowing? We are limited enough in our capacity to know and to understand, whatever methods we employ. As scientist and mathematician J. B. S. Haldane observed, "The universe is not only queerer than we suppose, but queerer than we *can* suppose." Science documents the facts of the natural world and develops theories that explain these facts. Religion addresses human purpose, meaning, and values through metaphor and myth. Many theologians and scientists believe that the present shift in our ways of thinking about reality is the result of the convergence of these different ways of knowing, enabling us to understand our reality in a holistic, integrated way.

Such an approach might seem anachronistic to transhumanists, but it is far more encouraging than the future offered by AI. Physician Deepak Chopra believes that a convergence is taking place between modern physics and the Hindu view of reality. The Vedas teach that time and space are projections on the screen of consciousness called Akasha, which forms a bridge between mind and matter. This idea of Akasha preceded quantum physics by millennia, but they both formulate an afterlife based inside, not outside, the universe. Similarly, Muslim Hamza Yusuf conceives of the end times in terms of modern physics. It will involve the cessation of thermodynamic energy, and the cosmos will fold back into itself.

Robert Russell, physicist, Christian theologian, and founder of the Center for Theology and Natural Sciences at the Graduate Theological Union in Berkeley, California, explores the history of the universe in theological terms informed by big bang cosmology and quantum theory. The big bang can be understood in terms of a Christian view of creation, but the far future is "freeze or fry": the universe will expand and cool to absolute zero, or collapse in on itself in unendingly higher temperatures. Neither option correlates with anything we have seen hinted at through analogies such as the Second Coming, or a Final Judgment, or a millennial age before an eternal heaven.

While Russell's model of the end times takes science seriously, he believes that God is free to act in human and cosmic history, and did so in Jesus's resurrection. He sees the resurrection as profound evidence that God created a universe that is transformable, and thus the future of the cosmos will not be that which science predicts. God made a new creation in Jesus that continued in the Christian community, and this required a permanent change in the laws of physics. In the end times, creation will be set free from the natural evil of decay and entropy. It will be transformed, and all creatures will live in community.

Understanding how this might come about requires a reformulation of time and eternity in terms of current physics and cosmology. Is time included in eternity, which also transcends it? Is eternity utterly beyond time? In considering these dizzying questions, Russell refers to the paradox of "the already and the not yet" that informs Christian notions of the Kingdom of God. As he explained to me, "You have to hold together the notion of a coming realm and a present realm." He uses the word *prolepsis*, which means "the manifestation in the present of the eschatological future." In prolepsis, God acts from the eternal future, reaching back into the present, as when he raised Jesus. We still live in time, which in a way is broken—we are unable to retrieve the past, and we cannot know the future until it arrives in the present. But in eternity, all moments, all the events in our lives, with their own past and future dimensions, will coexist and be available to us.

Russell reaches into his own life for an example of co-presence. When his mother died, he continued to live, so in that sense his experience was linear. But time is not limited to that. His mother's biggest fear was to be separated from him, to lose him, and he doesn't believe she could be in heaven if he were not there. "In the moment of her death, it's true that I was by her bedside and I survived her death, and it's also true that I greeted her in heaven when she died." Eternity renders these different stages of his experience "co-present"; his mother is risen, and she has him with her already, forever.

So how do we enter eternity? What happens when our bodies die? Russell believes that we go through the psychosomatic experience of death but that "When I die, God remembers me and God resurrects me with the New Creation. And in the New Creation, we embody all the moments of our lives, in eternity."

THE BELIEF THAT HUMAN LIFE, here and beyond, is not separate from the universe lies at the heart of the cosmic view of Jesuit scientist and philosopher Teilhard de Chardin and those who continue his work. Their conception of the universe does not follow the traditional story line of God's creation: our exile on earth due to our physical and flawed human nature, and God's final summons and judgment of souls in the end times. Instead, it tells an "inside" cosmic story in which the laws of nature are the "grammatical conditions for the arrival of surprising new events and meanings." The Teilhardian universe is composed not only of physical matter but also the accumulation of these events and meanings. What happened in the past is contained in the present and will contribute to the future in a story full of hope and anticipation.

Teilhard has expanded Darwin's theory of evolution to include infinitely more than random mutations and environmental pressures. For him, the cosmos is inhabited by God and humans, and has been disposed from the start to come alive through mind, religion, and morality. It is nothing less than the unfolding and development of consciousness whereby the universe is becoming aware of itself. The process of "convergence" holds evolution together and moves it forward, as it did when it generated what Teilhard called "the arrow of evolution," the human person. The ultimate Mover of this process—God—is not above but within it and up ahead, as we move toward ever greater unity in Christ, whose presence has from the beginning permeated the process.

The idea of humans propelling evolution toward its ultimate future requires shifting our understanding of the universe based in physical objects to one based in relationships, living as we do in a quantum universe with its webs of interactions. We are part of a larger integrated whole whose parts are codependent and coevolve. We should no longer flee the world into a spiritual reality separate from the physical but engage it in all its dimensions. The driving force of this engagement is love, from the beginning of the universe to its completion in the ultimate depth of love we call God. As Delio puts it, "Love is the law of evolution written on the human heart: we are created to love and to evolve in love."

Teilhard's God is engaged and relational, and his being and actions are one and the same. God is still the cause of creation of the cosmos, and God is still its future, but God is also the One emerging as we generate new life and wholeness. As theologian Richard Rohr writes, "God loves things by becoming them." God's first incarnation was creation itself, and the second was Jesus Christ. But instead of the necessary atonement for sin, which to Teilhard was evolution's inevitable growing pains, Jesus Christ's incarnation was planned from eternity as the self-revelation of a loving God. Indeed, the Eastern Fathers of the Church teach that the point of the incarnation, and the meaning of salvation, is to further the process of human divinization (*theosis*).

Teilhard and the theologians who carry on his work have not been entirely sanguine about the evolutionary process. They recognize forces that might reverse and fragment it. Losing our faith in God might cost us our energy for living, and thus for further evolution. The false primacy of mind over body persists, particularly in AI, thwarting the movement toward interrelatedness. All this runs entirely counter to what Teilhard sees as the sacred trajectory of evolution, in which love entwines all life-forms as the universe unfolds.

But for those who still harbor hope for the future, the dynamic, exploratory, open-ended unfolding in which we participate has profound implications for how we live our lives. When we seek knowledge and beauty, when we aspire to behave according to the good, we are expressing a cosmic restlessness that requires creativity in how we live. And we are realizing another layer of moral responsibility, not just in the care for creation through responsible stewardship but also in our own creativity in fostering its evolution.

TEILHARD DID NOT LEAVE US with a vision of the fullness of evolution, much less of heaven, and his vision is corporate rather than individual. As edifying as his ideas about the cosmos are, they left me wondering how to imagine what might lie beyond one's own death.

Fortunately I was able to ask Ilia Delio how to do so. She described earth and heaven as two sides of the same coin, not two separate distinct realities. Earth is reality for us in this realm, but the heavenly reality reaches beyond all limitations. There will be infinite possibilities as we let go of the limits of our earthly lives. We will be caught up in an unimaginably dynamic relationship of love, part of a God who is infinitely creating, and thus we will be transforming the cosmos. But we will not disappear— God has loved us into being for all eternity in our own unique personalities, and we will continue becoming even more ourselves, growing into the mystery of our own personhood. We will do this in the communion of saints—indeed we already do. The living are joined with those who have gone before: their memory, spirit, and energy touch us, they are embedded in us and inspire us to think and love in new ways. So for Delio, "Heaven is now, heaven is within. Let yourself be loved—that's finding heaven."

THIRTY-THREE

At the End of All
Our Exploring

With the drawing of this Love and the voice
of this Calling

We shall not cease from exploration
And the end of all our exploring
Will be to arrive where we started
And know the place for the first time.

· T. S. ELIOT

When I first went looking for heaven, I took for granted the deep gulf in modern Western society between the sacred and the secular that is clearly evident in debates between religious and scientific ways of knowing. But I found in the beliefs of traditional societies a sense of what it might be like to live in a world where religion was not isolated from other dimensions of life, where the spirit world and the natural world were one and the same. And as I studied the creative efforts to bring science and religion into a mutually beneficial conversation, and interviewed believers from different traditions, I sensed that a reintegration of the sacred with the rest of human experience might be taking place.

Religions are the treasury of God's revelations but too often are based on the assumption that revelation occurs only at particular times and places, and to special people. However, we finite beings have always lived in touch with the infinite, and God continues to reveal God's nature and our future. For many believers, faith is based less on dogma than on the ways it can guide us in our search for union with God. And we share hopes for a rewarding afterlife with many nonreligious people who believe our human nature transcends physical death. These hopes can never be controlled, not by philosophy or religion, by science or despair. They find expression in ongoing interpretation of traditional belief and in exploration of new modes of consciousness, and they are woven into present-day culture.

The great questions have not yet been answered—they require continual answering as we evolve. We still ask if belief in an afterlife with God is conceivable. In Marilynne Robinson's novel *Lila*, the main character worries about her miserable dead friend Doll and tells her minister husband that she is scared of God and dreams that Doll is trying to hide from Him. Her husband tries to comfort her: "If the Lord is more gracious than any of us can begin to imagine, and I'm sure He is, then your Doll and a whole lot of people are safe, and warm, and happy. And probably a little bit surprised. If there is no Lord, then things are just the way they look to us. Which is really much harder to accept. I mean, it doesn't feel right. There has to be more to it all, I believe."

"Well, but that's what you want to believe, ain't it," Lila replies.

"That doesn't mean it isn't true."

I BOTH WANT to believe it's true, and do. I have company—80 percent of Americans are pretty sure there is a heaven, and that they will be there with friends and family. We hear songs about it: from Paul Simon, who wants "a shot at redemption" and believes we all shall be "received in Graceland." And from Joni Mitchell, who declared that we are stardust, "billion-year-old carbon," that we have to "get ourselves back to the garden." Writer Frederick Buechner shares her nostalgia: "Like Adam, we have all lost Paradise; and yet we carry Paradise around inside of us in the form of a longing for, almost a memory of, a blessedness that is no more, or the dream of a blessedness that may someday be again."

The question of how we get to heaven—and the help we need—still concerns us, and we keep singing about it. The traditional spiritual "Swing Low, Sweet Chariot" looks ahead to liberation, to a band of angels coming to take us home on the brightest day when Jesus washes our sins away. And "If I get there before you do / Coming for to carry me home / I'll cut a hole and pull you through." John Newton's "Amazing Grace" tells of a wretch who was lost but now is found through grace, which has brought him through many dangers, toils, and snares and will lead him home. In a more vernacular vein, Randy Newman's "Harps and Angels" describes a bout of arrhythmia after which Newman hears harps and angels and a loving voice telling him it's not his time yet. The voice gives him sound advice: "Keep your business clean . . . you know exactly what I mean."

Movies have also envisioned the afterlife, often telling the story in vernacular terms. In *A Matter of Life and Death*, a dashing RAF pilot named Peter (played by David Niven) shares his last moments with a radio operator, then bails out of his burning plane without a parachute. But the conductor assigned to escort him to the afterlife misses him in the fog, and while others are processed by stern-looking women in a grim, colorless "training center" for the next world, Peter lands in a world saturated with color—our world—only to meet the radio operator, June (Kim Hunter), and immediately fall in love. On that basis, he resists his conductor's efforts to persuade him to give up and die.

Peter is granted the chance to plead his case in the afterlife, where a trial is held in a vast gray stony arena resounding with organ music. There is a seemingly endless audience of people from throughout history, and the judge is a bewigged and distinguished-looking man. (This is no heaven, and he is no god.) The judge opens the trial by declaring that judgment depends on both facts and conscience. A hostile prosecutor challenges Peter's right to continue to live on the basis of his being in love, and the jurors ask to hear from Peter and June themselves.

The court adjourns, and the judge and lawyers and jury go down the gray staircase to a place that is now in color, where June and Peter are grilled. She offers to die in his stead, and Peter watches her begin the ascent back up with the rest of the court, but of course it doesn't work: on earth, there is nothing stronger than love, and she runs back down into Peter's arms. Peter's appeal is granted and a new date in the distant future is set for his death. The judge's final words are that love is heaven and heaven is love.

In *Defending Your Life* people also face judgment, but in a much more pleasant setting and with much different consequences. It takes place in Judgment City, a kind of bardo where a person's next life is determined— a spanking-clean, efficient place where perky music seems always to be playing, the weather is forever clear, and you can eat all you want and never gain weight. Daniel Miller (played by Albert Brooks) arrives there after dying in a car crash and is installed in a hotel where white caftans and televisions are provided, so that he can watch sports and romances and games. He is also given a defense lawyer, who explains that he has had and will have many lifetimes. The point is to keep growing, as people on earth use only 3 percent of their brains, and little brains deal mainly with fear. The worst that can happen is that Daniel will have to go back to earth and try again (he's already been there twenty times).

In his hearings, Daniel is confronted with scenes from his life in which he was fearful—as a toddler witnessing his parents fighting, as a businessman too cautious to enter a deal that would have made him rich. But during this stressful time he also meets lovely Julia (Meryl Streep), who seems to be on a different track—her hotel is luxurious, and when he visits one of her hearings the mood is cordial as everybody watches a scene of her rescuing her children and animals from her burning house. Daniel and Julia are drawn to each other, and she declares her love and asks him to spend the night with her. But Daniel is reticent, afraid he'll screw up and ruin what they already have. He leaves a heartbroken Julia, only to regret it, and his efforts to contact her fail.

The next day is the culmination of Daniel's judgment process, in which he is shown the scene from the previous night and challenged about being fearful of love. His judges decree that he must return to earth, and so he is taken to the Destination Tram station by his lawyer, who advises him to follow his heart and seize opportunities. Daniel is locked into a seat on a tram full of disappointed-looking people, but as they pull out of the station he hears Julia shout from another tram full of happy-looking people. He busts out and runs the gauntlet through moving trams to reach Julia. Clinging to the outside of her tram he declares his love. It turns out his judges are watching, and they grant him a better fate. The door opens, Daniel and Julia kiss, the other passengers applaud, and the tram moves off into a tunnel beyond.

Once again, love has triumphed, as it does in *Babette's Feast*. The movie is a parable pointing the way to paradise and a taste of what is to come. Set in the late nineteenth century, it tells the story of two elderly spinster sisters (played by Birgitte Federspiel and Bodil Kjer) who carry on their minister father's work among the poor in a village on the coast of Denmark. They are served by Babette (Stéphane Audran), a refugee they have taken in, who works for them without pay. As the years go by, their small religious community becomes bitter and fractious. The sisters plan a celebration of their father's hundredth birthday, and Babette, who has recently won a lottery, insists on cooking a real French meal for them. The sisters are alarmed lest they be sinful in their enjoyment of such a feast, and swear the other community members to remain silent about the food. It is a wondrous repast: turtle soup, stuffed quail, luscious fruits, and the finest wines. A visiting general (Jarl Kulle), who had once been in love with one of the sisters, is inspired to speak from his heart: "Mercy and truth have met together. Righteousness and bliss shall kiss one another." He acknowledges that we tremble at the choices, the risks we must take in life. But eventually we come to realize they are not important, that mercy is infinite, and "we need only wait in confidence and receive it in gratitude."

The quarrelsome group, melting under the influence of food and wine and gracious words, make amends and bless each other. After dinner, one of the sisters sings of the glories of the world ending and of rest with God in the heavenly hall where he reigns. The guests take their leave and dance and sing of eternity being nigh and of their true home with God. The general lingers with his lost love and tells her that she has been with him every day of his life, and they promise to be present to each other not in flesh but in spirit.

Back in the kitchen, the sisters thank Babette and lament her imminent departure. She tells them that she will be staying; there is no one waiting for her in France, and she has spent her entire lottery fortune on the dinner. When they gently chide her for doing so, she reveals to them that she was once a celebrated chef and believes that a great artist is never poor. She understands that her great gift has brought harmony to the small community. Through the enjoyment of God's bounty, they have become grateful for the joys of this life and have been healed of their divisions and regrets. They understand they have had a taste of heaven.

WE STILL HEAR REPORTS from those who have gone beyond, although none are so eloquent as Dante's. Postmortem Doyle sent us revelations of the afterlife, and in Mitch Albom's novel *The First Phone Call from Heaven*, the dead call the living to say they are fine, not to worry, heaven is more wonderful than could be imagined. In his book *Heaven Is for Real: A Little Boy's Astounding Story of His Trip to Heaven and Back*, subsequently made into a movie, Todd Burpo recounts his small son's otherworldly journey while undergoing emergency surgery. The boy is greeted in heaven by an older sister his mother had miscarried, and stays with his great-grandfather in his own place. Heaven has grass and clouds and sky and mountains and animals just like earth, and is full of colors. There is a city that keeps getting bigger and bigger, you can hear all kinds of music, and you feel God's love so that you never want to leave.

This heaven is that of a four-year-old midwestern son of a part-time evangelical Christian minister, and it is no match for that of Ezekiel or Aquinas. But what else would it be? The grown children of a deceased undertaker in the television series *Six Feet Under* have a very different experience of the afterlife—they have lived longer, and their lives are complicated. Their late father visits them regularly, as do the dead they are burying, and their children who were never born. The dead seem to appear when the living require their perspective—their very long, and not always heartening, perspective.

EFFORTS TO GO BEYOND this earthly existence persist, often in new countercultural religious movements founded by charismatic leaders thought to possess great power and insight. Several cropped up toward the end of the last millennium. In the early 1990s, David Koresh's Branch Davidian was besieged by U.S. troops at the group's compound in Waco, Texas. Koresh believed that he was the seventh and final messenger angel described in the Book of Revelation, and that the Seventh Seal would soon be opened and would propel us toward final judgment. His followers eventually went up in flames: it was the end of their world, at least.

Around the same time, members of the Solar Temple, founded in Geneva in the 1980s, came to believe that the earth was soon to face a great catastrophe and that they needed to enter a higher spiritual plane. They burned themselves so that their bodies would be replaced with invisible forms existing in another dimension.

And then there was Heaven's Gate. Marshall Applewhite and Bonnie Nettles believed that they were the two witnesses in Revelation 11, superior beings from another planet. (Applewhite even thought he was Jesus's successor.) They sought to contact extraterrestrial beings and promised their followers that they would take them to "The Evolutionary Level above Human," which was none other than the Kingdom of God. By the mid-nineties, the group had come to realize they were all messengers come to show us the way out of our corrupt and suffering world and that their bodies were merely vehicles used to progress through evolutionary levels. They gave up all attachments—family, wealth, drugs, etc.—to be eligible to advance to another physical world in the universe, free of mammalian appetites.

"Graduation" from this world could occur through death by natural causes, violence, persecution, or accident, or collection by an alien spacecraft in which they would transform and perfect their bodies. In 1997, Applewhite declared the ultimate solution: a spacecraft was trailing the comet Hale-Bopp and the group needed to kill themselves in order to board it. He and thirty-eight of his followers ingested phenobarbital, applesauce, and vodka and then tied plastic bags over their heads so that they asphyxiated. Their bodies were found inside their Southern California community in March 1997. On April 1, 1997, the comet was visible all night to observers in the northern hemisphere. The spacecraft was never detected. But you can find the group's final statement on their website with instructions as to how we can follow them out of this world.

THE BELIEF IN MESSENGERS from beyond is not a new one. Throughout the ages, angels have protected and enlightened us, enforced God's will and battled against cosmic evil. The Sumerians called them "creatures from the sky," and in Persia the angel Vohu Manah brought God's message to Zoroaster. They were major actors in the Hebrew and Christian and Muslim traditions: Michael was the great protector in Daniel; Gabriel announced to Mary news of her miraculous conception. Jibril dictated the Qur'an, and someday Isra'fil will blow his horn at the Final Judgment. Most Americans have had a direct sense of their protection and look forward to being with them in heaven. Evangelist Billy Graham attested to a multitude of heavenly hosts in *Angels: God's Secret Agents*: "I am convinced that these heavenly beings exist and that they provide unseen aid on our behalf."

We find angels watching over us in Wim Wenders's movie *Wings of Desire*. But their task is neither glorious nor noble. Indeed, as critic Rita Kempley writes, "Angeling is lofty but lonely work. It is a thankless occupation—a billion years of sleepless nights, filled with human whining and existential dread. They can comfort souls, but they can't feel the wind on their wings or wiggle their toes. It's no wonder, then, that every once in a while, an angel defects," as one does at the end of the movie, having fallen in love with a very human trapeze artist.

———

It seems the veil between this life and the next is very thin—people have long claimed to encounter not only angels but unwelcome visitors in the form of zombies with no memory of their former lives and who do nothing but swarm and feed, or vampires, those unholy, undead creatures of the darkness who suck our very lifeblood. They are the unquiet dead, stuck perhaps in the bardos of their own limitations and obsessions. The living can wander these bardos as well—consider the fatuous weatherman (played by Bill Murray) in the movie *Groundhog Day* who keeps waking up to the same weather report, the same snippet of Sonny Bono's "I Got You Babe," February 2 all over again. And again. But there is a beautiful and sweet woman to be loved, and despite his cynicism, the weatherman begins to change. He reaches out to others and breaks out of himself, and time once again unfolds naturally. He is saved—he just had to learn to love, to *really* wake up.

We have heard this before from Jesus and the Buddha and so many others. As Elizabeth Barrett Browning wrote: "Earth's crammed with heaven / And every common bush afire with God; / But only he who sees, takes off his shoes, / The rest sit round it and pluck blackberries." The fact is, the assumptions we do not examine do not serve us well. In Flannery O'Connor's story "Revelation" the smug, moralistic Mrs. Turpin has a vision of a vast swinging bridge going up to heaven through a field of fire. A horde of souls was rumbling up, a motley bunch of white trash and freaks and lunatics all "shouting and clapping and leaping like frogs. And bringing up the end of the procession was a tribe of people whom she recognized at once as those who, like herself . . . had always had a little of everything and the God-given wit to use it right. She leaned forward to observe them closer. They were marching behind the others with great dignity, accountable as they had always been for good order and common sense and respectable behavior. They alone were on key. Yet she could see by their shocked and altered faces that even their virtues were being burned away."

In *THE LAST BATTLE*, the final book in his Narnia series, C. S. Lewis tells again the stories we now know well—of otherworld travelers (this time mid-twentieth-century English schoolchildren) and of the great final conflict. Forces gather on the side of evil hideous Tash, and of Aslan, the mighty loving lion. Aslan's forces seem doomed, but when their leader Tirian encounters Tash inside a stable, Aslan appears and dispatches Tash back to his own land. Tirian finds himself in the company of his comrades and others who have visited Narnia over the years. They tell of being on a train that took too fast a turn and of hearing a great bang, after which they found themselves in Narnia, greatly refreshed. Meanwhile, the inside of the stable has become a beautiful, gracious land with trees bearing delicious fruit. Oddly, there is also a door with no walls or roof, standing all by itself. Looking out, the friends see the dark old world; looking around, they realize their glowing world inside is bigger than the outside, and a young girl observes with wonder, "In our world too, a stable once had something inside it that was bigger than our whole world."

Aslan roars through the door, summoning Father Time, who blows his great horn. The sky fills with shooting stars, and creatures from all ends of the earth rush up to the door where Aslan stands, each gazing in his eyes. Those who look fearful and hateful disappear into a black shadow to his left; those who love him enter the door on his right. Outside dragons and lizards are tearing up forests; seas are rising to join with rivers to flow up to the door; the dying sun draws in the moon in a great explosion of fire. Aslan orders Father Time to make an end of things: he throws his horn into the sea, squeezes the sun to nothingness, and all is dark.

The door is shut, and our friends are summoned westward in the glorious country, which they now realize is Narnia. The old Narnia had been but a shadow, with a beginning and an end. This is different: "as different as a real thing is from a shadow or as waking life is from a dream." Indeed, they spy from a great distance their homeland, the real, inner England, where no good thing is destroyed. A noble unicorn in the company cries out what everyone is feeling: "I have come home at last! This is my real country! I belong here. This is the land I have been looking for all my life, though I never knew it till now."

The band presses on to magnificent golden gates that swing open to reveal an even more wondrous Narnia. It is time for celebration, although time does not seem to matter much, and there is a great gathering of friends and family and Narnians from past adventures. Aslan tells them that the dream of their old life is over, and now it is morning. Lewis can say no more than that "the things that began to happen after that were so great and beautiful that I cannot write them." It is the beginning of the real story that goes on forever, each chapter better than the last.

Death Is the
Mother of Beauty

e can write another chapter in our unfolding story, but we are far from any conclusion, and always will be. As physician and author Sir Thomas Browne observed, "A dialogue between two infants in the womb concerning the state of this world, might handsomely illustrate our ignorance of the next."

While writing this book, I was asked by several people whether it was to be a work of fact or of fiction—to which I could only reply: Your call! It is a history of hope, not an account of the afterlife itself. The facts are many: the grave goods, the works of art and literature, the vast historical record of mystical visions and religious and moral teachings. But these facts are inevitably determined by time and culture and are clearly inconclusive. And ideas about the afterlife are far beyond fiction—they are part of the ongoing collective exercise of the human imagination.

I began this book about heaven out of curiosity about what happens after death. I assumed it was straight ahead to the destinations—heaven or purgatory or hell—taught by my faith tradition, but my assumptions turned out to be largely unexamined. I had no idea of the variety and beauty of the afterlife taught by other faiths, nor the ways in which my encounter with them would change me. My studies led me to become a member of a much bigger family than I could have imagined—to feel a deep sense of belonging to the faith of all who keep watch, who glimpse beyond, who know that it is through love and compassion that they will find their way there. This has come as a comfort in a time when such faith is sometimes viewed as unenlightened.

There are no definitive answers to what lies ahead of us—I knew that in my bones when I started this book—but some things have become clear to me. It is not just a matter of personal fate or the fulfillment of a particular faith; it has also to do with the universe itself. We humans are an integral part of the universe; our destiny is shaped by it, and in turn we shape its destiny. We are becoming aware that our customary linear way of thinking is far too limiting, and our understanding of time is expanding to include many more dimensions than the past that is gone, the present that is here, the future that is not yet. We need new ways to observe and comprehend our human experience. We may find that understanding and achieving our destiny are one and the same.

We have always hoped for life to extend beyond our short time on earth, and as long as we hope, we will imagine life beyond. But I believe that we hope because we are already dimly aware that there is a future and that we are being called toward it. There may indeed be many futures, many afterlives. After all, there have been and are and will be many lives. Some long for a return to God in the Garden; some see the Way stretching forward to something new. Some do not see God in their future; for others, God is their future. Our far future will be determined by the way we live our lives now—and why not? Life, after all, continues. Through loving engagement with others, and with creation, we are already living in the kingdom to come.

We move straight ahead fueled by hope, our passage earned by lives well lived. But we do have to find our own way. First, we have to wake up and stay awake to the possibilities. We can reach beyond life now—through prayer and ritual, or meditation, or parapsychological exploration. We can be conscious, active participants in the great wave of human hope and imagination. That's all we can manage, but what company we keep! As G. K. Chesterton wrote, "Comradeship and serious joy are not interludes in our travel; but rather our travels are interludes in comradeship and joy. . . . All roads point to an ultimate inn . . . and when we drink again, it shall be from the great flagons in the tavern at the end of the world."

WE ALL ENCOUNTER DEATH, that which has inspired so many visions and opens the door beyond. I know my brother is out there, because he visited his loved ones in the days after he died. His widow saw at sunset a dolphin leap from the ocean, fins spread in the open air, Bill unbound by water or gravity. My own glimpse came in the Sierra high country, while I was resting on a hillside overlooking a long meadow. It was surrounded by mountains and cut through by a rushing stream. I noticed my husband, who was farther down, intently watching something in the trees near him. All of a sudden there burst forth a golden stag. He took the stream in one great leap, paused to look back at us, then bounded slowly across the meadow, into the trees on the other side.

So I trust I will join my brother in that ultimate inn, drinking from those flagons of wine, taking our sweet time figuring things out. We'll be surrounded by our family and friends from earth, and some we've just met from the communion of saints. The Christian vision of the afterlife, in heaven, is still the most resonant for me. I believe the Resurrection and the Kingdom of God to be the ultimate expression of hopes for eternal life—but then I'm shaped that way, and those hopes are becoming more vivid as I grow older.

Each parting contains more and more of the final goodbye, reminding me to cherish what I have and to be mindful of what is to come. The death I see in my future, not so far now, is the mother of beauty—and as I go forward, God draws near.

Portal by Nora Cain, 2018

Acknowledgments

I am fortunate to be associated with both university and faith communities. I would like to thank all those who advised me about traditions to study, books to read, and important figures whose work and thought would guide me in my research.

From Stanford University: David Abernethy, Shahzad Bashir, Steven Carter, the Reverend Glen Davis, Savas Dimopoulos, Nancy Greenfield, Rabbi Patricia Karlin-Neumann, the Reverend Patrick Labelle, O.P., Tanya Luhrmann, the Reverend Scotty McLennan, Jennifer Pegg, the Reverend Joanne Sanders, the Reverend Jane Shaw, Lee Yearley, Stanford Interfaith Student Discussion Group, and Catholic Community at Stanford *Conspiratio* Discussion Group.

From Santa Clara University: the Reverend Laura Brekke, the Reverend Paul Crowley, S.J., David Gray, Theresa Ladrigan-Whelpley, Akiba Lerner, David Pinault, Thomas Plante, David Pleins, the Reverend Michael Zampelli, S.J., Santa Clara University Interfaith Student Discussion Group, and Santa Clara University Ignatian Center Discussion Group.

From Georgetown University: Paul Elie, John Haught, the Reverend Daniel Madigan, S.J., and Mary Novak.

From the Graduate Theological Union: Robert Russell, Colleen Keyes, and Sister Marianne Farina, C.S.C.

From Villanova University: Ilia Delio, O.S.F.

From the University of Bristol: Ursula King.

I am grateful to friends old and new for sharing their knowledge and wisdom, in particular: Dean and Janine Applegate, Reza Aslan, Betsy and Kit Burton, Nora Cain, John Cornwell, Clare Fitzgerald and Pat Rice, Ron

ACKNOWLEDGMENTS

Hansen, Kathryn Harrison, Michael Herr, Bruce, the Reverend Tom Madden, Jeffrey Myers, Nethra, the Reverend Patrick O'Neil, O.P., the Reverend Timothy Radcliffe, O.P., Rick Ryan, George and Paula Saunders, Rabbi Elie Spitz, and Kristen Tracy.

Some of these friends granted me personal interviews about their beliefs in life beyond. I am also grateful to the people from various faith traditions who were willing to meet with a curious stranger to share their deepest hopes: Parvez Ahmed, Ann Cannon, Russell Hancock, Ishrat and Habibe Husain, Rashmita Jani, Swami Prasannatmandanda, Punita, Dr. Robert, and Simone.

I am especially grateful to my agent, Amanda Urban, and to Jacqueline Shost, who helped me through the editing process. And to my editor, Jake Morrissey: he asked me to write a book about heaven, and faithfully guided me along the way. I could not have done it without him.

Finally, many thanks to my family, who have sustained me throughout the writing of this book, in particular my daughter Mary Elizabeth, who edited many drafts, and my husband, guide to literature, and soul mate Tobias Wolff.

Notes

Introduction: At the Horizon of the Known

xv **"In every man's life there are moments"**: Heschel, *Man Is Not Alone: A Philosophy of Religion*, 165, 8.

Chapter 1. Seek and Ye Shall Find

3 **"I learn by going where I have to go"**: Roethke, "The Waking," *Collected Poems of Theodore Roethke*, 108.

5 **"As regards gods, I am unable"**: Ruse, *Atheism*, 10.

5 **"One elephant having a trunk"**: Chesterton, *Orthodoxy*, 60.

6 **"The extensive reach"**: Quoted in Heschel, *God in Search of Man*, 37–38.

7 **"You have made us"**: This is the most common translation of the passage from Augustine's *Confessions*, Book I.1.1.

7 **"the Spirit that comes from God"**: 1 Corinthians 2:12.

7 **ways of knowing**: Hincks, "Justified Reason: The Collaboration of Knowledge, Belief, and Faith."

7 **"collaboration with the mind of God"**: When I started writing this book, I felt compelled to make the case that exploring life beyond was a legitimate effort in an age when science has become the dominant way of knowing. For many people it's the only way to know anything at all, and they look to science for the answers sought previously through religion. As it turned out, research into the tension between science and faith served as a booster rocket for the project. Once I got it out of the way I could proceed without it. But for those who may be interested, here is what I found from philosophers and theologians as well as scientists.

Beyond the Greeks, there was for centuries no sustained tradition of argument against the existence of God in the Western world. In biblical times, among the Hebrews, it was faith that mattered. In medieval times, challenges to the existence of God would have been subject to social censure and punishment for heresy. However, the Protestant Reformation in the sixteenth century, with its repudiation of Catholicism, opened the door to alternative ways of thinking. By the seventeenth century, understandings of nature inherited from antiquity and the Middle Ages had changed dramatically as a result of scientific advances. With the rise of science and its methods for exploring nature came new ways of thinking, new basic principles, that did not rest on the foundations of religious dogma.

René Descartes was a transitional figure between pre-modern philosophy, which reflected religious belief; and modern philosophy, which reflects a scientific mindset. A believing Christian, Descartes claimed to be able to prove the existence of God, which cannot be separated from the essence or nature of a supreme perfect being. Further, it was Descartes's scientific rationalism that informed his view of all organisms as mechanisms, including the material human body in which an immaterial soul resides.

Our conception of the universe also underwent a profound change. Nicolaus Copernicus reconstructed the universe, positioning the sun at the center. Our world was no longer the center of a system of concentric spheres containing planets, stars, an outer sphere called the *primum mobile* through which God moved the universe, and beyond that the empyrean, the dwelling place of God. Giordano Bruno went even further, arguing that there is not one solar system, but billions; and that the universe is the way it is by accident. With just one solar system, God is busy coordinating the conditions that suit us; with billions, God doesn't have to be involved.

The principles of Isaac Newton made it possible to describe the orbits of heavenly bodies, as well as the force of attraction that made them move, in mathematical terms. The medieval view of the cosmos reflecting an orderly, God-suffused universe was replaced by a worldview in which the entire natural universe is controlled by the laws of nature, motion, and gravity. The widespread response to such notions of the universe and divine involvement was deism, which reflected a God who created the universe, set it in motion according to natural laws, and thenceforth did not intervene.

It would seem that we humans were now machines rather than organisms, no longer blessed citizens of an orderly universe ruled by an interested God: we had lost our place at its center and discovered laws that relieved God of his ongoing duties. But the tensions between these ways of knowing were far from being resolved, as I discovered in the life of Charles Darwin, as told by J. David Pleins in *The Evolving God*. Darwin's theories set forth in *On the Origin of the Species* widened the gulf between religious/philosophical and scientific explanations for things. He proposed that variations had occurred through the ages that would enable certain life-forms to survive, and that these variations were passed along to offspring. This process, which drives evolution, he called natural selection.

Natural selection was random, impersonal, the result of blind chance rather than the design of an engaged and loving God. But, contrary to contemporary popular assumptions, his theory doesn't prove that Darwin was an atheist. Darwin, who studied divinity at Cambridge, spent his life in serious consideration of theological questions and of religion itself, growing increasingly aware that evolution was not just about physical forms but had religious and moral dimensions. He even confessed "the impossibility of conceiving that this grand and wondrous universe, with our conscious selves, arose through chance." (See Pleins, *The Evolving God*, 92.)

The argument at that time was not between God and science or religion and evolution. Darwin had simply discovered a new law of nature designed by God. In the last sentence of *On the Origin of Species*, he refers to life having been originally breathed into forms by the Creator. And in his last years he wondered if science would indeed have the last word on this matter—or whether religion and science could learn to live in a productive, symbiotic relationship.

In our time, the chasm between religious belief and science has grown ever wider. Atheists argue that advances in science have demolished the belief in a God who created and sustains the universe, engages as a person with his creatures, and provides an eternal heavenly home for them. But we should not assume that science has all the answers, and certainly no final answers. As Nobel laureate Steven Weinberg writes, "Physical science has historically progressed not only by finding precise explanations of natural phenomena, but also by discovering what sorts of things *can* be precisely explained. These may be fewer than we had thought." (See Weinberg, "Physics: What We Do and Don't Know.")

Science cannot describe or explain the mysteries addressed by faith, the why rather than the how, the purpose rather than the details of physical phenomena. We have questions and yearnings and experiences that scientism can never explain. Why did we conceive of a God, and why do we continue to search for meaning? Why do mystics believe they have encountered God? Why do humans long for heaven, for enlightenment? Scientism, with its implicit atheism, its rejection of religion, metaphor, myth, is simply not enough: it is an incomplete and insufficient worldview.

7 **the path of faith:** In addition to making the case for writing a book on life beyond with reference to scientism, I also felt compelled to make the case for faith. Following Saint Augustine, I believe our search for God is a process shaped by the Being drawing us toward unity. In any time and for any person, God can be found through love, and truth, and beauty. For Bernard of Clairvaux, love returns always to its source, God, "as he knows that all who love him are made happy by their love of him." (See Hart, *Experience of God*, 276.) For Bernard Lonergan, the search for truth is an implicit search for God. For Rabbi Abraham Joshua Heschel it is in beauty that we begin to experience the sublime, the "silent allusion of things to a meaning" greater than ourselves. (See Heschel, *God in Search of Man*, 39.)

Whatever our capacities, whatever route we take toward God, we must seek if we are to find. Blaise Pascal believed that God can be expected to appear openly to those who truly search for him, but to remain hidden from those who do not. (See Shortt, *God Is No Thing*, 58.) Sadly, much in contemporary life is antithetical to such exploration: the reliance on scientism as a sufficient explanatory system; the false gods of money and power and individualism; the distractions of the digital age. Religion itself is diminished: unmoored from practice, from symbol and ritual and community, it has in various forms become political, dogmatic, corrupt, and violent.

The search can be daunting. Although there are rare instances of spontaneous spiritual experiences, it is generally the fruit of the concerted efforts by a person who wishes to live and grow in the spiritual life. One way is to follow a religious path, through observing rituals and ethical norms, engaging in spiritual exercises such as prayer, and living a life imbued with compassion. Such faithful practice can lead to "intimations of transcendence." (See Armstrong, "The Question: Should We Believe in Belief?") As we will see in the course of exploring hopes for the afterlife, such intimations take many forms, not only from faith to faith and individual to individual, but over the course of one's lifetime.

7 **The wise course:** O'Malley, "The Eye and I."

8 **"Truth inheres not in doctrine":** Wiman, *My Bright Abyss*, 109.

8 **"to shape into one":** Coleridge, quoted in Zaleski, *Otherworld Journeys*, 61.

10 **deep calls to deep:** Psalm 42:7 ("deep calls unto deep").

Chapter 2. Origins

11 **"Another world to live in":** Santayana, *Reason in Religion*, 6.

11 **human nature:** Although I have pointed out the limits of science with respect to the subject of life beyond, I found it essential in exploring the origins of spirituality and hopes for the future. Steven Mithen's *Prehistory of the Mind: A Search for the Origins of Art, Religion, and Science*, Robert Bellah's *Religion in Human Evolution: From the Paleolithic to the Axial Age*, and J. David Pleins's *The Evolving God: Charles Darwin on the Naturalness of Religion* were particularly helpful sources.

11 **our capacities developed through evolution:** There were stirrings of spirituality long before it was packaged in religion; it may even have predated humans. Wildlife biologist Laura Kehoe describes scientists observing a Western African subspecies of chimpanzee called *Pan troglodytes verus* in the wilds of the Republic of Guinea. The chimps marked certain trees with stones, piled stones for no evident purpose inside hollow tree trunks, and engaged in this behavior deliberately and repetitively. In other words, the chimps seemed to be enacting a ritual.

These behaviors may relate to male display, or they may be distantly related to practices of indigenous West African people who collect stones in sacred trees. (See Kehoe, "The Images of Chimps Thrilled Me.") A good dose of caution is warranted here, but we may be seeing the evidence that symbolic rituals may have their roots in animal behavior, an indication that the line between animals and humans is becoming less and less distinct: we share emotions, exhibit altruism, have distinct personalities, and solve problems. Perhaps we also share a sense of the sacred.

11 **ritual disposal of the dead:** Watson, "Ancient Fossils Found in African Cave Are Tantalizing Glimpse of Early Man."

12 **intimations of an afterlife:** Mooallem, "Neanderthals Were People, Too."

12 **Archaeologist Steven Mithen locates their origins in the brain:** Mithen, *Prehistory of the Mind*.

12 **describing a process where we went:** Steven Mithen sets forth three phases in the development of our brains, using the metaphor (tongue-in-cheek, surely) of a cathedral. In the first, pictured as the "nave," the mind functioned through a form of intelligence involving all-purpose learning and rules for making decisions. The second phase is illustrated by "chapels" along the "nave." Each chapel represents a different form of specialized intelligence regarding specific areas of behavior, beginning with social interaction. Additional chapels eventually evolved for intelligence in dealing with the natural world; for technical intelligence for making and using tools; and finally for linguistic intelligence.

This process is evident in *Homo habilis*, the oldest in the *Homo* genus, from about 1.5 to 2.4 million years ago. Their brains still had the same basic design as they did 6 million years ago, although the nave of generalized knowledge was larger and the chapel for social intelligence was more ornate. Chapels for interacting with the natural world and developing tools were still under construction. At this point, these areas would have been functioning in complete isolation from each other, with no communication. As *Homo habilis* evolved, the chapel for social intelligence became more capacious, enabled by the safety of group living and the beginnings of language.

Anywhere from 6 to 35 million years ago, the brain evolved to its third phase. The chapels were no longer entirely separate, and knowledge and ideas flowed between the areas of specialized intelligence, providing new ways to think and to act. One was foraging, indicating the ability to store information about various resources; another was the ability to attribute mental states to oneself and other people. For Mithen, consciousness came about when we became able to use our minds as models for others, and to predict their behavior.

13 **humans have always engaged in play:** Bellah, *Religion in Human Evolution*, 91.

13 **"possible worlds, multiple realities":** Robert Bellah points out that play seems to have its own internal value, as we play mostly just to play. The earliest form of play is simply the kind of things we humans do while caring for a baby, cooing and tickling and smiling. Similar behavior is found in the great apes; indeed it goes back millions of years, along with social and ethical patterns of behavior. It is fertile ground for a wide range of physical and behavioral capacities, such as verbal communication, which in turn give rise to innovation and creativity. When we humans adopted cooperative breeding, with group members sharing caregiving, there were important consequences: increased intelligence, social interaction, and the ability to understand others' feelings.

When we play, we manifest imagination and learning in a dynamic way—and fortunately, its benefits do not end in childhood. Play can become ritual—everything from Thanksgiving dinner to a solemn funeral—that sustains and enriches a culture. It celebrates the solidarity of the group, attends to the feelings of its members, and establishes its identity. Untold generations of loving caregivers have given us warmth and security; they have also given us history, culture, science, morality. Through play rooted in love, through its manifestations in human culture and expression, we find "possible worlds, multiple realities" whose "consequences we could not live without." (Bellah, *Religion in Human Evolution*, 91.) Our tendency to believe in a life beyond this one can be seen as part of a narrative trajectory beginning with play and language that sustains faith and lights our path forward.

13 **Many consider this development a product of evolution:** Evolutionary biology adds another dimension to our understanding of the origins of religion. Journalist Nicholas Wade argues that our ancestors acquired a set of genes that they passed on to us, genes as basic to our makeup as language or music. These genes were expressed in an instinct for faith that in turn has led to further fruitful adaptation such as morality. (See Haught, "Hard-wired for God?") Behaving in an altruistic manner, an individual risks her own genetic future so that the larger population of shared genes will survive.

Empathy too runs deep in our heritage, engaging brain areas over a hundred million years old. It evolved such that our ancestors not only felt with others but also understood what they might want and need. (See Bellah, *Religion in Human Evolution*, 72.) Empathy started in the body, not in imagination or reasoning: understanding followed bodily connections. The "theory of mind" holds that we have a capacity to know what others know or see, but it takes empathy to anticipate and appreciate what others need or feel. Advanced forms of knowing what others know may be unique to our species, but they pale in comparison to our capacity to share emotions.

Our capacity for religious faith, with its attendant feelings, thoughts, and actions, has been transmitted culturally as well, and endures because it has helped us survive. It has brought us together and given us a sense of shared identity, helped us to face and endure threats, and endowed us with a sense of meaning that inspires us to live moral lives. Insofar as religions, with all their benefits, point to life beyond, such belief may even promote the survival of our genes.

13 **"follows from the extreme difficulty":** Quoted in Pleins, *The Evolving God*, 98.

14 **no place for philosophy or a divinity:** Pleins, *The Evolving God*, 58.

14 **Consider the gravesite in Sungir:** Mithen, *Prehistory of the Mind*, 174–75.

15 **Les Trois Frères:** There are multiple images of the paintings at Les Trois Frères to be found online; see for example "The Sorcerer of Les Trois Freres," https://en.wikipedia.org/wiki/The_Sorcerer_(cave_art).

Chapter 3. The Sacred Fire

16 **"They had what the world has lost":** John Collier cited in Smith, *The World's Religions*, 382.

16 **how primal religions came about:** In addition to Bellah's *Religion in Human Evolution*, J. P. Couliano's book *Out of This World: Otherworldly Journeys from Gilgamesh to Albert Einstein* was enormously helpful in writing this and subsequent chapters. Throughout the writing of this book, Huston Smith's *World Religions* proved invaluable as a general reference.

17 **"universal, independent, endless existence":** Lubbock, *Origin of Civilisation*, quoted in Pleins, *The Evolving God*, 74.

17 **Donald sees the roots of religion:** The following is an expanded treatment of Merlin Donald's stages in the evolution of religious belief.

The earliest stage, dating back hundreds of millions of years, is characterized by episodic memory, which involves remembering and recalling events when encountering similar new events. At some later point still extremely distant in time, mimetic culture emerged, first in primates and later in humans. Mimetic culture is based on the ability to observe and learn from the actions of others, and to adapt it to your own purposes. Although it preceded language and is based on gesture—think dance—mimetic culture was essential to the evolution of language. It also gave rise to ritual, which predates religion but lies at its very heart. Ritual, which may be more efficient than language in transmitting emotions and modeling social roles, serves in religion to make beliefs feel real.

Physical evidence unfortunately is hard to come by—perhaps body paint and shell beads were used in rituals, along with the simple flutes that have been found from forty thousand years ago. Music seems ever-present in ritual, which almost certainly involved song and dance. (See Bellah, *Religion in Human Evolution*, 92.) But we can only surmise how ritual came about. Robert Bellah suggests it may be the result of the movement in hominid groups (at an unspecified point in time) from dominance hierarchies to more egalitarian social patterns. The development of capacities for paying attention and sharing intention with others would have resulted in higher levels of cooperation. Rituals would have celebrated the solidarity of the group through attending to the feelings of all members, and probably marking the identity of the group as opposed to other groups. (See Bellah, *Religion in Human Evolution*, 94.)

However it came about, Donald proposes that from mimetic culture arose not only ritual but also mythic or narrative culture, wherein cultural information is passed on through stories, first through oral and then through written expression. This is when our ancestors emerged from episodic consciousness; looked around themselves and realized a past, present, and future; and started telling stories about them.

Donald's theory dovetails with those who see play as precursor to ritual and religious belief. Historian Johan Huizinga found in "the primeval soil of play" not only ritual and myth but also the origin of law, commerce, art, and science. However, supernatural beings may not have figured so much as a sense of "a sacred order of things." (Quoted in Bellah, *Religion in Human Evolution*, 94.)

Similar to Huizinga, anthropologist Clifford Geertz defined religion as providing a model of "a general order of existence." This concept gave rise to other fields of human endeavor that sought truth about a general order. Art began and has flourished as a form of religious expression; philosophy provides belief systems; science has proposed general order through scientific cosmology and Darwinian evolutionary biology.

17 **"collective effervescence":** Émile Durkheim, quoted in Bellah, *Religion in Human Evolution*, 94.

18 **contemporary primal peoples:** There has been a tendency to take a superior attitude toward primal peoples, a modern human supremacism. Paleontologist Marcellin Boule described Neanderthals as "brutish" and "clumsy," indicating a lack of morals and a very low—bestial, even vegetative—level of functioning. Racial bias has also skewed our understanding: anthropologist Sir Arthur Keith justified colonialism by arguing that the modern white British were replacing the ancient brown man in Australia just as the newer, heartier *Homo sapiens* replaced the inferior Neanderthals. (See Mooallem, "Neanderthals Were People, Too.") In the twenty-first century, we still carry biases—often unconscious—about primal peoples, so the only respectful way to proceed is to explore their world through their own myths and narratives.

18 **In preliterate societies, anything that must be remembered:** The human capacity to sense the sacred—through nature, for example—can be limited by an exclusive reliance on writing and the clutter of useless information. Anthropologist Paul Radin believed that the invention of the alphabet caused a disorientation of our psychic life and our perception of external reality, and made thought and thinking the "exclusive proof of all verities." This never happened among primal peoples. (See Smith, *The World's Religions*, 369–70.)

18 **"ongoing, empowering seminar":** Smith, *The World's Religions*, 367, 369, 377.

19 **The longest continuous history:** Smith, 366–68.

20 **"It was immersion in the Earth":** O'Murchu, "What Will Mysticism in the 21st Century Look Like?"

20 **"death soul" that is freed at death:** Couliano, *Out of This World*, 34, 37.

22 **lost the secret of ascent:** Couliano, 37.

22 **shaman in a trance:** Zaleski, *Otherworld Journeys*, 13.

22 **"soul pursuit":** Couliano, *Out of This World*, 41.

23 **symbolic ascent through the seven levels of heaven:** Zaleski, *Otherworld Journeys*, 13.

23 **"sing into being":** Basso quoted in Bellah, *Religion in Human Evolution*, 141.

24 **Kalapalo shamans journey:** Bellah, *Religion in Human Evolution*, 138–45.

24 **to sing and dance into eternity:** Basso, *Kalapalo Indians of Central Brazil*, 58.
24 **their circle of life:** Neihardt, *Black Elk Speaks* contains illustrations of Black Elk's visions by his childhood friend Standing Bear.
25 **"While I stood there I saw":** Quoted in Neihardt, *Black Elk Speaks*, 26.
25 **"the outer world"; "the visions and ceremonies":** Quoted in Neihardt, 127.
25 **"as from a lonely hilltop":** Quoted in Neihardt, 1, 169, 1.
26 **to life beyond and back again:** I was moved by Black Elk's story, the great beauty of his visions but also by his modesty: he claimed no credit for his extraordinary experiences. As it happened, his was a small part in a great tragedy; he failed in his mission, as his times faded into ours.

My grandmother loved to tell stories of her childhood on the prairie in Nebraska. One of my favorites was about the day word came to her one-room schoolhouse that the great Lakota chief Sitting Bull (with whom Black Elk fought at the Battle of Little Bighorn) had been shot, and how awed the children were, and how their families came soon after to take them home.

Black Elk eventually became a Catholic—like my grandmother and all her descendants—and served as a catechist from 1904 until his death in 1950. His renown among his people for his inspired preaching, endurance of great suffering, and great holiness is such that a case is being made for him to become a Catholic saint. If I ever find the everywhen, I will ask him how he came to share our vision of what lies beyond. But by then I may know the answer.

Chapter 4. An Imagined World

29 **"You save the one":** Cited in Bellah, *Religion in Human Evolution*, 245.
29 **an imagined world:** In this chapter and those following, I owe an enormous debt to Alan Segal for his masterly book *Life after Death: A History of the Afterlife in Western Civilization*, a treasure trove of information and insight.
29 **"The more I try":** Quoted in Bellah, *Religion in Human Evolution*, 227.
30 **"You came to save me":** Bellah, *Religion in Human Evolution*, 245.
31 **new life after death:** Segal, *Life after Death: A History of the Afterlife in Western Civilization*, 46.
32 **As for common people:** Bellah, *Religion in Human Evolution*, 243.
33 **A'aru, the Field of Reeds:** Mark, "Egyptian Afterlife—The Field of Reeds."
34 **trials recorded in the epic:** Couliano, *Out of This World*, 53.
35 **When Enkidu dies:** Segal, *Life after Death*, 85.
35 **unfit for eternal wakefulness:** Zaleski, *Otherworld Journeys*, 15.

Chapter 5. The Realm of Endless Light

36 **"The soul of the Righteous":** Zoroastrian text *Hadokht*, cited in Couliano, *Out of This World*, 109.
36 **Mesopotamian otherworld travelers:** An important source for the information about otherworld travelers in this and subsequent chapters is Carol Zaleski's *Otherworld Journeys: Accounts of Near-death Experience in Medieval and Modern Times*.
37 **"rush . . . to defile him from the nose of the dead":** Quoted in Segal, *Life after Death*, 188–89.
37 **"Thus does the evil one's conscience":** Quoted in Zaleski, *Otherworld Journeys*, 66.
39 **"the feeling of abiding in the middle of plants":** Quoted in Couliano, *Out of This World*, 109.
39 **Viraz then meets his daena:** Couliano, 110.
39 **"satisfied their husbands and lords":** Quoted in Couliano, 111.
39 **"in the form of a naked whore":** Quoted in Couliano, 111.

Chapter 6. As Though It Were a Dream

42 **"Souls of Poets dead and gone":** John Keats, "Lines on the Mermaid Tavern," https://www.berfois.com/2019/02/lines-on-the-mermaid-tavern-john-keats/.
42 **"The gods of Olympus":** Calasso, *The Marriage of Cadmus and Harmony*, 54.
43 **various schools of Greek philosophy:** Segal, *Life after Death*, 222–23.
43 **"Happy is he among men":** Quoted in Segal, *Life after Death*, 217.
44 **"poor feckless ghosts"; "your life shall ebb away":** Homer, *The Odyssey*, 132, 134.
44 **"All people are like this":** Homer, 136.
46 **"After having got rid of the foolishness":** Plato, quoted in Stanford, *Heaven: A Guide to the Undiscovered Country*, 40.
47 **"those things which in times past":** Plato, quoted in Segal, *Life after Death*, 235.
47 **"the true heaven, the true light and the true earth":** Plato, quoted in Segal, 233.
48 **"captive Greece took captive":** Horace, Epistles 2, http://www.authorama.com/works-of-horace-9.html.

Chapter 7. The Eternal Covenant

53 **"He set knowledge before them":** Ecclesiasticus 17:11–12 (Jerusalem Bible translation). The book of Ecclesiasticus appears in the Roman Catholic canon but not in Jewish or Protestant canons.
53 **radical amazement:** Heschel, *God in Search of Man*, 46.
54 **"For behold! I am creating a new heaven":** Isaiah 65:17–18.
54 **"Enoch walked with God":** Genesis 5:24.

54 Immortality was offered to Elijah: 2 Kings 2:11.
55 "As the one dies so dies the other": Ecclesiastes 3:19–20.
55 "Whatever it is in your power to do": Ecclesiastes 9:10.
55 "Like the appearance of the bow": Ezekiel 1:28.
57 "His garment was like white snow": Daniel 7:9.
57 "the kingship and dominion and grandeur of all the kingdoms": Daniel 7:27.
57 "will be radiant like the bright expanse of sky": Daniel 12:3.
58 "hope in the resurrection of the dead"; "a dispute broke out": Acts 23:6–9.
58 In a lengthy vision, the book of Ezekiel describes: Ezekiel 40–48.
59 "would enjoy the goodness of the Lord": Psalm 27:13.
61 "The souls of those who have given themselves": Philo, quoted in Segal, *Life after Death*, 373.

Chapter 8. No Eye Has Seen It

62 "All the prophets prophesied": Yohanan bar Nappaha, quoted in Segal, *Life after Death*, 624.
62 A body of literature emerged: *The Norton Anthology of World Religions*, edited by Jack Miles, is an important source of information for anyone seeking to understand the range of religious belief of the world's great religions. It was an essential reference for this and subsequent chapters.
63 integration of body and soul: Spitz, *Does the Soul Survive?*, 48.
63 belief that we are all martyrs: Segal, *Life after Death*, 603.
63 "Everyone who walks in blamelessness": Rabbi Joshua, quoted in Segal, 635.
63 "benevolence of the eternal God": Quoted in Segal, 613.
63 Mishnah Sanhedrin 10: Segal, 604.
64 the martyrdom of Israel itself: Segal, 605.
64 "All the prophets prophesied": Yohanan bar Nappaha, quoted in Segal, 624. See also Isaiah 64:4.
64 The blessed would sit around on thrones: Segal, 624.
65 "In this world, one has the trouble": Segal, 626.
65 "How great is the goodness": Segal, 627.
65 "The Holy One . . . will burrow the earth": Rabbi Simai, quoted in Segal, 628.
66 In his vision, Ezekiel had witnessed: *The Norton Anthology of World Religions*, vol. 2, 284–87.
66 "This Enoch, whose flesh was turned to flame": Scholem, *Major Trends in Jewish Mysticism*, 67.
67 tour of the heavenly family of angels: Segal, *Life after Death*, 517.
67 passwords and incantations: Couliano, *Out of This World*, 168.
68 Future World of Reward: *The Norton Anthology of World Religions*, vol. 2, 322.
68 "Soul requires the good acts": Saadia, quoted in Spitz, *Does the Soul Survive?*, 29.
68 microcosm of the whole universe: Spitz, 51–52.
69 There would be no miracles: *The Norton Anthology of World Religions*, vol. 2, 456.

Chapter 9. The Gates of the Imagination

70 "God can only be known and grasped": Daniel Chanan Matt in *Zohar*, 32.
70 "to recover the tradition": *Zohar*, 26.
70 a new interpretation of their struggle: Daniel Chanan Matt's translation and introduction to *Zohar: The Book of Enlightenment* and Joseph Dan's *Kabbalah: A Very Short Introduction* were the principal sources for the information in this chapter.
71 "One generation goes": Ecclesiastes 1:4.
71 "written it from his own mind": Moses de León, quoted in Dan, *Kabbalah*, 32.
72 "God knows that my intention is good": *Zohar*, 22.
72 "When the desire arose": *Zohar*, 165–67.
72 only Rabbi Shimon survives: The tale of Rabbi Shimon in the Zohar is similar to that of Rabbi Akiva. Both were revered early second-century rabbis, and Rabbi Shimon is said to have been a disciple of Rabbi Akiva. Rabbi Shimon is credited by many orthodox Jews for having written the Zohar during that time.
74 For Luria, existence did not begin: Dan, *Kabbalah*, 74–77.
76 "Truly, all souls must undergo transmigration": Zohar, quoted in Spitz, *Does the Soul Survive?*, 80.
76 the history of every soul: Dan, *Kabbalah*, 83.

Chapter 10. Today

78 "Where is our Kingdom": Rabbi Kook, quoted in Shavit, *My Promised Land*, 204.
79 "I cannot but think of the sons of Israel": Quoted in Shavit, *My Promised Land*, 32.
80 "And in my going out to meet you": Yehudah Halevi, "Where Will I Find You," https://www.poetryfoundation.org/poetrymagazine/poems/55427/where-will-i-find-you.
80 "embrace the presence": Heschel, *The Sabbath*, 29.
83 "Citizens of two realms": Heschel, *Man Is Not Alone*, 8–9.

NOTES

Chapter 11. Jesus on Earth

87 **"Behold, I am sending My messenger":** Malachi 3:1.

89 **"The Lord of Hosts":** Isaiah 25:6.

89 **"until the day I drink":** Matthew 26:29.

89 **One must seek first God's kingdom:** Matthew 6:33.

90 **parable of the Good Samaritan:** Luke 10:29–37.

90 **"Go and do likewise":** I am indebted to my brother William C. Spohn for his interpretation of the Good Samaritan parable in *Go and Do Likewise: Jesus and Ethics*. He is the one I look forward to having a glass of wine with, having been my guiding light on this earth and beyond.

90 **"Whatsoever you do for the least of these":** Matthew 25:40, traditional translation.

91 **"For now we see through a glass, darkly":** 1 Corinthians 13:12, traditional translation.

91 **shine like the sun:** Matthew 13:43.

91 **"And concerning the resurrection of the dead":** Matthew 22:31–32.

91 **on the third day be raised:** Matthew 16:21.

91 **"The God of our ancestors":** Acts 22:14–15.

92 **"Through the Law I am dead to the Law":** Galatians 2:19.

92 **Those who converted:** 1 Corinthians 15:44.

92 **"grow brighter and brighter":** 2 Corinthians 3:18.

92 **"Death came through one man":** 1 Corinthians 15:21.

93 **emboldening her:** John 20:11–18.

93 **"give me your hand; put it into my side"; "My Lord and my God":** John 20: 27–28.

93 **two of his followers journey:** Luke 24:13.

93 **he disappears from their sight:** Luke tells the story of the encounter two disciples have on their way to the village of Emmaus. (See Luke 24:31.) They are walking along, talking about the events of recent days, when a man joins them, someone who doesn't seem to know about what happened to Jesus of Nazareth. The disciples are taken aback and speak of their leader as a great prophet whom they had hoped would be the one to set Israel free. He was crucified but apparently his body was no longer in the tomb. The man then recounts scriptural prophecies concerning the Christ who was to suffer to enter his glory. As it is getting late, they stop at an inn. When they are at table, the stranger takes the bread and says the blessing; then he breaks it and hands it to them. Their eyes are opened and they recognize him—but he has already vanished from their sight.

The story of the road to Emmaus is the story of every Christian making her way through life. It tells of confusion and loss—loss of a loved one, loss of treasured belief, loss of a clear way forward. But the story also tells of companions on the way—some of whom we recognize, some of whom we don't—and of taking a rest from the journey, gathering at table with friends. It tells of simple things like bread and blessing that mean far more than we expect. It tells of a rare and precious flash of recognition of Jesus himself through which we realize that Jesus walks with us always. But then, of course, he disappears—we may have had a glimpse of the kingdom up the way, but we are still on the road.

93 **"I am with you always":** Matthew 28:20.

Chapter 12. Staying Alert

94 **"So stay awake":** Matthew 25:13.

94 **carried up to heaven:** Luke 24:51.

94 **open to all:** Colossians 3:11.

95 **"between us and you a great gulf":** Luke 16:26.

95 **"one like a son of man":** Revelation 1:13–15.

96 **"Holy, holy, holy is the Lord God":** Revelation 4:8.

96 **"a Lamb that seemed to have been sacrificed":** Revelation 5:6.

96 **"there was silence in heaven":** Revelation 8:1. See Brown, *An Introduction to the New Testament*, 788. There are multiple online sources for Bergman's interpretation of this passage, e.g., https://churchlifejournal.nd.edu/articles/the-afterlife-of-bergmans-the-seventh-seal/.

96 **a woman clothed with the sun:** Revelation 12:1–6.

97 **Finally, John beholds a great white throne:** Revelation 20:11–12.

97 **"Very soon now, I shall be with you again":** Revelation 22:12–13.

100 **There was also a version of the divine realm:** Arendzen, "Gnosticism." See also Cuba, "Seventh Heaven" and the unattributed "The Magick of the Seven Heavens." These sources give a sense of the variety and complexity of Gnostic belief.

101 **"those things which neither eye has seen":** Irenaeus, *Against the Heresies*, quoted in McDannell and Lang, *Heaven: A History*, 53, echoing Paul in 1 Corinthians 2:9.

101 **"What is raised is this flesh":** Tertullian, quoted in Pagels, *The Gnostic Gospels*, 4–5.

102 **Paul refers to creation:** Romans 8:25–26.

Chapter 13. Augustine's Vision

103 **"With so many witnesses":** Hebrews 12:1.
104 **Christian views of heaven:** Anyone looking for Western conceptions of heaven should start with Colleen Mc-Dannell and Bernhard Lang's *Heaven: A History*. In this and several subsequent chapters, it was the source not only for information but for important ways to think about heaven or the afterlife.
104 **heaven would be theocentric:** McDannell and Lang, *Heaven: A History*, 31.
104 **when Peter tells Jesus that the disciples have given up everything:** Mark 10:29–30.
104 **"it is a good thing for a man":** 1 Corinthians 7:1,9.
104 **"he who has preserved [chastity]":** Ambrose, quoted in Stanford, *Heaven: A Guide to the Undiscovered Country*, 93.
105 **On the death of the body:** McDannell and Lang, *Heaven: A History*, 56–57.
106 **"beyond all corporeal objects and the heaven itself":** Augustine, *Confessions*, 171.
106 **"At that moment we extended":** Augustine, 172.
106 **"Grant me chastity and continence":** Augustine, 145.
106 **"I was astonished to find":** Augustine, 127.
107 **Those in power are mastered:** Augustine, *City of God*, Book XIV, Chapter 28.
107 **The Christian community will dwell in a renewed heaven:** Augustine, Book XX, Chapter 16.
109 **It was purported to be the original account:** McDannell and Lang, *Heaven: A History*, 61.
109 **"I must boast. . . . I know a man":** Quoted from Zaleski, *Otherworld Journeys*, 26.
110 **companions sharing faith and joy:** Hebrews 12:1.
110 **"In each generation she passes":** Wisdom 7:27.
111 **"Both sexes will rise":** Augustine, quoted in McDannell and Lang, *Heaven: A History*, 62–63.
112 **"Late have I loved Thee":** Augustine, *Confessions*, 201.

Chapter 14. Many Heavens

113 **"The dull spirit rises up":** "Abbot Suger's Memoirs."
113 **"By our ascending actions":** *Rule of Benedict*, Chapter 7:5, 57. See also Ecclesiasticus, 21–23.
115 **the threat of hell:** Stanford, *Heaven*, 123.
116 **Black-spotted souls are detained:** Zaleski, *Otherworld Journeys*, 69.
116 **violence and plundering:** Gardiner, *Visions of Heaven and Hell before Dante*, 135.
118 **processions and rituals and rich clothing:** McDannell and Lang, *Heaven: A History*, 74–77.
119 **"The work which shines here":** "Abbot Suger's Memoirs."
119 **the empyrean will become a house of light:** McDannell and Lang, *Heaven: A History*, 83–84.
119 **"Wherefore in order that the happiness of the saints":** Quoted in Aquinas, *Treatise on the Last Things*: "Whether the blessed in heaven will see the sufferings of the wicked?"
120 **"The more love of God someone will have":** Aquinas, quoted in McDannell and Lang, *Heaven: A History*, 90.

Chapter 15. They Had Love Always

122 **"Theologians may quarrel":** Meister Eckhart, from https://www.goodreads.com/quotes/582851-theologians -may-quarrel-but-the-mystics-of-the-world-speak.
122 **"graced wisdom that enabled her spirit":** Julian, quoted in Rolf, *Julian's Gospel*, 372.
122 **God revealed to Julian:** Veronica Mary Rolf, "Love, Longing, and Pity," August 28, 2015, https://www.juliansvoice.com/veronicas-blog/love-longing-and-pity.
122 **"with joy and cheer":** Julian of Norwich, *Revelations*, 85.
123 **"all shall be well":** See Rolf, *Julian's Gospel*, 383, for Middle English.
123 **"abide in one another":** Hadewich, quoted in Russell, A *History of Heaven*, 146.
124 **"Thus comes to pass":** Quoted in McDannell and Lang, *Heaven: A History*, 101.
125 **Benson Madonna:** Both paintings, Antonello da Messina's *Madonna and Child*, commonly called the Benson Madonna (1475), and the unattributed *Enthroned Madonna and Child*, are in the National Gallery of Art in Washington, D.C. Images and further information are available at https://www.nga.gov/collection/art-object-page.37.html and https://www.nga.gov/collection/art-object-page.37004.html.
126 *Madonna of the Magnificat*: Sandro Botticelli, *Madonna del Magnificat* (1481), Uffizi Gallery, Florence, Italy. Image and further information are available at https://www.uffizi.it/opere/madonna-col-bambino-e-angeli-madonna -del-magnificat and elsewhere online.
126 *The Divine Comedy*: Jeffrey Burton Russell's interpretation of Dante's *Divine Comedy* in A *History of Heaven: The Singing Silence* was a principal source in this chapter. The translations of Dante are all Russell's except for the final one by Peter Stanford, whose *Heaven: A Guide to the Undiscovered Country* was also very helpful.
126 **"what God sings":** Quoted in Russell, A *History of Heaven*, 165.
127 **"to reverse the ancient exile of our language":** Peter Hawkins, quoted in Russell, 153–54.
127 **"God's love that in the beginning":** Dante, quoted in Russell, 158.
128 **There seems to be a hierarchy of souls:** Russell, 169–70.
129 **hazardous to the pilgrim:** Russell, 165.
129 **"In order to represent or image":** Dante, quoted in Russell, 176.
129 **wrought by both heaven and earth:** Russell, 177.

NOTES

130 **"I saw . . . I saw . . . I saw":** Dante, quoted in Russell, 181.
131 **"O eternal light":** Dante, quoted in Russell, 184.
131 **"At this point high imagination failed":** Dante, quoted in Stanford, *Heaven*, 194.
131 **"the tongues of flames are in-folded":** Eliot, *The Complete Poems and Plays of T. S. Eliot*, 198.
132 **lush paradisal gardens:** See, for instance, *Paradise* (unattributed), detail of *The Last Judgment*, Santa Maria in Piano, Loreto Aprutino, Italy. Reproduced in McDannell and Lang, *Heaven: A History*, 117.
132 *Compendium of Revelations* **testified:** McDannell and Lang, *Heaven: A History*, 119.
132 **"believed in the immortality of the soul and that some celestial abode awaits":** Petrarch, quoted in McDannell and Lang, 124.
133 **"They had love always":** Tibullus, quoted in McDannell and Lang, 124.
133 **"without error":** Lorenzo Valla, quoted in McDannell and Lang, 128.
135 **an angel embraces a man:** See Fra Angelico, *Last Judgment* (c. 1431), Museo San Marco, Florence, Italy. Detail reproduced in McDannell and Lang, *Heaven: A History*, 130.
135 **"According to a rough estimate":** Celso Maffei, quoted in McDannell and Lang, *Heaven: A History*, 136.
135 **Giotto's *Last Judgment*:** Giotto, *The Last Judgment* (c. 1305), Arena Chapel, Padua, Italy. Image available at www.artbible.info and other online sources.

Chapter 16. Predestination for Glory

136 **"In my Father's house are many mansions":** John 14:2, King James Version.
136 **mankind being exalted:** Michelangelo, *Risen Christ* (1521), Santa Maria Sopra Minerva, Rome, Italy. Image and information available at www.michelangelo.org and other online sources.
137 **objected that so much nudity was not fitting:** Giorgio Vasari, *Artists of the Renaissance*, 274.
138 **"We are not made for fleeing human company":** Quoted in McDannell and Lang, *Heaven: A History*, 151.
138 **Luther denied free will:** Stanford, *Heaven: A Guide to the Undiscovered Country*, 208–9.
139 **Christians can be confident:** John Calvin, "The Institutes of the Christian Religion," in *The Norton Anthology of Religion*, vol. 2, 1106.
139 **"There is no divine authority":** Martin Luther, 95 Theses, nos. 27 and 36, https://www.luther.de/en/95thesen.html.
139 **"ants, bugs, and all unpleasant, stinking creatures":** Luther, quoted in McDannell and Lang, *Heaven: A History*, 153.
139 **"ministries and superiorities of the Church":** McDannell and Lang, 154.
140 **"To be in Paradise":** Calvin, quoted in McDannell and Lang, 155.
140 **"the vision of God":** Quoted in Stanford, *Heaven*, 211–12.
140 **"the greatest enhancement of the glory":** Polti, quoted in McDannell and Lang, *Heaven: A History*, 160.
140 **separate communities for men and women:** Stanford, *Heaven*, 214.
140 **fifty-eight examples:** McDannell and Lang, *Heaven: A History*, 160.
140 **a painting of the Last Judgment:** Peter Paul Rubens, *The Last Judgment*, 1615–617, in the Alte Pinakothek, Munich, Germany. Reproduced in McDannell and Lang, *Heaven: A History*, 179. Image available at https://en.wikipedia.org/wiki/The_Small_Last_Judgement_(Rubens).
141 **"quickens us to the attentiveness of contemplation":** Francis de Sales, quoted in Mursell, *The Story of Christian Spirituality*, 225.
141 **"predestination for glory":** Quoted in McDannell and Lang, *Heaven: A History*, 166.
142 **"In my Father's house are many mansions":** John 14:2, King James Version.
142 **"thought remains in the outskirts":** Teresa of Ávila, quoted in Stanford, *Heaven*, 212.
143 **God alone suffices:** Teresa of Ávila, "Nada te turbe." https://www.getfed.com/nada-te-turbe-teresa-avila-poem-5760/.
145 **"Blessed are they that do his commandments":** Bunyan, *The Pilgrim's Progress*, 187.
145 **"Hail, good woman, I bring thee tidings":** Bunyan, 328.
146 **a union of pure spirit in pure desiring:** Milton, *Paradise Lost*, Book VIII, lines 622–28.
146 **fuller than the love of God:** William Blake, *Satan Watching the Endearments of Adam and Eve*, 1808. Reproduced in McDannell and Lang, *Heaven: A History*, 233. Online image available at https://emuseum.huntington.org/objects/111/illustration-5-to-miltons-paradise-lost-satan-watching-t.
146 **taking their solitary way:** Milton, *Paradise Lost*, Book XII, lines 648–49.
146 **"Nature has no place in glory":** Joseph Hall, quoted in McDannell and Lang, *Heaven: A History*, 173.
147 **"the angels . . . would certainly be seduced from their innocence":** John Dunton, quoted in Stanford, *Heaven*, 236.
147 **"tunes up our dull and drooping souls":** Richard Baxter, quoted in McDannell and Lang, *Heaven: A History*, 174.
147 **"Finish then thy New Creation":** Quoted in *The Norton Anthology of World Religions*, vol. 2, 1197.
148 **death will be swallowed up:** 1 Corinthians 15:52–54.
148 **he shall reign forever and ever:** Revelation 11:15, 19:6.
148 **"Worthy is the Lamb that was slain":** Cf. Revelation 5:12–14.

149 **"Not one good thing wilt Thou withhold":** Quoted in https://www.musixmatch.com/lyrics/NTYCYPCD /How-Lovely-Is-Thy-Dwelling-Place and other online sources.

Chapter 17. Eternal Progress

150 **"That's what eternities are for":** Author interview with Russell Hancock.

150 **"to prevent so negative an attitude":** Swedenborg, quoted in McDannell and Lang, *Heaven: A History*, 181.

151 **Swedenborg trained himself to go into a trance:** Van Dusen, *The Presence of Other Worlds*, 27.

151 **"All my experience in heaven":** Swedenborg, *Afterlife*, xiii.

151 **"heaven is yoked with earth":** Swedenborg, quoted in McDannell and Lang, *Heaven: A History*, 193.

151 **"correspond to the goods and truths they have from the Lord":** Swedenborg, quoted in Stanford, *Heaven*, 239.

152 **Luther is put out:** McDannell and Lang, *Heaven: A History*, 188.

152 **"turn blue in the face, almost to die":** Swedenborg, quoted in McDannell and Lang, 201.

152 **concentrate solely on God:** McDannell and Lang, 201.

153 **the Countess Elizabeth Gyllenborg-Stjerncrona:** McDannell and Lang, 218.

153 **"no birth and no death":** Peter Ackroyd, quoted in Stanford, *Heaven*, 245.

153 **"I am under the direction":** Stanford, 246.

153 **Blake wrote *The Marriage of Heaven and Hell*:** William Blake, *The Marriage of Heaven and Hell*. Most of the plates have been reproduced online by the British Library, https://bl.uk/collection-items/the-marriage-of-heaven -and-hell-by-william-blake.

154 **"The road of excess"; "Prudence is"; "have the vanity to speak of themselves":** Blake, *The Marriage of Heaven and Hell*, plates 7, 12, 13.

154 **all the old falsehoods:** Blake, plates 21, 22.

154 **"The works of this visionary":** Blake, quoted in McDannell and Lang, *Heaven: A History*, 235.

154 **"Whenever any Individual Rejects Error":** McDannell and Lang, 235.

154 **"primordial man and woman":** McDannell and Lang, 243.

155 **"each family would truly present":** McDannell and Lang, 269.

155 **"studying the character of God":** McDannell and Lang, 266.

155 **"beautiful home, and my husband":** McDannell and Lang, 267.

155 **"mean little ten-cent heaven":** Mark Twain, quoted in Stanford, *Heaven*, 255–56.

155 **"feel-good" religion:** Russell, *Paradise Mislaid*, 64.

156 **"by the creeds or superstitious notions":** Joseph Smith, quoted in Givens, *Wrestling the Angel*, 38.

156 **"crooked, broken, scattered, and imperfect language":** Joseph Smith to William W. Phelps, November 27, 1832, https://www.deseret.com/2010/1/26/20374629/scribes-recorded-prophet-s-crooked-broken-language.

159 **"It can well be said that the resurrection and millennium":** Gordon Allred, quoted in McDannell and Lang, *Heaven: A History*, 317.

159 **fire-infused glass:** Revelation 15:2.

159 **"As man expands toward divinity":** B. H. Roberts, quoted in Givens, *Wrestling the Angel*, 46.

160 **God himself continues to grow:** McDannell and Lang, *Heaven: A History*, 320.

160 **the terrestrial and the telestial:** *Doctrine and Covenants* 132:16–17, 76:97–98, 76:81–90, 98–112; 88:100–101. www.churchofjesuschrist.org.

Chapter 18. God's New Creation

161 **"All the way to heaven":** The Reverend Greg Boyle, S.J., founder of Homeboy Industries, as related to me by a member of a discussion group sponsored by the Ignatian Center, Santa Clara University.

161 **God promised in Genesis:** Genesis 12:1–3.

161 **regathering of God's people:** Matthew Hagg, "Robert Jeffress, Pastor Who Said Jews Are Going to Hell, Led Prayer at Jerusalem Embassy," https://www.youtube.com/watch?v=jSGSSisCT7E.

162 **"At the trumpet of God":** 1 Thessalonians 4:16-17.

164 **"the eye through which I see God":** Meister Eckhart https://cac.org/meister-eckhart-part-ii-2015-07-16/.

164 **"all the way to heaven":** The Reverend Greg Boyle, S.J.

164 **"Lord, I believe":** Mark 9:24, King James Version.

165 **choir practice in a jeweler's shop:** This saying attributed to George Orwell is ubiquitous but it has proved impossible to find its exact source. It appears on page 402 in *A Chilli Too Far* by Brian Kennett, with no source given.

165 **heaven for Christians is pure relationship:** Author interview with the Reverend Tom Madden.

166 **The great cloud of Christian witnesses:** Hebrews 12:1.

Chapter 19. The Path to the Afterlife

169 **"O ye who believe!":** Qur'an 4:136.

169 **Muhammad's revelations were to change:** For someone who knew little about Islam, John Esposito's *Islam: The Straight Path* was an invaluable introduction. Nerina Rustomji's *The Garden and the Fire: Heaven and Hell in Islamic Culture* was the source for much of my understanding of Islamic afterlife. Also, I am indebted to Daniel

Madigan, S.J., for his kind advice as to how to approach Islam and for his invaluable article, "Death and Afterlife in Islamic Thought."

170 **"Proclaim! In the name of thy Lord":** Qur'an 96:1-5.
170 **Arabic, is the language of God:** In the chapters about Islam, I use the word *God* in most instances. I use the word *Allah* when this more personal term is appropriate and when I am quoting the Qur'an.
172 **God breathed his Spirit:** Qur'an 15:29.
172 **"It is Allah Who Gives you life":** Qur'an 45:26.
172 **"Let them Delight in it":** Qur'an 6:113.
172 **"O son of Adam, you will die alone":** Hasan al-Basri, quoted in Smith, *The World's Religions*, 240.
172 **"Allah raised him up Unto Himself":** Qur'an 4:158.
173 **everything will perish but the face of God:** Qur'an 28:88.
174 **The Qur'an stresses individual responsibility:** Yusuf, "The Afterlife."
174 **It will be an evil fate:** Qur'an 18:29.
174 **It was thought that souls of prophets and martyrs:** For an excellent treatment of Islamic views of the afterlife, see Madigan, "Morto e dopo morte nel pensiero islamico" (Death and Afterlife in Islamic Thought), 89–103.

Chapter 20. Companions of the Garden

176 **"To those who do right is a goodly reward":** Qur'an 10:26.
177 *Liber Scalae:* This text was in wide circulation during Dante's time, and it is likely that he was familiar with this Muslim view of paradise.
177 **"be brought nigh to the Righteous":** Qur'an 50:31.
178 **"The Garden and the Fire":** Muhammad, quoted in Rustomji, *The Garden and the Fire*, 36.
178 **"Glory be to Allah Who did take His servant":** Qur'an 17:1.
179 **the steed Buraq, "the animal whose every stride":** Ibn Ishaq, quoted in Rustomji, *The Garden and the Fire*, 29.
180 **"A good spirit from a good body!":** Muhammad, quoted in Rustomji, 33–34.
182 **"Prayer at appointed hour":** Muhammad, quoted in Rustomji, 60.
182 **"Such will be their entertainment":** Qur'an 56:56.
183 **"They are what is between his jaws":** Muhammad quoted from Rustomji, *The Garden and the Fire*, 51.
183 **"If you have always been good":** Muhammad, quoted in Rustomji, 56.
184 **"neither pass water":** Rustomji, 84 (verb tense shift in original).
184 **"We live forever and never pass away":** Rustomji, 96.
185 **with a face that would light the morning:** Rustomji, 113.
185 **while the houris remained:** Rustomji, 114–15.
186 **"the greatest bliss is the Good Pleasure of Allah":** Qur'an 9:72.
186 **"Some faces, that day":** Qur'an 75: 22–23.
186 **They will experience supreme bliss:** Madigan, "Death and Afterlife in Islamic Thought," 9.

Chapter 21. The Goal of You All Is Allah

187 **"If Allah had so willed":** Qur'an 5:48.
188 **"In [Paradise] there is what no eye has seen":** Muhammad, quoted in Madigan, "Death and Afterlife in Islamic Thought," 8.
188 **He despised physical delights:** Madigan, "Death and Afterlife in Islamic Thought."
189 **"He loves them and they love Him":** Qur'an 5:54, and Rumi, "The Love and the Beloved," quoted in Smith, *The World's Religions*, 260.
189 **"the science of the relation":** Al-Ghazali, quoted in Smith, *The World's Religions*, 262.
190 **their lower self having been killed in interior struggle:** Madigan, "Death and Afterlife in Islamic Thought," 10.
190 **By his own account, al-Bistami crossed multiple seas:** Segal, *Life after Death*, 657.
191 *The Unveiling of Secrets:* Baqli, *The Unveiling of Secrets: Diary of a Sufi Master*, 23, 42.
192 **"Worldly desires were trying to keep me chained":** Al-Ghazali, quoted in Esposito, *Islam: The Straight Path*, 127.
192 **"I saw clearly that the mystics were men":** Esposito, *Islam: The Straight Path*, 128.

Chapter 22. For God to Decide

193 **"We are nearer to him":** Qur'an 50:16.
193 **Islam was facing great challenges:** Smith, *The World's Religions*, 266–67.
193 **freedom for Muslims to continually reinterpret the Qur'an:** Esposito, *Islam: The Straight Path*, 261.
193 **through a violent and terrorist form of jihad:** Esposito, 240.
194 **"Fight in the cause of Allah"; "And slay them wherever ye catch them":** Qur'an 2:190, 2:191. Passages edited for context.
194 **"But if the enemy Incline towards peace":** Qur'an 8:61. Passage edited for context.

NOTES

194 **"Let those fight in the cause of Allah"**: Qur'an 4:74. Passage edited for context.
195 **"One who prays for martyrdom sincerely"**: Quoted in Segal, *Life after Death*, 659.
195 **"Each time we sleep with a *houri*"**: Al-Suyuti, quoted in Ibn Warraq, "Virgins? What Virgins?," 2.
196 **The word *hur* refers to white raisins**: Ibn Warraq, referring to Luxenburg, *Die Syro-Aramaische Lesart des Koran*, 3.
196 **Over the centuries, women's role in religious practice**: Esposito, *Islam: The Straight Path*, 271.
196 **Women are to be elevated**: Yusuf, "Sacred Nature of Women."
197 **the question of what women can look forward to in paradise**: Shameem, "Men Get Hoor Al'Een in Jannah . . . but . . . What Do We Get?"
200 **her death will be her wedding night**: A loose reference to Rumi, "Wedding Night," at https://www.poem ofquotes.com/mawlawirumi/wedding-night.php.

Looking East
205 **"Seekers, listen"**: Kabir, quoted in Heehs, *Indian Religions*, 365.
205 **"All religions resemble each other"**: Jean-Frédéric Bernard, quoted in *The Norton Anthology of World Religions*, vol. 1, 26.
206 **"independently valid paths"**: Heim, *Salvations: Truth and Difference in Religion*, 4.
207 **"now only dimly perceived"**: Joseph DiNoia, O.P., quoted in Heim, 160.

Chapter 23. Life after Life after Life
209 **"Only that yogi"**: Quoted in Smith, *The World's Religions*, 46–47.
210 **thereafter pervades the universe**: Kapoor, "Creation and Consciousness."
210 **The Hindu cosmos contains multiple worlds**: Smith, *The World's Religions*, 72.
210 **Human life fades**: *The Norton Anthology of World Religions*, vol. 1, 238.
211 **the Golden Age will begin anew**: *The Norton Anthology of World Religions*, 241.
212 **"the beyond within"**: Quoted in Smith, *The World's Religions*, 22. See pages 26–50 for discussion of yogas.
212 **"Only that yogi"**: Bhagavad Gita, quoted in Smith, *The World's Religions*, 46–47.
213 **according to the law of karma**: *The Norton Anthology of World Religions*, vol. 1. See pages 242–44 for discussion of karma.
213 **"You won't remove the fierce karma"**: Cuntarar, quoted in *The Norton Anthology of World Religions*, vol. 1, 326.
214 **good and bhakti could expand infinitely**: *The Norton Anthology of World Religions*, vol. 1, 235.
214 **a flowering of ecstatic poetry**: Hirsch, 66–67. See also https://poets.org/weeks-poetry-term-bhakti-poetry.
214 **"Heaven and hell are for the ignorant"**: Kabir, quoted in Heehs, *Indian Religions*, 365.
215 **"Brahma, Vishnu and Shiva died"**: *The Norton Anthology of World Religions*, vol. 1, 415.
215 **"I've built a house"**: Tukaram, quoted in *The Norton Anthology of World Religions*, vol. 1, 485.
216 **we are fully absorbed into the One**: Swami Adiswarananda, "Hinduism: Death and Life Beyond Death."

Chapter 24. Gone to God
217 **"Although he is Unity"**: Prema Chaitanya, quoted in Smith, *The World's Religions*, 73.
217 **One of the most famous is the trip**: Dharma, "Arjuna Goes to Heaven."
219 **"although he is Unity"**: Prema Chaitanya, quoted in Smith, *The World's Religions*, 73.
221 **"Whatsoever you do for the least of these"**: Matthew 25:40, traditional translation.
222 **we just have to improve our consciousness**: Yogananda, "The New Path," chapter 32.
223 **Kriya Yoga**: Yogananda at https://www.ananda.org/kriya-yoga/.

Chapter 25. The Path to Enlightenment
225 **"Life and death are in the mind"**: Sogyal Rinpoche, *The Tibetan Book of Living and Dying*, 47.
227 **a hierarchy of realms**: *The Norton Anthology of World Religions*, vol. 1, 736–40.
230 **a moral slip will be diluted by a refined nature**: Harvey, *An Introduction to Buddhist Ethics*, 26, 15, 17.
230 **three refuges, three sources of inspiration**: Harvey, 8.
231 **eightfold path to cessation**: Harvey, 37.
231 **Meditation aimed at insight**: *The Norton Anthology of World Religions* vol. 1, 876.
232 **produces "clear comprehension"**: Harvey, *An Introduction to Buddhist Ethics*, 11.
232 **Such cultivation of the mind**: *The Norton Anthology of World Religions*, vol. 1, 1274.
232 **"All conditioned things"**: The Buddha, quoted in *The Norton Anthology of World Religions*, vol. 1, 842.
233 **"Having crossed over to the other shore"**: *The Norton Anthology of World Religions*, vol. 1, 897.
233 **"state of awareness"**: *The Norton Anthology of World Religions*, vol. 1, 1124.
233 **universal salvation**: *The Norton Anthology of World Religions*, vol. 1, 961.
234 **the departing soul arrives safely in the Pure Land**: "Nectar Ritual Painting" in Samsung Museum, Korea. Reproduced in Leidy, *The Art of Buddhism*, 294. Similar images available at www.kavenyou.com, antiquealive.com and other online sources.
234 **This Pure Land is described**: *The Norton Anthology of World Religions*, vol. 1, 1004; see pages 998–1007 for "Discourse on the Land of Bliss."

236 **the moment of faith in Amitabha:** *The Norton Anthology of World Religions*, vol. 1, 1293—94.

Chapter 26. The Clear Light

237 **"Our innermost essence":** Sogyal Rinpoche, *The Tibetan Book of Living and Dying*, 12.
237 **remarkably specific ways:** The principal source for this chapter is Sogyal Rinpoche's *The Tibetan Book of Living and Dying*.
237 **our passage through death:** Sogyal Rinpoche, 11.
237 **"our innermost essence":** Sogyal Rinpoche, 12.
237 **Knowledge of this true "nature of mind":** Sogyal Rinpoche, 48.
238 **Every person has a vast store of seeds:** *The Norton Anthology of World Religions*, vol. 1, 1393.
238 **"Empower us to produce"; "Empower us to be reborn":** Lama Lobsang Chökyi Gyaltsen, quoted in *The Norton Anthology of World Religions*, vol. 1, 1396—97.
239 **to become enlightened during this lifetime:** Sogyal Rinpoche, *The Tibetan Book of Living and Dying*, 114.
239 **the ultimate revelation, the Clear Light:** Sogyal Rinpoche, 260.
240 **"fish writhing on hot sand":** Coleman and Jinpa, *The Tibetan Book of the Dead*.
241 **the power of Amitabha:** Sogyal Rinpoche, *The Tibetan Book of Living and Dying*, 235—37.
241 **"a year's rainfall of tears":** Dawa Drolma, *Delog*, 39.
242 **"I awoke from the deep sleep of ordinary consciousness":** Dawa Drolma, 116.
242 **"inexpressible, unimaginable sense of infinite cosmic order":** Dawa Drolma, 119—20.
242 **"not meant to tarry":** Quoted in Saunders, *Lincoln in the Bardo*, 31.

Chapter 27. If We Could Only Awaken

244 **"Our Buddha nature":** Author interview with Paula Saunders.
244 **well suited to modernity:** *The Norton Anthology of World Religions*, vol. 1, 1418.
249 **"God has made different religions":** Smith, *The World's Religions*, 74.
249 **"walking each other home":** Ram Dass and Bush, *Walking Each Other Home*.

Chapter 28. Voices from Beyond

253 **"We want a religion":** Arthur Conan Doyle, quoted in McDannell and Lang, *Heaven: A History*, 294.
253 **to study paranormal phenomena in a scientific way:** Abrahamsen, *Paranormal*, 42.
253 **"We want a religion":** Doyle, quoted in McDannell and Lang, *Heaven: A History*, 294.
253 **In his influential book:** William James's *The Varieties of Religious Experience: A Study in Human Nature* is a wise and wonderful exploration of the nature of human religiosity. Everyone remotely interested in such things should read it.
254 **"the feelings, acts and experiences":** James, 22.
254 **"by their fruits ye shall know them":** Quoted in James, *The Varieties of Religious Experience*, 14, echoing Matthew 7:16.
254 **"His contentment with the finite":** James, 70.
254 **"They are essentially religions of deliverance":** James, 119.
254 **his own over-belief:** James, 378—79.
255 **"seems to diffuse through the tissues":** Roach, *Spook*, 124.
255 **Emerging technologies:** Roach, 195.
256 **"personalities which have left this earth":** Roach, 204.
256 **like a newborn babe:** Abrahamsen, *Paranormal*, 53.
256 **"last week's dinner":** Doyle, quoted in Abrahamsen, 69.
256 **"every religion is linked to one or another":** Doyle, quoted in Abrahamsen, 142—43.
257 **"She prayed so earnestly for the light":** Bertha Berner, quoted in Johnston, "Mrs. Stanford and the Netherworld."
258 **"My dear uncle I am pleased":** Pegg, "Remnants of a Spiritualist's Belief."
258 **"Unfortunately, so far, we have met only with charlatans":** James Lathrop Stanford, quoted in Johnston, "Mrs. Stanford and the Netherworld."
258 **"after a long silence":** Bertha Berner, quoted in Johnston.

Chapter 29. The Beyond Within

259 **"The beyond within":** Smith, The *World Religions*, 22.
259 **"Science without religion is lame":** Einstein, *Ideas and Opinions*, 45—46.
259 **Scientific materialists, who believe:** Hart, *The Experience of God*, 153.
259 **"We have to recognize that we are spiritual beings":** Alexander and Tompkins, *The Map of Heaven*, xxiii.
259 **the result of our unconsciously synthesizing and harmonizing:** Segal, *Life after Death*, 341.
260 **"spooky action at a distance":** This quote of Einstein's is ubiquitous but its exact source is unclear.
260 **"Quantum theory and a vast body of supporting experiments":** Radin, quoted in Pearson, *Opening Heaven's Door*, 74.
260 **"neuroplasticity," whereby brain cells change:** Chopra, *Life after Death*, 223.

NOTES

261 **"where mysticism meets science":** Hagerty, *Fingerprints of God*, 14.
261 **"If we had a keen vision and feeling":** Eliot, *Middlemarch*, 162.
261 **conventionality as a sign of authenticity:** Zaleski, *Otherworld Journeys*, 85.
262 **when a society sees itself as besieged by change:** Zaleski, 100.
262 **a brain scan for spiritual experience:** Hagerty, *Fingerprints of God*, 75.
262 **research on stress, genetics, and meditation is yielding valuable information:** In this chapter I relied on Barbara Bradley Hagerty's *Fingerprints of God: What Science Is Learning about the Brain and Spiritual Experience*, an engaging and highly informative study of current neuroscientific research on religious experience. Michael Pollan's *How to Change Your Mind: What the New Science of Psychedelics Teaches Us about Consciousness, Dying, Addiction, Depression, and Transcendence* examines the use of drugs to facilitate or enhance spiritual experience.
263 **some regard them as a "touch of God":** Hagerty, *Fingerprints of God*, 77.
263 **a "God spot" in our brains:** Wolff, *Not Less Than Everything*, 165.
263 **"forth at pleasure into endless space":** Longinus, quoted in Heschel, *God in Search of Man*, 37–38.
263 **we are wired for spirituality:** Hagerty, *Fingerprints of God*, 85–87.
263 **Mary Roach, author of the book:** Roach, *Spook*, 221–23.
263 **areas of the brain are involved in spiritual experience:** Fischer, "Distinct 'God Spot' in the Brain Does Not Exist, MU Researcher Says."
263 **Work on the physiology of seizures:** Hagerty, *Fingerprints of God*, 132–33.
264 **The transcendent state of mystical experience:** Hagerty, 173–75.
264 **Newburg surmises that the monks and nuns go beyond:** Hagerty, 178–79.
264 **There is a long history of people using psychedelic substances:** Pollan, *How to Change Your Mind*, 103.
264 **In 1962, psychiatrist Walter Pahnke conducted the "Good Friday Experiment":** Pollan, "The Trip Treatment."
265 **"'God' might be the only word":** Pollan, *How to Change Your Mind*, 285.
265 **"To fathom Hell or go angelic":** Humphry Osmond, quoted in Pollan, *How to Change Your Mind*, 163.

Chapter 30. Beyond Time-Space
266 **"There are more things in heaven and earth":** William Shakespeare, *Hamlet*, act 1, scene 5.
266 **an audio technology called Hemi-Sync:** The Hemi-Sync Catalog, 1.
267 **"the peak of uncontrolled thought":** Monroe, *Ultimate Journey*, 17.
267 **"food chain predator system":** Monroe, 63.
267 **"There"—beyond time-space:** Monroe, 86.
267 **This is the "I-There" of Monroe:** Monroe, 176.
268 **"the density of the molecular surroundings":** Buhlman, *The Secret of the Soul*, 141.
268 **"a transparent vacuum without a circumference or center":** Buhlman, *The Secret of the Soul*, 124.
269 **The dozen or so people:** In order to be accepted for the William Buhlman workshop, I agreed not to use any Monroe Institute materials for my own purposes, nor to divulge it to others. I draw instead on my own notes and reactions to the three nights and two days I spent there, and on material from Buhlman's *The Secret of the Soul*.

Chapter 31. The Vastly Alerted Mind
273 **"The individual nearing death may":** Russell Noyes and Roy Kletti, quoted in Zaleski, *Otherworld Journeys*, 174.
273 **"the transition from physical life":** Monroe, *Ultimate Journey*, 265.
274 **"The vastly alerted mind":** Quoted in Zaleski, *Otherworld Journeys*, 174.
274 **Atheists, agnostics, fundamentalists:** Zaleski, 177.
274 **cardiologist Pim van Lommel:** Roach, *Spook*, 267.
274 **Eben Alexander (who documented his own NDE in *Proof of Heaven*):** Abrahamsen, *Paranormal*, 35–36.
274 **psychiatrist Bruce Greyson suggests:** Roach, *Spook*, 283.
275 **a five-stage continuum:** Zaleski, 106.
275 **And then there is the light itself:** Pearson, *Opening Heaven's Door*, 126.
276 **"Anyone who has seen a little":** Pope Gregory I, quoted in Pearson, *Opening Heaven's Door*, 126.
276 **"Into this One":** Pearson, 132–33.
277 **individual accountability:** Pearson, 150.
277 **the same neural activity he observed:** Hagerty, *Fingerprints of God*, 236–37.
277 **Others find themselves:** Bush and Greyson, "Distressing Near-Death Experiences."

Chapter 32. The Universe Awakening
282 **"The Christian of the future":** Karl Rahner, "The Spirituality of the Church of the Future," *Theological Investigations*, vol. 20, 149.
283 **"possible to repackage the mind":** Delio, *The Unbearable Wholeness of Being*, 157.
283 **"But this year, it became":** Mozur, "Google's AlphaGo Defeats Chinese Go Master in Win for A.I."
284 **"Biology is not destiny":** Bart Kosko, quoted in Delio, *The Unbearable Wholeness*, 161.
284 **An episode of the *Black Mirror* television series:** "San Junipero," *The Black Mirror*.
285 **"You gave us insufficient evidence!":** Bertrand Russell, quoted in Irwin, "God Is a Question, Not an Answer."

NOTES

285 **Why do humans long for heaven?:** I am indebted to John Haught and Ilia Delio for their personal guidance and for their extraordinary scholarship that opens up the worldview of Teilhard de Chardin and carries it forward in inspiring ways. Robert Russell was very helpful in making sense of esoteric, even mysterious, ideas about time and life beyond.

285 **"The universe is not only queerer":** J. B. S. Haldane, quoted in Bryson, *A Short History of Nearly Everything*, 17.

285 **Akasha:** Chopra, *Life after Death*, 211.

285 **cessation of thermodynamic energy:** Yusuf, "The End of Time."

287 **an "inside" cosmic story:** Haught, *Science and Faith*, 62.

287 **the cosmos is inhabited by God:** Haught, "Teilhard, Big History, and Religion: A Look Inside," 1.

287 **development of consciousness:** Delio, *The Unbearable Wholeness of Being*, 38.

288 **The ultimate Mover:** Delio, 125–26.

288 **the ultimate depth of love:** Delio, 41.

288 **"Love is the law":** Delio, 184.

288 **"God loves things":** Rohr, *The Universal Christ*, 16.

288 **human divinization:** Rohr, "Divinization."

289 **"Heaven is now":** Author interview with Ilia Delio.

Chapter 33. At the End of All Our Exploring

290 **"With the drawing of this Love and the voice of this Calling":** T. S. Eliot, "Little Gidding" from *Four Quartets*, *The Complete Poems and Plays of T. S. Eliot*, 198.

291 **present-day culture:** Greg Garrett's *Entertaining Judgment: The Afterlife in Popular Imagination* is not only a valuable resource but a delightful exploration of life beyond as expressed in contemporary popular culture.

291 **"That doesn't mean it isn't true":** Robinson, *Lila*, 142–43 (my italics).

291 **with friends and family:** Garrett, *Entertaining Judgment*, 102.

291 **"a shot at redemption"; "received in Graceland":** Simon, "You Can Call Me Al" and "Graceland," *Graceland*.

291 **"billion-year-old carbon"; "get ourselves back to the garden":** Mitchell, "Woodstock," *Ladies of the Canyon*.

291 **"Like Adam, we have all lost Paradise":** Quoted in Garrett, *Entertaining Judgment*, 105.

292 **"Harps and Angels":** Newman, "Harps and Angels."

294 **"Mercy and truth have met together":** Psalm 85:10; also from the story "Babette's Feast" by Isak Dinesen (Karen Blixen).

295 **The First Phone Call from Heaven:** Garrett, *Entertaining Judgment*, 21.

296 **two witnesses:** Revelation 11:1–14.

297 **group's final statement:** http://www.heavensgate.com/misc/pressrel.htm.

297 **Gabriel announced to Mary:** There are countless depictions of the Annunciation. A fine example is Simone Martini and Lippo Memmi, *Annunciation with Saint Margaret and Saint Ansanus* (1333), Uffizi Gallery, Florence, Italy. Image available at https://www.uffizi.it/en/artworks/annunciation-with-st-margaret-and-st-ansanus and elsewhere online.

297 **Most Americans have had a direct sense:** Garrett, *Entertaining Judgment*, 72.

297 **"I am convinced that these heavenly beings exist":** Billy Graham, quoted in Garrett, *Entertaining Judgment*, 63.

297 **"Angeling is lofty but lonely work":** Rita Kempley, quoted in Garrett, 78.

298 **"Earth's crammed with heaven":** Browning, "Aurora Leigh," 487.

298 **"shouting and clapping and leaping like frogs":** O'Connor, *Complete Stories*, 508.

299 **"In our world too":** Lewis, *The Last Battle*, 177.

299 **The old Narnia had been but a shadow:** Lewis, 212–13.

300 **"the things that began to happen":** Lewis, 228.

Afterword: Death Is the Mother of Beauty

301 **"Death is the mother of beauty":** Wallace Stevens, "Sunday Morning," www.poetryfoundation.org/poetrymagazine/poems/13261/sunday-morning/.

301 **"A dialogue between two infants":** Enright, *Oxford Book of Death*, 171.

303 **"Comradeship and serious joy":** Chesterton, *Charles Dickens: The Last of the Great Men*, 215.

Bibliography

"Abbot Suger's Memoirs." *Athena Review* 4, no. 2. http://www.athenapub.com/AR/14suger.htm.

"About Interstate Industries Inc. d/b/a Monroe Products." The Hemi-Sync Catalog. Faber, VA: Monroe Institute, 2015.

Abrahamsen, Valerie A. *Paranormal: A New Testament Scholar Looks at the Afterlife.* Manchester Center, VT: Shires, 2015.

Adiswarananda, Swami. "Hinduism: Death and Life Beyond Death." *Teachings.* https://ramakrishna.org/lifeanddeath.html.

Alexander, Eben, and Ptolemy Tompkins. *The Map of Heaven: How Science, Religion, and Ordinary People Are Proving the Afterlife.* New York: Simon & Schuster, 2014.

Alighieri, Dante. *The Divine Comedy.* Translated by John D. Sinclair. New York: Oxford University Press, 1961.

Aquinas, Thomas Saint. *The Summa Theologica of St. Thomas Aquinas Part III (Supplement).* Fathers of the English Dominican Province, 1922.

———. *Treatise on the Last Things.* Fathers of the English Dominican Province, 1921. Kindle edition.

Arendzen, J. "Gnosticism." *The Catholic Encyclopedia.* New York: Robert Appleton, 1909. https://www.newadvent.org/cathen/06592a.htm.

Armstrong, Karen. *A History of God: The 4,000-Year Quest of Judaism, Christianity and Islam.* New York: Alfred A. Knopf, 1993.

———. "The Question: Should We Believe in Belief?" *The Guardian,* July 12, 2009.

Augustine, Saint. *City of God,* Book XIV, Chapter 28. Translated by Marcus Dods. From *Nicene and Post-Nicene Fathers, First Series,* vol. 2. Edited by Philip Schaff. Buffalo, NY: Christian Literature Publishing, 1887. Revised and edited by Kevin Knight. https://www.newadvent.org/fathers/1201.htm.

———. *The Confessions of Saint Augustine.* Translated by Henry Chadwick. Oxford: Oxford University Press, 2008.

———. *The Retractions (The Fathers of the Church,* vol. 60). Translated by Sister Mary Inez Bogan. Washington, DC: Catholic University of America Press, 1999.

Baqli, Ruzbihan. *The Unveiling of Secrets: Diary of a Sufi Master.* Translated by Carl W. Ernst. Chapel Hill, NC: Parvardigar Press, 1997.

Basso, Ellen B. *The Kalapalo Indians of Central Brazil.* New York: Holt, Rinehart and Winston, 1973.

Bellah, Robert N. *Religion in Human Evolution: From the Paleolithic to the Axial Age.* Cambridge, MA: Belknap Press of Harvard University Press, 2011.

Benedict, Saint. *The Rule of St. Benedict.* Translated by Anthony C. Meisel and M. L. del Mastro. New York: Doubleday, 1975.

Blair, Sheila S., and Jonathan M. Bloom. *Images of Paradise in Islamic Art.* Hanover, NH: Hood Museum of Art: Dartmouth College, 1991.

Blake, William. *The Marriage of Heaven and Hell: In Full Color.* New York: Dover, 1994.

Brown, Raymond E. *An Introduction to the New Testament.* New York: Doubleday, 1997.

Browning, Elizabeth Barrett. *Aurora Leigh.* Athens: Ohio University Press, 1992.

Bryson, Bill. *A Short History of Nearly Everything.* New York: Broadway Books, 2003.

Buhlman, William. *Adventures in the Afterlife.* Millsboro, DE: Osprey, 2013.

———. *The Secret of the Soul: Using Out-of-Body Experiences to Understand Our True Nature.* San Francisco: HarperSanFrancisco, 2001.

Bunyan, John. *The Pilgrim's Progress.* London: Simpkin, Marshall, 1856. Google Books.

Burpo, Todd, and Lynn Vincent. *Heaven Is for Real: A Little Boy's Astounding Story of His Trip to Heaven and Back.* Nashville: Thomas Nelson, 2010.

Bush, Nancy Evans, and Bruce Greyson. "Distressing Near-Death Experiences." *Psychiatry* 55, no. 1 (February 1992), 95–110.

Calasso, Roberto. *The Marriage of Cadmus and Harmony.* New York: Vintage, 1993.

Campbell, Joseph. *Myths to Live By.* New York: Viking, 1972.

Chervin, Ronda, Richard Ballard, and Ruth Ballard. *What the Saints Said about Heaven: 101 Holy Insights on Everlasting Life.* Charlotte, NC: Tan, 2011.

Chesterton, G. K. *Charles Dickens, The Last of the Great Men.* Milwaukee: Wiseblood Books, 2013.

———. *Orthodoxy.* Moscow: Canon Press, 2020.

BIBLIOGRAPHY

Chopra, Deepak. *Life after Death: The Burden of Proof.* New York: Three Rivers Press, 2006.

Citrin, Rabbi Paul. *Lights in the Forest: Rabbis Respond to Twelve Essential Jewish Questions.* New York: Central Conference of American Rabbis, 2014.

Coleman, Graham, and Thupten Jinpa. *Tibetan Book of the Dead.* London: Penguin UK, 2007.

Couliano, Ioan P. *Out of This World: Otherworldly Journeys from Gilgamesh to Albert Einstein.* Boston: Shambhala, 1991.

Craven, Margaret. *I Heard the Owl Call My Name.* New York: Dell, 1980.

Cuba, Gary. "Seventh Heaven." http://www.thefoggiestnotion.com/seventh_heaven.htm.

Dan, Joseph. *Kabbalah: A Very Short Introduction.* New York: Oxford University Press, 2007.

Darwin, Charles. *On the Origin of Species by Means of Natural Selection.* London: John Murray, 1859.

Dawa Drolma, Delog. *Delog: Journey to Realms Beyond Death.* Junction City, CA: Padma, 1995.

Delio, Ilia. *The Emergent Christ: Exploring the Meaning of Catholic in an Evolutionary Universe.* Maryknoll, NY: Orbis Books, 2011.

————, ed. *From Teilhard to Omega: Co-creating an Unfinished Universe.* Maryknoll, NY: Orbis Books, 2014.

————. *The Unbearable Wholeness of Being: God, Evolution, and the Power of Love.* Maryknoll, NY: Orbis Books, 2016.

Dharma, Krishna. "Arjuna Goes to Heaven" (taken from the Mahâbhârata, Book 1, Chapter 25). 1999. http://vahini.org /Discourses/d9-arjunagoestoheaven.html.

Dionysius the Areopagite. *The Celestial Hierarchy.* Kindle Edition.

Doctrine and Covenants 132:16–17; 76:97–98; 76:81–90, 98–112; 88:100–101. Church of Jesus Christ of Latter-day Saints. www.churchofjesuschrist.org.

Donahue, John R. *The Gospel in Parable: Metaphor, Narrative, and Theology in the Synoptic Gospels.* Philadelphia: Fortress Press, 1988.

Doyle, Arthur Conan. *The History of Spiritualism.* London: Cassell, 1926.

Einstein, Albert. *Ideas and Opinions.* New York: Three Rivers Press, 1982.

Eire, Carlos M. N. *A Very Brief History of Eternity.* Princeton, NJ: Princeton University Press, 2010.

Eknath, Easwaran, trans. *The Bhagavad Gita.* Petaluma, CA: Nilgiri, 1985.

————. *The Upanishads.* Petaluma, CA: Nilgiri, 1987.

Eliot, George. *Middlemarch.* Ware, UK: Wordsworth Editions, 1994. Google Books.

Eliot, T. S. *The Complete Poems and Plays of T. S. Eliot.* London: Faber and Faber, 1969.

Enright, D. J., ed. *The Oxford Book of Death.* Oxford: Oxford University Press, 1983.

Esposito, John L. *Islam: The Straight Path.* New York: Oxford University Press, 2011.

Faruqi, al, Isma'il R. *Islam.* Beltsville, MD: Amana, 1984.

Fischer, Brad. "Distinct 'God Spot' in the Brain Does Not Exist, MU Researcher Says." News Bureau, University of Missouri, April 18, 2012. www.munewsarchives.missouri.edu.

Gardiner, Ellen, ed. *Visions of Heaven and Hell before Dante.* New York: Italica Press, 1989.

Garrett, Greg. *Entertaining Judgment: The Afterlife in Popular Imagination.* New York: Oxford University Press, 2015.

Givens, Terryl. *Wrestling the Angel: The Foundations of Mormon Thought: Cosmos, God, Humanity.* New York: Oxford University Press, 2015.

Givens, Terryl, and Fiona Givens. *The God Who Weeps: How Mormonism Makes Sense of Life.* Crawfordsville, IN: Ensign Peak, 2012.

Gregory the Great. *The Dialogues of Gregory the Great.* Toronto: Public Domain, 2016. Kindle Edition.

Greyson, Bruce. "Biological Aspects of Near-Death Experiences." *Perspectives in Biology and Medicine* 42, no. 1 (Autumn 1998). Online version at Project Muse, Perspectives in Biology and Medicine. http://www.muse.jhu.edu.

Haag, Matthew. "Robert Jeffress, Pastor Who Said Jews Are Going to Hell, Led Prayer at Jerusalem Embassy." *The New York Times*, May 19, 2018.

Hagerty, Barbara Bradley. *Fingerprints of God: What Science Is Learning about the Brain and Spiritual Experience.* New York: Riverhead Books, 2010.

Hart, David Bentley. *The Experience of God: Being, Consciousness, Bliss.* London: Yale University Press, 2013.

Harvey, Peter. *An Introduction to Buddhist Ethics: Foundations, Values, and Issues.* Cambridge, UK: Cambridge University Press, 2000.

Haught, John F. "Hard-wired for God?" *Commonweal Magazine*, April 5, 2010. www.commonwealmagazine.org/hard -wired-god.

————. *Resting on the Future: Catholic Theology for an Unfinished Universe.* New York: Bloomsbury Academic, 2015.

————. *Science and Faith: A New Introduction.* New York: Paulist Press, 2012.

————. "Teilhard, Big History, and Religion: A Look Inside." *The Teilhard Studies* 71 (Fall 2015). http://www.teilhard dechardin.org/mm_uploads/71-Teilhard_Big_History_and_Religion.pdf.

Heehs, Peter, ed. *Indian Religions: A Historical Reader of Spiritual Expression and Experience.* New York: New York University Press, 2002.

Heim, S. Mark. *Salvations: Truth and Difference in Religion.* Maryknoll, NY: Orbis Books, 1995.

Heschel, Abraham Joshua. *God in Search of Man: A Philosophy of Judaism.* New York: Farrar, Straus & Giroux, 1955.

————. *Man Is Not Alone: A Philosophy of Religion.* New York: Farrar, Straus & Giroux, 1976.

————. *The Sabbath.* New York: Farrar, Straus & Giroux, 1951.

Hincks, Adam D. "Justified Reason: The Collaboration of Knowledge, Faith, and Belief." *America Magazine*, September 22, 2014. https://www.americamagazine.org/issue/justified-reason.

BIBLIOGRAPHY

Hirsch, Edward. *A Poet's Glossary*. Boston: Harcourt, 2014.

Holloway, Mark. *Heavens on Earth: Utopian Communities in America, 1680–1880*. New York: Dover, 1966.

Homer, *The Odyssey*. Translated by Samuel Butler. Roslyn, NY: Walter J. Black, 1944.

Ibn Warraq. "Virgins? What Virgins?" *The Guardian*, January 11, 2002. https://www.theguardian.com/books/2002/jan/12/books.guardianreview5.

Irwin, William. "God Is a Question, Not an Answer." *The New York Times*, March 26, 2016. https://opinionator.blogs.nytimes.com/2016/03/26/god-is-a-question-not-an-answer.

James, William. *The Varieties of Religious Experience: A Study in Human Nature*. San Bernardino, CA: Renaissance Classics, 2014.

Johnson, Elizabeth A. *Friends of God and Prophets: A Feminist Theological Reading of the Communion of Saints*. New York: Continuum, 1998.

———. *Quest for the Living God: Mapping Frontiers in the Theology of God*. New York: Continuum, 2007.

Johnston, Theresa. "Mrs. Stanford and the Netherworld." *Stanford Magazine*, May/June 2000. https://stanfordmag.org/contents/mrs-stanford-and-the-netherworld.

Jones, Alan. *Ramblings of a Rational Mystic*. Morrisville, NC: Lulu Press, 2011. Google Books.

Julian of Norwich. *Revelations of Divine Love*. London: Penguin, 1966.

Kaplan, Aryeh. *Sefer Yetzirah: The Book of Creation*. San Francisco: Red Wheel/Weiser, 1997.

Kapoor, Desh. "Creation and Consciousness." *Drishtikone*, September 27, 2009. https://www.patheos.com/blogs/drishtikone/2009/09/creation-and-consciousness/.

Kehoe, Laura. "The Images of Chimps Thrilled Me: Do They Show Evidence of Spirituality in the Wild?" *The Guardian*, March 5, 2016. https://www.theguardian.com/science/2016/mar/06/chimps-more-human-than-we-think.

Kennet, Brian. *A Chilli Too Far*. booksmango, 2012. Google Books.

Kurian, George Thomas, and Mark A. Lamport, eds. *Encyclopedia of Christian Education*, vol. 3. Lanham, MD: Rowan & Littlefield, 2015. Google Books.

Lee, Sherman. *A History of Far Eastern Art*. New York: Prentice Hall and Harry N. Abrams, 1964.

Leidy, Denise Patry. *The Art of Buddhism: An Introduction to Its History and Meaning*. Boston and London: Shambala, 2008.

L'Engle, Madeleine. "The Glory." "randomness and ruminations," November 14, 2012. https://melissareyes.wordpress.com/2012/11/14/the-glory-by-madeleine-l-engle/.

Lerner, Akiba. *Redemptive Hope: From the Age of Enlightenment to the Age of Obama*. New York: Fordham University Press, 2015.

Lewis, C. S. *The Last Battle*. New York: Harper, 2002.

Lumpkin, Joseph. *The Books of Enoch: A Complete Volume Containing: 1 Enoch (The Ethiopic Book of Enoch), 2 Enoch (The Slavonic Book of Enoch), 3 Enoch (The Hebrew Book of Enoch)*. Blountsville, AL: Fifth Estate, 2011.

Luxenberg, Christoph. *Die Syro-Aramaische Lesart des Koran*. Berlin: Hans Schiler, 2007.

Madigan, Daniel, S.J. "Morte e dopo morte nel pensiero islamico" (Death and Afterlife in Islamic Thought). In *Homo moriens: Saggi sull'aldilà e sul destino ultimo dell'uomo*, ed. A. Lambertino, 89–103. Parma: Monte Università Parma, 2004.

"The Magick of the Seven Heavens." http://www.archangels-and-angels.com/misc/seven_heavens.html.

Mark, Joshua J. "Egyptian Afterlife—The Field of Reeds." *Ancient History Encyclopedia*, March 28, 2016. https://www.ancient.eu/article/877/egyptian-afterlife---the-field-of-reeds/.

Matt, Daniel Chanan, trans. *Zohar: The Book of Enlightenment*. Mahwah, NJ: Paulist Press, 1983.

McDannell, Colleen, and Bernhard Lang. *Heaven: A History*. New Haven, CT: Yale University Press, 1988.

McGrath, Alister E. *A Brief History of Heaven*. Malden, MA: Blackwell, 2003.

Mechthild of Magdeburg. *The Flowering Light of the Godhead*. Mahwah, NJ: Paulist Press, 1998.

Meisel, Anthony C., and M. L. del Mastro. *The Rule of St. Benedict*. New York: Doubleday, 1975.

Miles, Jack, ed. *The Norton Anthology of World Religions*. New York: W. W. Norton, 2015.

Miller, Lisa. *Heaven: Our Enduring Fascination with the Afterlife*. New York: Harper, 2010.

———. *Visions of Heaven: A Journey through the Afterlife*. Des Moines: Time Books, 2014.

Milton, John. *Paradise Lost: And, Paradise Regained*. New York: Signet Classic, 2001.

Mithen, Steven J. *The Prehistory of the Mind: A Search for the Origins of Art, Religion, and Science*. London: Thames and Hudson, 1996.

Monroe, Robert A. *Ultimate Journey*. New York: Harmony Books, 1994.

Mooallem, Jon. "Neanderthals Were People, Too." *The New York Times*, January 11, 2017.

Moody, Raymond A. *Life after Life*. New York: HarperCollins, 1975.

Mookerjee, Ajit. *Ritual Art of India*. Rochester, VT: Inner Traditions, 1998.

Mozur, Paul. "Google's AlphaGo Defeats Chinese Go Master in Win for A.I." *The New York Times*, May 23, 2017.

Mursell, Gordon, ed. *The Story of Christian Spirituality*. Oxford, UK: Lion, 2001.

Neihardt, John G. *Black Elk Speaks*. Lincoln: University of Nebraska Press, 2014.

Nochlin, Linda. *Realism*. Harmondsworth, UK: Penguin, 1971.

O'Connor, Flannery. *Complete Stories*. New York: Farrar, Straus & Giroux, 1971.

O'Malley, William, S.J. "The Eye and I." *America Magazine*, December 10, 2007, https://www.americamagazine.org/issue/637/article/eye-and-i.

O'Murchú, Diarmuid. *Quantum Theology*. New York: Crossroad, 1997.

BIBLIOGRAPHY

———. "What Will Mysticism in the 21st Century Look Like?" *National Catholic Reporter*, January 10, 2017. https://www.ncronline.org/blogs/soul-seeing/what-will-mysticism-21st-century-look.

Pagels, Elaine H. *Beyond Belief: The Secret Gospel of Thomas*. New York: Random House, 2003.

———. *The Gnostic Gospels*. New York: Random House, 1979.

Pearson, Patricia. *Opening Heaven's Door: What the Dying Are Trying to Say about Where They're Going*. New York: Simon & Schuster, 2015.

Pegg, Jenny. "Remnants of a Spiritualist's Belief." *Stanford Magazine*, September/October 2012. https://stanfordmag.org/contents/remnants-of-a-spiritualist-s-belief.

Perkins, Rodney, and Forrest Jackson. *Cosmic Suicide: The Tragedy and Transcendence of Heaven's Gate*. Dallas: Pentaradial Press, 2016. Kindle edition.

Peters, Ted, Robert J. Russell, and Michael Welker. *Resurrection: Theological and Scientific Assessments*. Grand Rapids, MI: W. B. Eerdmans, 2002.

Phelps, Elizabeth Stuart. *The Gates Ajar*. London: Sampson Low, Son, & Maerston, 1869. Google Books.

Pleins, J. David. *The Evolving God: Charles Darwin on the Naturalness of Religion*. New York: Bloomsbury Academic, 2013.

Pollan, Michael. *How to Change Your Mind: What the New Science of Psychedelics Teaches Us about Consciousness, Dying, Addiction, Depression, and Transcendence*. New York: Penguin, 2018.

———. "The Trip Treatment." *The New Yorker*, February 9, 2015.

Proctor, James D. *Science, Religion, and the Human Experience*. Oxford: Oxford University Press, 2005.

Rahner, Karl, S.J. "The Spirituality of the Church of the Future." In *Theological Investigations*, vol. 20. New York: Crossroad, 1981.

Ram Dass and Mirabai Bush. *Walking Each Other Home*. Boulder: Sounds True, 2018.

Roach, Mary. *Spook: Science Tackles the Afterlife*. New York: W. W. Norton, 2005.

Robinson, Marilynne. *Lila*. New York: Farrar, Straus & Giroux, 2014.

Roethke, Theodore. *The Collected Poems of Theodore Roethke*. Garden City, NY: Doubleday, 1966.

Rohr, Richard. "Divinization." *Daily Meditations*. Center for Action and Contemplation, April 29, 2019, https://cac.org/divinization-2019-04-29/.

———. *The Universal Christ: How a Forgotten Reality Can Change Everything We See, Hope For, and Believe*. New York: Convergent, 2019.

Rolf, Veronica Mary. *Julian's Gospel: Illuminating the Life and Revelations of Julian of Norwich*. Maryknoll, NY: Orbis Books, 2013.

———. "Love, Longing, and Pity." *Veronica's Blog*, Julian's Voice, August 28, 2015, https://www.juliansvoice.com/veronicas-blog/love-longing-and-pity.

Rohr, Richard. "Divinization." *Daily Meditations*. Center for Action and Contemplation, April 29, 2019. https://cac.org/divinization-2019-04-29/.

Ruse, Michael. *Atheism: What Everyone Needs to Know*. New York: Oxford University Press, 2015.

Russell, Jeffrey Burton. *A History of Heaven: The Singing Silence*. Princeton, NJ: Princeton University Press, 1997.

———. *Paradise Mislaid: How We Lost Heaven—and How We Can Regain It*. Oxford: Oxford University Press, 2006.

Russell, Robert J. *Time in Eternity: Pannenberg, Physics, and Eschatology in Creative Mutual Interaction*. Notre Dame, IN: University of Notre Dame Press, 2012.

Rustomji, Nerina. *The Garden and the Fire: Heaven and Hell in Islamic Culture*. New York: Columbia University Press, 2009.

Santayana, George. *Reason in Religion*. New York: Dover, 1982.

Saunders, George. *Lincoln in the Bardo*. New York: Random House, 2017.

Scheindlin, Raymond P. *A Short History of the Jewish People: From Legendary Times to Modern Statehood*. New York: Macmillan, 1998.

Schlitz, Marilyn. *Death Makes Life Possible: Revolutionary Insights on Living, Dying, and the Continuation of Consciousness*. Boulder, CO: Sounds True, 2015.

Scholem, Gershom G. *Major Trends in Jewish Mysticism*. New York: Schocken Books, 1995.

Segal, Alan F. *Life after Death: A History of the Afterlife in Western Religion*. New York: Doubleday, 2004.

Shameem, Asma bint. "Men Get Hoor Al'Een in Jannah . . . But . . . What Do We Get??!!" In *Women and Family*, https://www.farhathashmi.com/articles-section/women-and-family/men-get-hoor/.

Shavit, Ari. *My Promised Land: The Triumph and Tragedy of Israel*. New York: Spiegel & Grau, 2013.

Shortt, Rupert. *God Is No Thing: Coherent Christianity*. London: C. Hurst, 2016.

Smith, Francis R. *The World Is Charged: The Transcendent with Us*. New York: Crossroad, 2003.

Smith, Huston. *The World's Religions: Our Great Wisdom Traditions*. San Francisco: HarperSanFrancisco, 1991.

Smith, Jane I., and Yvonne Yazbeck Haddad. *The Islamic Understanding of Death and Resurrection*. Albany: State University of New York Press, 1981.

Smith, Joseph. *The Book of Mormon: An Account*. Salt Lake City, UT: Church of Jesus Christ of Latter-day Saints, 1950.

———. "The Joseph Smith Papers." www.josephsmithpapers.org.

Sogyal, Rinpoche, Patrick Gaffney, and Andrew Harvey, eds. *The Tibetan Book of Living and Dying*. San Francisco: HarperSanFrancisco, 1992.

Spilka, Bernard, Peter C. Hill, and Ralph W. Hood. *The Psychology of Religion: An Empirical Approach*. New York: Guilford Press, 2003.

BIBLIOGRAPHY

Spitz, Elie Kaplan. *Does the Soul Survive?: A Jewish Journey to Belief in Afterlife, Past Lives, and Living with Purpose.* Woodstock, VT: Jewish Lights, 2000.

Spohn, William C. *Go and Do Likewise: Jesus and Ethics.* New York: Continuum, 1999.

Stanford, Peter. *Heaven: A Guide to the Undiscovered Country.* New York: Palgrave Macmillan, 2002.

Swedenborg, Emanuel, and Donald Rose. *Afterlife: A Guided Tour of Heaven and Its Wonders.* West Chester, PA: Swedenborg Foundation, 2006.

Teilhard de Chardin, Pierre. *The Divine Milieu.* New York: HarperCollins, 2001.

———. *The Phenomenon of Man.* New York: Harper Perennial, 2008.

Teresa of Ávila, Saint. *Interior Castle.* PDF version: https://www.documentacatholicaomnia.eu/03d/1515-1582,_Teresa_d%27Avila,_The_Interior_Castle_ Of_The_Mansions,_EN.pdf.

van Dusen, Wilson. *The Presence of Other Worlds: The Psychological/Spiritual Findings of Emanuel Swedenborg.* West Chester, PA: Chrysalis, 2004.

Vasari, Giorgio. *Artists of the Renaissance.* Translated by George Bull. New York: Viking, 1978.

Virgil, *The Aeneid.* Translated by Robert Fitzgerald. New York: Random House, 1983.

Walker, Benjamin. *Gnosticism: Its History and Influence.* Wellingborough, UK: Aquarian Press, 1983.

Watson, Traci. "Ancient Fossils in African Cave Are Tantalizing Glimpse of Early Man." *USA Today,* September 10, 2015. https://www.usatoday.com/story/news/2015/09/10/fossils-humans-cave-ancient-bones/71966570/.

Weinberg, Steven. "Physics: What We Do and Don't Know." *New York Review of Books,* November 7, 2013. https://www.nybooks.com/articles/2013/11/07/physics-what-we-do-and-dont-know/.

Wiman, Christian. *My Bright Abyss: Meditation of a Modern Believer.* New York: Farrar, Straus & Giroux, 2013.

Wolff, Catherine, ed. *Not Less Than Everything: Catholic Writers on Heroes of Conscience from Joan of Arc to Oscar Romero.* New York: HarperOne, 2013.

Wright, N. T. *Surprised by Hope: Rethinking Heaven, the Resurrection, and the Mission of the Church.* New York: HarperOne, 2008.

Yogananda. *Autobiography of a Yogi.* Los Angeles: Self-Realization Fellowship, 1969.

———. *Karma and Reincarnation.* Nevada City, CA: Crystal Clarity, 2007.

———. "The New Path." https://www.ananda.org/free-inspiration/books/the-new-path/chapter-32/.

Yusuf, Hamza. "The Afterlife." October 1, 2011. https://islamondemand.com/the-afterlife-hamza-yusuf/ and https://www.youtube.com/watch?v=LzwmRc86Yy8.

———. "The End of Time." March 15, 2015. https://islamondemand.com/the-end-of-time-hamza-yusuf/ and https://www.youtube.com/watch?v=44o1qrbyo1U.

———. "Sacred Nature of Women." July 30, 2016. https://islamio.com/en/watch/sacred-nature-of-women-shaykh-hamza-yusuf-beautiful/.

Zaleski, Carol. *Otherworld Journeys: Accounts of Near-death Experience in Medieval and Modern Times.* New York: Oxford University Press, 1987.

Zaleski, Carol, and Philip Zaleski. *The Book of Heaven: An Anthology of Writings from Ancient to Modern Times.* Oxford: Oxford University Press, 2000.

Sacred Texts
The Holy Qur'ān. Text, translation, and commentary by Abdullah Yusuf Ali. Beltsville, MD: Amana, 2009.

The Jerusalem Bible. London: Darton, Longman & Todd, 1974.

Tanakh: The Holy Scriptures. Philadelphia/Jerusalem: Jewish Publication Society, 1985.

TV Series, Songs, Movies
"San Junipero." *Black Mirror.* Season 3, episode 4. October 21, 2016. Netflix, www.netflix.com.

Six Feet Under. HBO, June 3, 2001–August 21, 2005. www.hbo.com.six-feet-under.

Bono, Sonny. "I Got You Babe." *Look at Us,* 1965.

Mitchell, Joni. "Woodstock." *Ladies of the Canyon.* Reprise Records, 1970.

Newman, Randy. "Harps and Angels." *Harps and Angels.* Nonesuch, 2008.

Simon, Paul. "You Can Call Me Al." *Graceland.* Warner Bros. Records, 1986.

Babette's Feast. Dir. Gabriel Axel. Nordisk Film, 1987.

Defending Your Life. Dir. Albert Brooks. Geffen Film Company, 1991.

Groundhog Day. Dir. Harold Ramis. Trevor Albert/Harold Ramis, 1993.

A Matter of Life and Death. Dir. Michael Powell and Emeric Pressburger. The Archers/J. Arthur Rank, 1946.

Wings of Desire. Dir. Wim Wenders. Road Movies/Filmproduktion/Argos Films/Westdeutscher Rundfunk, 1988.

Illustration Credits

Index

INDEX

INDEX